ISRAEL'S VICIOUS CIRCLE

Israel's Vicious Circle

Ten years of writings on Israel and Palestine

Uri Avnery

Edited by Sara R. Powell

Pluto Press

First published 2008 by Pluto Press
345 Archway Road, London N6 5AA

www.plutobooks.com

Copyright © Uri Avnery 2008

The right of Uri Avnery to be identified as the author of this work has been
asserted by him in accordance with the Copyright, Designs and Patents Act 1988.

British Library Cataloguing in Publication Data
A catalogue record for this book is available from the British Library

ISBN   978 0 7453 2823 2

Library of Congress Cataloging in Publication Data applied for

10 9 8 7 6 5 4 3 2 1

Designed and produced for Pluto Press by
Curran Publishing Services, Norwich
Printed and bound in the United States of America

*All footnotes and commentary outside the original essays are by Sara Powell
(ed.). They do not necessarily represent Uri Avnery's views.*
 *All articles were originally written in Hebrew by Uri Avnery for an Israeli
audience; they were originally edited in the English translation by Chris Costello.
"Truth against truth" by Uri Avnery was originally published in pamphlet form
by Gush Shalom.*

RACHEL

Wife, editor of the original Hebrew text, invaluable critic

"I remember thee, the kindness of thy youth, the love of thine espousals, when thou wentest after me in the wilderness, in a land that was not sown." (Jeremiah 2:2)

Contents

Foreword

In the early days of the State of Israel, one of our most prominent journalists was an editor who always strove to give the public exactly what it wanted to hear. More than once, when he had inadvertently diverged from the public mood, he presented the opposite view the very next day. In some cases, he even switched his positions the same day, from one edition to another.

Abba Eban, the sharp-tongued Israeli foreign minister, once threatened him: "If you don't stop attacking me, I shall publish a collection of all your articles!" The attacks stopped at once.

In the spring of 1954, I started a weekly column with the Hebrew title *Hanidon*, which can be rendered as "re:," "concerning," "in the matter of." Not having missed a single week since then, I must have published something like 2,810 articles, comprising some 4 million words. If somebody threatened to publish all of them, I would just tell them: "Make sure you don't omit any."

I am in the happy position of having nothing to fear from such a threat. I have not trimmed my views to match the general mood. I have never believed that it is a commentator's job to "reflect" public opinion. Rather, it is our duty to tell the truth, as we see it.

In the old days, that was the role of the prophet. In biblical times, a prophet was not a person who foretold the future, but one who stood at the gate of the town and berated the people for their faults and the rulers for their misdeeds.

This did not make for popularity. One of these unfortunates, Jeremiah, cried out: "Woe is me, my mother, that thou hast borne me a man of strife and a man of contention to the whole earth! I have neither lent on usury, nor men have lent to me on usury, yet every one of them does curse me." (Jeremiah 15:10)

When Judea was in danger of being defeated by Babylon, the ministers beseeched the king: "Let this man be put to death, for thus he weakeneth the hands of the men of war ... this man seeketh not the welfare of this people but the hurt." So they took him and threw him into a dungeon full of mire. (Jeremiah 38:4)

Far be it from me to compare myself to such an august figure, but he has served me as a model to emulate. I have always admired his courage and his steadfastness, even though he was a bit of an egomaniac. Humility hardly goes with the job, neither then or now.

This book consists of essays written during the last few years. They were not penned in the proverbial ivory tower by a detached professor. They were composed in the thick of the struggle, by someone very much involved. Perhaps I would phrase some sentences differently today. I was certainly wrong in some assessments. But I have not asked the editor of this volume to change, add or omit a single word. For all of them give testimony to the emotions and thoughts of the moment.

A few words about myself: I am an Israeli. I consider myself an Israeli patriot. Those who seek the destruction of the State of Israel will find no comfort here. All my criticism, even when extreme—especially when extreme—stems from love.

From the first hour of the state, when I heard the Declaration of Independence on the radio as my unit was preparing for battle, I was in opposition—not because I am "against," but because I am "for." In my mind's eye, I see an alternative model of the state. In the words of Thoreau, I hear a different drummer. A drummer calling for a different Israel, an Israel one can be proud of—moral, democratic, secular, progressive, egalitarian, not lording it over another people, at peace with its neighbors, an integral part of the region which is our extended fatherland, in the front line of humanity's struggle for a better world.

I believe in this other Israel. I believe that it will come about. I hope that I shall see it with my own eyes. With the approach of my 85th birthday, there is not too much time left.

Uri Avnery
Tel Aviv, spring 2008

Introduction by Sara R. Powell

My name is Sara Powell and I am honored to have been asked to edit a compilation of Uri Avnery's writings. Avnery is the pre-eminent Israeli peace activist—co-founder of Gush Shalom, the largest Israeli peace organization, and largely responsible for the fact that Palestinian and Israeli officials are able to negotiate with each other for an end to their decades-long conflict. His is one of the most powerful voices calling out to other Israelis to pay attention to what is being done in their name and to take responsibility for it. Moreover, through translating his essays into English, and making them available through collections such as this, and on the Internet, Avnery is introducing many citizens of the world to a situation that has been frequently misrepresented and misunderstood. The fact that his is an Israeli voice documenting the problems of Israeli occupation makes his observations difficult to refute. His life and his work authenticate the unpopular truth he tells, and his engaging style draws in even those who have no direct interest in the region. Moreover, he has been—and continues to be—actively, physically engaged in (sometimes dangerous) demonstrations and direct action for many years. He has also been—and continues to be— an inspiration for all those interested in peace and justice in Israel and Palestine.

I first became aware that there was an issue surrounding Palestinians and Israelis as a small child in Beirut, Lebanon, in the early 1960s. My notions of the situation were, of course, fuzzy and unformed; I only knew that there were nice people I knew who, because they were Palestinian, could not go back home. The issue was discussed at the family dinner table, but I absorbed little of the details of the debate.

Later, as an adolescent in Tehran, Iran, in the late 1960s and early 1970s, I learned more about the issue in school—where we studied the history of the region, Israel and various Palestinian organizations,

1

including Fatah, the Popular Front for the Liberation of Palestine (PFLP) and the Popular Democratic Front for the Liberation of Palestine (PDFLP)—and in the tension that revolved around US embassy life (my father was a career Foreign Service Officer working for the US Department of State).[1] I watched as the Embassy began to fortify itself, as ticking packages were treated like bombs only to be revealed as toy clocks mailed by doting grandparents. I remember the first searches at airports. It was the age of the letter bomb. It was the age of hijacking.

It was during this time that my growing political awareness—especially following close on the worldwide youth movements that peaked in 1968, the shock of the Israeli success in the 1967 war, and the effect of the relatively new Palestine Liberation Organization (PLO) particularly under the leadership of Yassir Arafat—as well as my own experience in the Middle East led me to a lifelong interest in the region in general, and to interest and activism specifically with regard to the issue of Palestine and Israel.

Like Uri Avnery, I have a passionate interest in educating the public with regard to an ongoing critical situation and contributing whatever I can to finding a just solution. It is my honor to be able to present this volume of Avnery's monumental contribution to this cause.

The image of the vicious circle is a theme Uri Avnery uses often in his essays on the various relationships between Israel and the rest of the world, particularly Palestine, and it is apt. There are vicious circles of attack, counter-attack and escalation. There are vicious circles of peace process, failure to progress and renewed animosity. There are even vicious physical circles in the sense of the Separation Wall surrounding Palestinian territory or of unwelcoming Arab governments surrounding the state of Israel. However, by spring 2008, it has become clear that the circles have become spirals—downward spirals—and that they are even more vicious. All aspects of the situation themselves spiral viciously through Avnery's writing, forming an intertwined, subtle picture of the whole.

Although I have endeavored to present a full picture, this book is not meant to be a definitive history of the Arab–Israeli conflict. It is a compilation of (mostly) recent essays by one of the major figures participating in the attempt to break the cycle of violence and counter-violence that has continued throughout virtually the entire existence of Israel. Sometimes an official participant and sometimes an ex-officio contributor, Uri Avnery has performed many roles from his earliest days as a teen activist in the Irgun through his young adulthood as a member of the army to the last few decades as a peace activist. Avnery served in the Knesset, co-founded Gush Shalom, and was the first Israeli to have contact with the PLO. He has been advocating that Israel conduct negotiations with the PLO for a comprehensive peace that includes Palestine's aspirations for its own state ever since, but his efforts toward peace started during his youth.

In my attempt to edit the unique voice of Avnery my goal was to introduce a broader audience to one of the most prominent and thoughtful participants in the decades-long Israeli fight for a state and its concomitant occupation of Palestine—itself a unique world situation—with a selection that exemplifies his position, and to place both Avnery and the situation between Palestine and Israel in the larger Middle East context to which it belongs, as well as to place it in a global context. Avnery works to educate the public that Israel and Palestine are caught in a vicious circle, largely—though not entirely—kept within the circle by Israeli policy and Israeli action. Moreover, he makes the point that the situation is one of the most critical in a region becoming more and more desperate, which is in itself part of a global order that seems to be spinning out of control. For the reader already familiar with Avnery, I have tried to choose work that represents both some of the best of his oeuvre and pieces that present an overall view of his almost lifelong mission of bringing peace with justice to Palestine and Israel, and with the hope that this project may play some part in the advancement of that goal. I share Avnery's views that a just peace must be achieved in the near future.

In order to appreciate the singular perspective of Avnery's views, it is necessary to read the brief autobiographical sketches and personal remembrances that he often uses as an introductory allegory to the political analysis that comprises his weekly column.

The reader learns about Avnery's parents, his own "angry young man" period during the late 1940s, his growing sensitivity to the "other": the indigenous Palestinians. Avnery tantalizes his readers with hints of secret, intense—life and death—meetings. His autobiographical books read almost like novels.

What really grips the reader, though, is that this is no fiction and that Avnery bluntly describes what he has witnessed, and actively participated in, over the past 70 years.

He joined the Zionist underground—Avnery says terrorist—organization in 1938, just shy of his 15th birthday, as an ardent nationalist. After three years he left the organization because of its anti-Arab political stance and its methodology. By 1946 he founded the *Eretz Yisrael Hatzira*, or Young Palestine, movement and edited its publication *ba-Ma'avak* (Struggle). His was among the first in a bevy of Israeli voices calling for unity and cooperation between the Zionist immigrant community trying to wrest out a homeland and the native Palestinians, among whom he saw another oppressed community akin to his own. Despite his desire for a Semitic alliance between the Jewish and Arab communities (he proposed an essentially formal alliance of a Semitic region), he joined the army at the onset of the Israeli War of Independence, the Palestinian *Nakba*.

Although always a Zionist in the sense that he adheres to the idea of a Jewish nation state, Avnery continued his quest for peace and mutual respect between the two peoples now inhabiting the historic land of Palestine, predicated on the idea of two states—Palestinian and Israeli—as Semitic allies. This idea of a Semitic alliance forms an essential part of Avnery's views on Zionism. He considers himself a post-Zionist, a term he coined to describe those in favor of a Jewish nation state in the context of being part of a regional Semitic whole, secular with a culturally Jewish character, as opposed to early Zionism, which saw the Jewish nation state as an essentially European state, a bulwark against the barbarous hordes as expressed in Vladimir Ze'ev Jabotinsky's article "The iron wall," which Avnery discusses in his October 2007 article in this volume, "The mother of all pretexts." In his essay "Omelets into eggs," included here, Avnery presents his views on Zionism; for a full discussion of Avnery's theory, see his book, *Israel Without Zionists: A Plea for Peace in the Middle East* (Macmillan, 1968). In addition to his participant/eyewitness perspective, it is this post-Zionism—his Jewish nationalism coupled with his ardent support of Palestinian rights and nationalism—that makes Avnery's voice so unique.

In beginning the collection with essays focused on Judaism, Zionism, and anti-Semitism, I have tried to place Avnery within the context of the thought that shaped him, and even now is at the root of his fundamental belief system. He has completely internalized the concept synonymous with post-Holocaust Zionism—"never again"—as, of course, all peoples and governments should. He is in the minority, though, through his inclusive interpretation of "never again." He means never again for anyone, not just a select few.

Seen through Avnery's Israeli eyes, his graphic depiction of Israel's occupation of Palestine is striking. In his inimitable forthright style, Avnery tells it like he sees it—bleak, cruel, corrupting, even sadistic. Avnery does not mince words to spare his country, but neither does he spare Palestinians from censure. Any person, with no previous knowledge of the situation in Israel and Palestine, could read Avnery and absorb a good sense of the nature of the issue, without the usual spin of either narrative. That is one reason his voice is so important. Even an expert, though, can gain insight from Avnery's unique eyewitness/participant status.

Often the press misrepresents and the world misunderstands the situation in Palestine and Israel. Avnery not only paints a vivid picture of the grim occupation, he tells an enraging story of power and duplicity in the negotiation process toward peace. It is indeed a vicious circle as each Palestinian concession becomes the base point for the next round of talks, and the percentage of historic Palestine left for a state dwindles steadily, both on the ground and around the negotiating table.

Though there are those on both sides of the issue who fight the status quo, Israel, powerful in its own right, receives virtually unqualified support from the United States—the world's current evil empire at the height of its power and madness. Nonetheless, voices like Avnery's are rippling through the world. Access to the Internet has raised awareness of this issue in particular, but of world issues in general, throughout a great deal of the world's population. It is in the US empire where the effects of this dissemination of knowledge about the hitherto little-known (because vastly misrepresented) issue of Palestine and Israel are having the greatest effect.

Following on polls that are finding a growing sympathy for Palestinians, Israel is scrambling to regain its spot as the victim deserving of special treatment. Every trick, from a "rebranding campaign" touting the wonders of being an Ethiopian Israeli soccer player (when Ethiopian Jews face racism in Israel) to the nasty, vicious attacks by groups like Campus Watch on intellectuals speaking a truth about the current nature of the Israeli state, is being vigorously pursued in the attempt to keep Palestinians isolated and powerless. Nonetheless, the situation is changing. World public opinion is shifting. The question is: Will it shift enough, quickly enough, to throw the vicious circle off its course?

The circle must break; the world is reaching a crisis point that cannot entirely be avoided, and the situation in Israel and Palestine is a central issue. How it will play out remains to be seen. I do not agree with all Avnery's positions, most notably his position with regard to the question of one or two states. I tend toward one state because the two peoples are intricately and inextricably entwined on the same land, because the right of return is a moral and legal right, and because I am repelled by the notion of any state built on exclusivity, including the one in which I live.

Concomitantly, I also think that Israelis—many of whom know no other home—cannot and should not be displaced; Palestinian Arabs have no inherent right to exclusivity either. In several of his writings, including a May 2007 piece "One state: solution or Utopia," which concludes Chapter 1, Avnery alludes to an ideal notion of internationalism wherein borders and nationalism are no longer relevant. While agreeing that the notion is idealist, I think ideals are worth working toward. I think Avnery would agree. However, in the world of realpolitik, Avnery argues that the Jewish state is central to most Israelis, and indeed, many Jews worldwide. In addition to the above-mentioned remarks, Avnery's essay "A new consensus," also included in this volume, sheds further light on his position.

Of course, the only tenable peace will have to be arrived at by the parties involved—Israel and Palestine—and the world should support whatever deal the majority of both sides agree to, always providing of course that negotiations are fair. Avnery's voice has always been strong in demanding good faith.

I have great admiration and respect for Avnery's courage, fortitude and unwavering commitment to bringing peace with justice to the troubled peoples of Israel and Palestine. I have endeavored to be true to Avnery in this collection while telling the truth as I see it, too. The footnotes and all commentary outside the original essays are my additions to the work. I hope this collection of his essays contributes to peace in Avnery's home and am honored and grateful to have been given the opportunity to contribute whatever small amount I could. I am especially grateful to Uri Avnery for his work, both written and active, to Roger van Zwanenberg for his trust and encouragement, and to the Washington Report on Middle East Affairs for so much. Further thanks go to Chris Costello who has volunteered many hours to edit Avnery's English translations from his original Hebrew, and who generously sent me copies of some of his work. Any deficiencies within this book, however, are my own. Avnery's voice speaks for itself. I hope here, it speaks to you.

SRP

"Truth Against Truth"
A Completely Different Look at the
Israeli–Palestinian Conflict
An Introduction by Uri Avnery

- The Arabs believed that the Jews had been implanted in Palestine by Western imperialism, in order to subjugate the Arab world. The Zionists, on the other hand, were convinced that the Arab resistance to the Zionist enterprise was simply the consequence of the murderous nature of the Arabs and of Islam.
- The Israeli public must recognize that besides all the positive aspects of the Zionist enterprise, a terrible injustice has been inflicted on the Palestinian people.
- This requires a readiness to hear and understand the other side's position in this historical conflict, in order to bridge the two national experiences and unify them in a joint narrative.

The tyranny of myths

1. The violent confrontation that broke out in October 2000 and was called the "al-Aqsa Intifada" is but another stage of the historical conflict that began with the creation of the Zionist Movement at the end of the nineteenth century.
2. A fifth generation of Israelis and Palestinians has already been born into this conflict. The entire mental and material world of this generation has been shaped by this confrontation, which dominates all spheres of their lives.
3. In the course of this long conflict, as in every war, an enormous mass of myths, historical falsifications, propaganda slogans, and prejudices has accumulated on both sides.
4. The behavior of each of the two sides to the conflict is shaped by their historical narrative, the way they view the history of the conflict over the last 120 years. The Zionist historical version and

7

the Palestinian historical version contradict each other entirely, both in the general picture and in almost every detail.

5.   From the beginning of the conflict up to the present day, the Zionist/Israeli leadership has acted in total disregard of the Palestinian narrative. Even when it wished to reach a solution, such efforts were doomed to failure because of ignorance of the national aspirations, traumas, fears, and hopes of the Palestinian people. Something similar happened on the other side, even if there is no symmetry between the two sides.

6.   The settlement of such a prolonged historical conflict is possible only when each side is able to understand the mental-political world of the other and is ready to speak as equal to equal, "eye to eye." Contemptuous, power-oriented, overbearing, insensitive, and ignorant attitudes prevent an agreed solution.

7.   "Leftist" Israeli governments that, at times, aroused much hope were afflicted with such attitudes as much as "rightist" ones, causing a wide gap between their initial promise and their disastrous performance. (An example is Ehud Barak's term in office.)

8.   A large part of the old peace movement (also known as "the Zionist left" or "the sane camp"), such as Peace Now, is also beset by some of these attitudes, and so collapses in times of crisis.

9.   Therefore, the first task of a new Israeli peace camp is to free itself from false and from one-sided views.

10. This does not mean that the Israeli narrative should automatically be rejected and the Palestinian narrative unquestioningly accepted, or the other way round. But it does require a readiness to hear and understand the other side's position in this historical conflict, in order to bridge the two national experiences and unify them in a joint narrative.

11. Any other way will lead to a perpetuation of the conflict, with periods of ostensible tranquility and conciliation frequently interrupted by violent hostilities between the two nations and between Israel and the Arab world. Given the pace of development of weapons of mass destruction, further rounds of hostility could lead to the annihilation of both sides to the conflict.

The root of the conflict

12. The core of the conflict is the confrontation between the Israeli-Jewish nation and the Palestinian-Arab nation. It is essentially a national conflict, even if it has religious, social, and other aspects.

13. The Zionist Movement was essentially a Jewish reaction to the emergence of the national movements in Europe, all of which were more or less anti-Semitic. Having been rejected by the European nations, some of the Jews decided to establish themselves as a separate nation and, following the new European model, to set up a national state of their own, where they could be masters of their own fate.

14. Traditional and religious motives drew the Zionist Movement to Palestine (*Eretz Israel* in Hebrew) and the decision was made to establish the Jewish state in this land. The maxim was: "A land without a people for a people without a land." This maxim was not only conceived in ignorance, but also reflected the general arrogance towards non-European peoples that prevailed in Europe at that time.

15. Palestine was not an empty land—not at the end of the nineteenth century, nor at any other period. At that time, there were half a million people living in Palestine, 90 percent of them Arabs. This population objected, of course, to the incursion of foreign settlers into their land.

16. The Arab National Movement emerged almost simultaneously with the Zionist Movement, initially to fight the Ottoman Empire and later the colonial regimes built on its ruins at the end of World War I. A separate Arab-Palestinian national movement developed in the country after the British created a separate state called "Palestine," and in the course of the struggle against Zionist infiltration.

17. Since the end of World War I, there has been an ongoing struggle between two national movements, the Jewish-Zionist and the Palestinian-Arab, both of which aspire to accomplish their goals—which are entirely incompatible—within the same territory. This situation remains unchanged to this day.

18. As persecution of the Jews in Europe intensified, and as the countries of the world closed their gates to the Jews attempting to flee the inferno, so the Zionist Movement gained strength. Nazi anti-Semitism turned the Zionist Utopia into a realizable modern enterprise by causing a mass immigration of trained manpower, intellectuals, technology, and capital to Palestine. The Holocaust, which took the lives of about 6 million Jews, gave tremendous moral and political force to the Zionist claim, leading to the establishment of the State of Israel.

19. The Palestinian nation, witnessing the growth of the Jewish population in their land, could not comprehend why they should

be expected to pay the price for crimes committed against the Jews by Europeans. They violently objected to further Jewish immigration and to the acquisition of land by the Jews.

20. The struggle between the two nations in the country appeared in the emotional sphere as the "war of the traumas." The Israeli-Hebrew nation carried with them the old trauma of the persecution of the Jews in Europe: massacres, mass expulsions, the Inquisition, pogroms and the Holocaust. They lived with the consciousness of being an eternal victim. The clash with the Arab-Palestinian nation appeared to them as just a continuation of anti-Semitic persecution.

21. The Arab-Palestinian nation carried with them the memories of the long-lasting colonial oppression, with its insults and humiliations, especially when compared with the background of the historical memories from the glorious days of the Caliphs. They, too, lived with the consciousness of being victims, and the *Nakba* (catastrophe) of 1948 appeared to them as the continuation of the oppression and humiliation by Western colonialists.

22. The complete blindness of each of the two nations to the national existence of the other inevitably led to false and distorted perceptions that took root deep in their collective consciousness. These perceptions continue to affect their attitudes toward each other to the present day.

23. The Arabs believed that the Jews had been implanted in Palestine by Western imperialism, in order to subjugate the Arab world and control its natural resources. This conviction was supported by the fact that the Zionist Movement, from the outset, strove for an alliance with at least one Western power, in order to overcome Arab resistance (Germany in the days of Herzl, Britain from the time of the Uganda plan and the Balfour Declaration until the end of the Mandate, the Soviet Union in 1948, France from the 1950s until the 1967 war, the United States from then on). This resulted in practical cooperation and a community of interests between the Zionist enterprise and imperialist and colonialist powers, directed against the Arab national movement.

24. The Zionists, on the other hand, were convinced that the Arab resistance to the Zionist enterprise—which was intended to save the Jews from the flames of Europe—was simply the consequence of the murderous nature of the Arabs and of Islam. In their eyes, Arab fighters were "gangs," and the uprisings of the time were "riots."

25. Actually, the most extreme Zionist leader, Vladimir (Ze'ev) Jabotinsky, was almost alone in having recognized by the 1920s that the Arab resistance to the Zionist settlement was an inevitable, natural, and, from its own point of view, just reaction of a "native" people defending their country against foreign invaders. Jabotinsky also recognized that the Arabs in the country were a distinct national entity and derided the attempts to bribe the leaders of other Arab countries in order to put an end to the Palestinian Arab resistance. However, Jabotinsky's solution was to erect an "iron wall" against the Arabs and to crush their resistance by force.

26. These completely contradictory perceptions of the facts permeate every single aspect of the conflict. For example, the Jews interpreted their struggle for "Jewish Labor" as a progressive social effort to transform a people of intellectuals, merchants, middlemen, and speculators into one of workers and farmers. The Arabs, on the other hand, saw it as a racist effort by the Zionists to dispossess them, to exclude them from the labor market, and to create on their land an Arab-free, separatist Jewish economy.

27. The Zionists were proud of their "redemption of the land." They had purchased it at full price with money collected from Jews around the world. *Olim* (new immigrants, literally pilgrims), many of whom had been intellectuals and merchants in their former lives, now earned their living by hard manual labor. They believed that they had achieved all this by peaceful means and without dispossessing a single Arab. For the Arabs this was a cruel narrative of dispossession and expulsion: the Jews acquired lands from Arab absentee landowners living in the cities of Palestine and abroad, and then forcibly evicted the peasants who had been farming this land for generations. To help them in this effort, the Zionists engaged the Turkish and, later, the British police. The Arab masses looked on in despair as their land was taken from them.

28. Against the Zionist claim of having successfully "made the desert bloom," the Arabs cited the testimonies of European travelers who had, for several centuries, described Palestine as a comparatively populous and flourishing land, the equal of any of its regional neighbors.

Independence and disaster

29. The contrast between the two national versions reached a peak in the war of 1948, which was called "the War of Independence" or

even "the War of Liberation" by the Jews, and "*al Nakba*," the catastrophe, by the Arabs.

30. As the conflict intensified in the region, and with the resounding impact of the Holocaust, the United Nations decided to divide the country into two states, Jewish and Arab. Jerusalem and its environs were to remain a separate entity, under international jurisdiction. The Jews were allotted 55 percent of the land, including the unpopulated Negev desert.

31. Most of the Zionist Movement accepted the partition resolution, convinced that the crucial issue was to establish a firm foundation for Jewish sovereignty. In closed meetings, David Ben-Gurion never concealed his intention to expand, at the first opportunity, the territory given to the Jews. That is why Israel's Declaration of Independence did not define the state's borders and Israel has not defined its borders to this day.

32. The Arab world did not accept the partition plan and regarded it as a vile attempt by the United Nations, which at the time was essentially a club of Western and Communist nations, to divide a country that did not belong to it. Handing over more than half of the country to the Jewish minority, which comprised a mere third of the population, made it all the more unforgivable in their eyes.

33. The war initiated by the Arabs after the partition plan was, inevitably, an "ethnic" war: a war in which each side seeks to conquer as much land as possible and evict the population of the other side. Such a campaign (which later came to be known as "ethnic cleansing") always involves expulsions and atrocities.

34. The war of 1948 was a direct continuation of the Zionist–Arab conflict, and each side sought to fulfill its historical aims. The Jews wanted to establish a homogeneous national state that would be as large as possible. The Arabs wanted to eradicate the Zionist Jewish entity that had been established in Palestine.

35. Both sides practiced ethnic cleansing as an integral part of the fighting. Almost no Arabs remained in the territories captured by the Jews and no Jews at all remained in territories captured by the Arabs. However, as the territories captured by the Jews were very large while the Arabs managed to conquer only small areas (such as the Etzion Bloc, the Jewish quarter in the Old City of Jerusalem), the result was one-sided. (The ideas of "population exchange" and "transfer" were raised in Zionist organizations as early as the 1930s. Effectively this meant the expulsion of the Arab population from the country. On the other side, many

among the Arabs believed that the Zionists should go back to wherever they came from.)

What happened in 1948 was an "ethnic" war, as described above.

36. The myth of "the few against the many" was created on the Jewish side to describe the stand of the Jewish community of 650,000 against the entire Arab world of over 100 million. The Jewish community lost 1 percent of its people in the war. The Arab side saw an entirely different picture: a fragmented Arab population with no national leadership to speak of, with no unified command over its meager forces, poorly equipped with mostly obsolete weapons, facing an extremely well-organized Jewish community that was highly trained in the use of the weapons that were flowing to it (especially from the Soviet bloc). The neighboring Arab countries betrayed the Palestinians, and when they finally did send their armies into Palestine, they mainly operated in competition with each other, with no coordination and no common plan. From the social and military points of view, the fighting capabilities of the Israeli side were far superior to those of the Arab states, which had hardly emerged from the colonial era.

37. According to the United Nations plan, the Jewish state was supposed to receive 55 percent of Palestine, in which the Arabs would constitute almost half of the population. During the war, the Jewish state expanded its territory and ended up with 78 percent of the area of Palestine, which was left almost empty of Arabs. The Arab populations of Nazareth and some villages in the Galilee area remained almost by chance; the villages in the Triangle were given to Israel as part of a deal by King Abdullah of Trans-Jordan, and their Arab inhabitants could not, therefore, be driven out.

38. In the war, some 750,000 Palestinians were uprooted. Some of them found themselves in the battle zone and fled, as civilians do in every war. Some were driven away by acts of terror, such as the Deir-Yassin massacre.[2] Others were systematically expelled in the course of the ethnic cleansing.

39. No less important than the expulsion itself is the fact that the refugees were not allowed to return to their homes when the fighting was over, as is usual after a conventional war. Quite the contrary, the new State of Israel saw the removal of the Arabs very much as a blessing and proceeded to completely erase some 450 Arab villages. New Jewish villages were built on the ruins, often

adopting a Hebrew version of the former name. The abandoned neighborhoods in the towns were filled with masses of new immigrants. In Israeli textbooks, all mention of the former inhabitants was eliminated.

A Jewish state

40. The signing of the armistice agreements at the beginning of 1949 did not put an end to the historical conflict. On the contrary, it raised it to a new and more intense level.

41. The new State of Israel dedicated its early years to the consolidation of its character as a homogeneous "Jewish state." Huge areas of land were expropriated from the "absentees" (the refugees who were not allowed back), from those officially designated as "present absentees" (Arabs who had stayed in Israel but were not accorded Israeli citizenship) and even from the Arab citizens of Israel, most of whose lands were taken over. On these lands, a dense network of Jewish communities was created. Jewish immigrants were invited and even induced to come en masse. This great effort increased the state's population several times over in just a few years.

42. At the same time, the state pursued a vigorous policy of obliterating the Palestinian national entity. With Israeli assistance, the monarch of Trans-Jordan, Abdullah, assumed control over the West Bank and since then there has been, in effect, an Israeli military guarantee for the existence of what became the Hashemite Kingdom of Jordan.

43. The main rationale for the alliance between Israel and the Hashemite Kingdom, which has already existed for three generations, is to prevent the establishment of an independent and viable Palestinian state, which was—and still is—considered by the Israeli leadership a potential obstacle to the realization of the Zionist objective.

44. A historic change occurred at the end of the 1950s on the Palestinian side when Yassir Arafat and his associates founded the Palestinian Liberation Movement (Fatah), not only to conduct the fight against Israel but also to free the Palestinian cause from the hegemony of the Arab governments. It was no accident that this movement emerged after the failure of the great pan-Arab wave, whose most renowned representative was Gamal Abd-el-Nasser. Up to this point many Palestinians had hoped to be absorbed into a united pan-Arab nation. When this hope faded away, the separate national Palestinian identity reasserted itself.

45. In the early 1960s, Gamal Abd-el-Nasser set up the Palestinian Liberation Organization (PLO), mainly in order to forestall independent Palestinian actions that might involve him in an undesired war with Israel. The organization was intended to impose Egyptian control on the Palestinians. However, after the Arab debacle in the June 1967 war, Fatah, under Yassir Arafat, took control over the PLO, which has been the sole representative of the Palestinian people ever since.

The Six-Day War

46. Like everything else that has happened in the last 120 years, the June 1967 war is seen in a very different light by the two sides. According to the Israeli myth, it was a desperate war of defense, which miraculously left a lot of land in Israel's hands. According to the Palestinian myth, Israel drew the leaders of Egypt, Syria, and Jordan into a war Israel was interested in, which was aimed right from the beginning at capturing what was left of Palestine.

47. Many Israelis believe that the "Six-Day War" is the root of all evil and that it was only then that the peace-loving and progressive Israel turned into a conqueror and an occupier. This conviction allows them to maintain the absolute purity of Zionism and the State of Israel up to that point in history, and preserve their old myths. There is no truth to this legend.

48. The war of 1967 was yet another phase of the old struggle between the two national movements. It did not change the essence; it only changed the circumstances. The essential objectives of the Zionist Movement—a Jewish state, expansion, and settlement—were furthered by the addition of yet more territory. The particular circumstances of this war made complete ethnic cleansing impossible, but several hundred thousand Palestinians were nevertheless expelled.

49. The 1947 partition plan allotted to Israel 55 percent of Palestine; an additional 23 percent was captured in the 1948 war and now the remaining 22 percent, across the "Green Line" (the pre-1967 armistice line), was also captured. In 1967 Israel inadvertently united under its rule all the parts of the Palestinian people that remained in the country (including some of the refugees).

50. As soon as the war ended, the movement to settle the occupied territories began. Almost all the Israeli political factions participated in this movement, from the messianic-nationalistic "Gush Emunim" to the "leftist" United Kibbutz Movement. The

first settlers were supported by most politicians, left and right, from Yigal Alon (advocate of the Jewish settlement in Hebron) to Shimon Peres (the Kedumim settlement).

51. The fact that all governments of Israel cultivated and advanced the settlements, albeit to different extents, proves that the urge to implant new settlements was particular to no specific ideological camp and extended to the entire Zionist Movement. The impression that only a small minority has been driving the settlement activity forward is an illusion. Only an intense effort of all parts of the government, including all ministries, from 1967 onwards, could have produced the legislative, strategic, and budgetary infrastructure required for such a long-lasting and expensive endeavor.

52. The legislative infrastructure operates on the misleading assumption that the Occupation Authority is the owner of "government-owned lands," although these are the essential land reserves of the Palestinian population. It goes without saying that the settlement activity contravenes international law.

53. The dispute between the proponents of "Greater Israel" and those of "territorial compromise" is essentially a dispute about the way to achieve the shared basic Zionist aspiration: a homogeneous Jewish state in as large a territory as possible, but without a "ticking demographic bomb." The proponents of "compromise" emphasize the demographic issue and want to prevent the inclusion of the Palestinian population in the Israeli state. The "Greater Israel" adherents place the emphasis on the geographic issue and believe—privately or publicly—that it is possible to expel the non-Jewish population from the country (code name: "Transfer").

54. The general staff of the Israeli army played an important role in the planning and building of the settlements. It created the map of the settlements (identified with Ariel Sharon): blocs of settlements and bypass roads along lateral and longitudinal axes, chopping the West Bank and the Gaza Strip into pieces and imprisoning the Palestinians in isolated enclaves, each of which is surrounded by settlements and the occupation forces.

55. The Palestinians employed several methods of resistance, mainly raids across the Jordanian and Lebanese borders and attacks inside Israel and throughout the world. These acts are considered "terror" by Israelis, while the Palestinians see them as the legitimate resistance of an occupied people. While the Israelis considered the PLO leadership, headed by Yassir Arafat, as a

terrorist headquarters, it gradually came to be internationally recognized as the "sole legitimate representative" of the Palestinian people.

56. At the end of 1987, when the Palestinians realized that these actions were not putting an end to the settlement momentum, which was gradually pulling the land out from under their feet, they launched the intifada: a spontaneous grassroots uprising of all sectors of the population. In this ("first") intifada, 1,500 Palestinians were killed, among them hundreds of children; these casualties amounted to several times the number of Israeli losses, but the intifada put the "Palestinian problem" back on the Israeli and international agenda.

The peace process

57. The October 1973 war, which commenced with the surprise initial successes of the Egyptian and Syrian forces and ended with their defeat, convinced Yassir Arafat and his close associates that the realization of Palestinian national aspirations by military means was impossible. He decided to create a political option that would lead to an agreement with Israel and enable the Palestinians, through negotiations, to establish an independent state in at least a part of the country.

The urge to implant new settlements was particular to no specific ideological camp and extended to the entire Zionist Movement. It was an intense effort of all parts of the government.

58. To prepare the ground for this, Arafat initiated contact with Israeli personalities who could influence public opinion and government policy. His emissaries (Said Hamami and Issam Sartawi) met with Israeli peace pioneers, who at the end of 1975 established the "Israeli Council for Israeli-Palestinian Peace."

59. These contacts, which gradually became more extensive, as well as the growing Israeli fatigue with the intifada, the official Jordanian disengagement from the West Bank, the changing international situation (the collapse of the Communist Bloc, the Gulf War) led to the Madrid Conference and, later, to the Oslo Agreement.

The Oslo Agreement

60. The Oslo Agreement had positive and negative features.

61. On the positive side, the agreement brought Israel to its first official recognition of the Palestinian people and its national

leadership, and brought the Palestinian national movement to its recognition of the existence of Israel. In this respect, the agreement—and the exchange of letters that preceded it—were of paramount historical significance.

62. In effect, the agreement gave the Palestinian national movement a territorial base on Palestinian soil, the structure of a "state in the making," and armed forces: facts that would play an important role in the ongoing Palestinian struggle. For the Israelis, the agreement opened the gates to the Arab world and put an end to Palestinian attacks, as long as the agreement was effective.

63. The most substantive flaw in the agreement was that the final aim was not spelled out, allowing the two sides to continue to aim for entirely different objectives. The Palestinians saw the interim agreement as a highway to the end of the occupation and to the establishment of a Palestinian state in all the occupied territories (which altogether constitute 22 percent of the area of the former Palestine between the Mediterranean Sea and the Jordan River). On the other hand, successive Israeli governments regarded it as a way to maintain the occupation in large sections of the West Bank and the Gaza Strip, with the Palestinian "self-government" filling the role of an auxiliary security agency protecting Israel and the settlements.

64. Since the final aim was not defined, the Oslo agreement did not mark the beginning of the process to end the conflict but, rather, a new phase of the conflict.

65. Because the expectations of both sides were so divergent and each remained entirely bound to its own national "narrative," every section of the agreement was interpreted differently. Ultimately, many parts of the agreement were left unimplemented, mainly by Israel (for example, the third withdrawal and the four safe passages between the West Bank and the Gaza Strip).

66. Throughout the period of the "Oslo Process," Israel continued its vigorous expansion of the settlements, primarily by creating new settlements under various guises, expanding existing ones, building an elaborate network of "bypass" roads, expropriating land, demolishing houses, uprooting plantations and other measures. The Palestinians, for their part, used the time to build up their strength, both within the framework of the agreement and outside it. In fact, the historical confrontation continued unabated under the guise of negotiations and the "peace process," which became a substitute for actual peace.

67. In contradiction to his image, which was cultivated extensively

after his assassination, Yitzhak Rabin continued furthering expansion "on the ground," while simultaneously engaging in the political process for the achievement of peace according to Israeli perceptions. As a disciple of the Zionist "narrative" and its mythology, he suffered from cognitive dissonance when his sincere desire for peace clashed with his conceptual world. This became apparent when he refrained from removing the Jewish settlement in Hebron after the Goldstein massacre of praying Muslims. It appears that he began to internalize some parts of the Palestinian narrative only towards the end of his life.

68. The case of Shimon Peres is much more damning. He created for himself the international image of a peacemaker and even adjusted his language to reflect this image ("the New Middle East") while remaining essentially a traditional Zionist hawk.

   This became clear in his short and bloody period as Prime Minister after the assassination of Rabin in 1995 and, again, in his joining the Sharon government in 2001 and accepting the role of spokesman and apologist for Sharon.

69. The clearest expression of the Israeli dilemma was provided by Ehud Barak, who came to power thoroughly convinced of his ability to cut the Gordian knot of the historical conflict in one dramatic stroke, in the fashion of Alexander the Great. Barak approached the issue in total ignorance of the Palestinian narrative, showing utter contempt for its significance. He drew up his proposals in complete disregard of the Palestinian side and presented them as an ultimatum. He was shocked and enraged when the Palestinians rejected them.

70. In his own eyes and in the eyes of the entire Israeli public, Barak "turned every stone" and made the Palestinians "more generous offers than any previous Prime Minister." In exchange, he demanded that the Palestinians sign a declaration that these offers constitute the "end to the conflict." The Palestinians considered this absurd, since Barak was asking them to give up their basic national aspirations, such as the right of return and sovereignty over East Jerusalem, including the Temple Mount. Moreover, the annexation of territories that were presented by Barak as negligible percentages (such as the "Settlement Blocs") amounted, according to Palestinian calculations, to an actual annexation of 20 percent of the West Bank to Israel.

71. In the Palestinian view, they had already made their decisive concession by agreeing to establish their state beyond the Green Line, in a mere 22 percent of their historical homeland. Therefore,

they would only accept minor border changes in the context of territorial swaps. The traditional Israeli position is that the territories acquired by it in the course of the 1948 war were beyond dispute, and the required compromise concerns only the remaining 22 percent.

72. Thus, as with most terms and concepts, the word "concession" has different meanings for the two sides. The Palestinians believe that they already "conceded" 78 percent of their land when they agreed in Oslo to accept a mere 22 percent of it. The Israelis believe that they are "conceding" when they agree to "give" the Palestinians parts of that 22 percent.

Camp David, 2000: ignorance and arrogance

As a result of Camp David, the dividing line between the Zionist "right" and "left" almost disappeared. The slogan "We have no partner" was adopted by all.

73. Things came to a head at the Camp David Summit in the summer of 2000, which was imposed on Arafat against his will and without any time for preparations. Barak's demands, presented at the summit as Clinton's, were that the Palestinians agree to end the conflict by relinquishing the right of return and any return of refugees to Israel, accept complicated arrangements for East Jerusalem and the Temple Mount without obtaining sovereignty over them, agree to the annexation by Israel of large settlement blocs on the West Bank and the Gaza Strip, accept an Israeli military presence in other large areas (such as the Jordan valley), and agree to Israeli control over the borders between the Palestinian state and the rest of the world. There was no possibility that any Palestinian leader could sign such an agreement and convince his people to accept it, and thus the summit ended without results. Soon after, the careers of Clinton and Barak also came to an end, while Arafat was received by the Palestinians as a hero who had withstood the pressure of Clinton and Barak and not surrendered.

The al-Aqsa Intifada

74. The breakdown of the summit, the elimination of any hope for an agreement between the two sides and the unconditional pro-Israeli stance of the United States inevitably led to another round of violent confrontations, which became known as "the al-Aqsa Intifada." For the Palestinians, it is a justified national uprising

against a protracted occupation with no end in sight that has allowed the continued pulling out of their land from under their feet. For the Israelis, it is an outburst of murderous terrorism. The perpetrators of these attacks appear to the Palestinians as national heroes and to the Israelis as vicious criminals who must be liquidated.

75. The official media in Israel frequently dropped the term "settlers" and, by command from above, started to refer to them as "residents," so that any attack on them looked like a crime against civilians. The Palestinians see the settlers as the spearhead of a dangerous enemy who is dispossessing them of their land, and who must be resisted and attacked.

76. In the course of the al-Aqsa Intifada, a large part of the Israeli "Peace Camp" collapsed, demonstrating the shallow-rootedness of many of its convictions. Since it never undertook a real revision of the Zionist narrative and never internalized the fact that there exists a Palestinian narrative, too, it found the Palestinian behavior quite inexplicable, especially after Barak had "turned every stone and made more generous offers than any previous Prime Minister." The only remaining explanation was that the Palestinians had deceived the Israeli Peace Camp, that they had never really intended to make peace and that their true purpose is to throw the Jews into the sea, as the Zionist right has always claimed. The conclusion: "We have no partner."

77. As a result, the dividing line between the Zionist "right" and "left" almost disappeared. The leaders of the Labor Party joined the Sharon Government and became his most effective apologists (as did Shimon Peres for example) and even the formal leftist opposition became ineffective. This proved again that the original Zionist narrative is the decisive factor unifying all parts of the political system in Israel, making the differences between them lose their significance in times of crisis.

78. The al-Aqsa Intifada (also called the "Second Intifada") raised the intensity of the conflict to a new level. In its first three years, about 2,600 Palestinians and 800 Israelis were killed. The Israeli military operations turned the lives of the Palestinians into hell, cut towns and villages off from each other, destroyed their economy and brought many to the verge of hunger. The extra-judicial execution of Palestinian militants ("targeted liquidations"), often killing civilian bystanders, became routine. Incursions into Palestinian towns and villages, in order to kill or arrest suspects, also became daily occurrences.

Yassir Arafat, the leader of the Palestinian liberation struggle, effectively imprisoned in his Ramallah compound (the "Mukata'ah") under constant threat to his life, became the supreme symbol of the resistance to the occupation.

79. Contrary to the expectations of the Israeli military and political leadership, the extreme military and economic pressure did not break the Palestinian population. Even in the most extreme circumstances, they managed to maintain some semblance of normal life and found means to fight back. The most effective and appalling weapon was the suicide bombing, which brought the bloody confrontation into the center of Israeli cities. The intifada also caused other damage to Israel, paralyzing tourism and stopping foreign investment, deepening the depression, causing the national economy to contract and social services to collapse, thereby widening the social gap and increasing domestic tensions in Israel

80. As a response to the attacks, and especially the suicide bombings, which had a severe impact on public morale, the leaders of the "Zionist Left" demanded a physical barrier between Israel and the Palestinian territories. At first, the "Zionist right" opposed this "Separation Fence," fearing that it would create a political border in close proximity to the Green Line. But Ariel Sharon soon realized that he could exploit the idea of the fence for his own purposes. He started to build the barrier along a path that was in accord with his aims, cutting deep into the Palestinian territories, joining the large settlement blocs to Israel and confining the Palestinians in isolated enclaves, under effective Israeli control.

81. By the end of the third year of the al-Aqsa Intifada, definite signs of war fatigue, as well as opposition to the growing brutality of the occupation, could be detected among the Israeli public. Such indications included the refusal movement among youngsters called up for army service, the revolt of 27 air-force pilots, the refusal of the elite general staff commando unit to take part in "illegal and immoral" operations, the joint statement made by four former security service chiefs against the continuation of the occupation, the publication of the peace principles of Sari Nusseibeh and Ami Ayalon, the Geneva Initiative of Yossi Beilin and Yassir Abed-Rabbo, the ongoing struggle against the Separation Wall, and the change of positions and style of politicians and commentators.

82. Following the US invasion of Iraq at the beginning of 2003, the United States became more sensitive to the negative consequences

of the Israeli–Palestinian conflict. Owing to the domestic pressures exerted in the United States by the powerful Jewish and Fundamentalist Christian lobbies, which have a lot of influence in George W. Bush's White House, the ability of the American administration to work for a solution is very limited. In spite of this, a "Quartet" consisting of the United States, the European Union, Russia, and the UN succeeded in presenting a so-called "Roadmap to Peace."

83. The Roadmap of 2003 is afflicted with the same basic fault as the Oslo Declaration of Principles of 1993. Although, unlike Oslo, it does define an aim ("Two states for two peoples"), it does not spell out where the borders of the future Palestinian state are going to be, thus emptying the "map" of its principal meaning. Ariel Sharon was able to accept the Roadmap (with 14 reservations that emptied it of its main content) since he was quite ready to confer the designation of "Palestinian state" on the Palestinian enclaves that he wants to set up in 10 percent of the country.

84. The Oslo experience, and of course the new experiment of the Roadmap, confirm conclusively that a document that sets out interim stages is valueless unless it clearly spells out from the outset the details of the final peace agreement. In the absence of such a definition, there is no possibility at all that the interim stages will be realized. When each side is striving for a different final aim, the confrontation is bound to flare up again at every interim stage.

85. Well knowing that there is no chance at all for the actual realization of the Roadmap, Sharon announced at the end of 2003 his plan for "unilateral steps." This is a code-name for the annexation of about half of the West Bank to Israel and the confining of the Palestinians in isolated enclaves, connected only by roads, tunnels, and bridges that can be cut off at any time. The plan is constructed in such a way that none of the Palestinian population will be added to Israel, and no land reserves remain for the Palestinian enclaves. Since the plan does not require any negotiation with the Palestinians, but claims to bring "peace and security" to the Israeli citizens, it is able to exploit the growing Israeli longing for a solution without disturbing any Israeli's prejudices and hatred against the Palestinians.

86. The general attack of the Sharon government and the army leadership on the population in the occupied territories (extension of the settlements, establishment of new settlements called

"outposts," building the "separation fence" and settler-only
"bypass roads," incursions of the army into Palestinian towns,
"targeted liquidations," demolition of homes, and uprooting of
plantations), on the one hand, and the lethal Palestinian attacks
inside Israel on the other hand, put the Palestinian citizens of
Israel in an intolerable position.

87. The natural inclination of the Arab citizens of Israel to help their
brethren on the other side of the Green Line conflicts with their
desire to be accepted as equal citizens of Israel. At the same time,
the fear and hatred of the Jewish population in Israel against all
"Arabs" is growing, and threatens the foundations of equality and
civil rights. These processes came to a head in the events of
October 2000, immediately after the outbreak of the al-Aqsa
Intifada, when the Israeli police opened lethal fire on Arab
citizens.

88. These processes, together with the re-emergence of the
"demographic problem" on the Israeli agenda, cast new doubt on
the "Jewish democratic state" doctrine. The internal
contradiction between these two attributes, which has not been
resolved since the founding of the State of Israel either in theory
or in practice, is more conspicuous than ever. The exact meaning
of the term "Jewish state" has never been spelled out, nor the
status of the Arab-Palestinian minority in a state officially defined
as "Jewish." The demand to turn Israel into a "state of all its
citizens" and/or to give defined national rights to the Arab-
Palestinian minority is being heard more and more, and not only
from Arab citizens.

89. As a result of all these processes, the conflict is becoming less and
less an Israeli–Palestinian confrontation, and more and more a
Jewish–Arab one. The support extended by the vast majority of
the Jewish Diaspora to Israel, irrespective of its actions, and the
adherence of the Arab and Muslim masses to the Palestinian
cause, irrespective of the attitude of their leaders, have
consolidated this phenomenon. The assassination of Hamas
leaders Sheikh Ahmed Yassin in March 2003 and Abd-al-Aziz
al-Rantisi three weeks later fanned the flames even more.

A new peace camp

90. The new peace movement must be based on the understanding
that the conflict is a clash between the Zionist-Israeli movement,
whose "genetic code" directs it to take over the entire country and

to drive out the non-Jewish population, and the Palestinian national movement, whose "genetic code" directs it to halt this drive and set up a Palestinian state in the entire country. This can be seen as the clash between "an irresistible force" and an "immovable object."

91. The task of the Israeli peace movement is to stop the historical clash, overcome the Zionist-Israeli "genetic code," and cooperate with the Palestinian peace forces, in order to enable a peace through historic compromise that will lead to reconciliation between the two peoples. The Palestinian peace forces have a similar task.

92. For this, diplomatic formulations of a future peace agreement are insufficient. The Israeli peace movement must be inspired by a new spirit that will touch the hearts of the other people, create faith in the possibility of peace and win the hearts of the Israeli sectors that are held captive by the old myths and prejudices. The peace movement must address the hearts and the minds of the entire Israeli public.

93. The small and consistent Israeli peace movements that held on and continued the struggle, when most of the peace camp collapsed in the wake of the Camp David debacle and the outbreak of the al-Aqsa Intifada, must play a decisive role in this process.

94. These movements can be likened to a small wheel with an autonomous drive which turns a bigger wheel, which in turn activates an even bigger wheel, and so on, until the whole machinery springs into action. All the past achievements of the Israeli peace forces were attained that way, such as Israeli recognition of the existence of the Palestinian people, the wide public acceptance of the idea of a Palestinian state, the readiness to start negotiations with the PLO, to compromise on Jerusalem, and so on.

95. The new peace camp must lead public opinion towards a brave reassessment of the national "narrative" and rid it of falsities. It must sincerely strive to unite the historical versions of both peoples into a single "narrative," free from historical deceptions and acceptable to both sides.

96. While doing this, it must also help the Israeli public to recognize that, besides all the great and positive aspects of the Zionist enterprise, a terrible injustice has been inflicted on the Palestinian people. This injustice, most extreme during the *Nakba*, obliges us to assume responsibility and correct as much of it as possible.

97. A peace agreement is valueless unless both sides are able to accept

it in spirit and in practice, in as much as it satisfies the basic national aspirations and does not offend national dignity and honor.

98. In the existing situation, there is no solution but the one based on the principle of "Two states for two peoples," meaning peaceful coexistence in two independent states, Israel and Palestine.

99. The idea voiced sometimes that it is possible and desirable to replace the two-state with a one-state solution in all the territory between the Mediterranean Sea and the Jordan, either as a bi-national or non-national state, is unrealistic. The vast majority of Israelis will not agree to the dismantling of the State of Israel, much as the vast majority of Palestinians will not give up the establishment of a national state of their own. This illusion is also dangerous, since it undermines the struggle for the two-state solution, which can be realized in the foreseeable future, in favor of an idea that has no chance of realization in the coming decades. This illusion can also be misused as a pretext for the existence and extension of the settlements. If a joint state were set up, it would become a battlefield, with one side fighting to establish its supremacy by the expulsion of the other side.

100. The new peace camp must formulate a peace plan based on the following principles:

   a. The occupation will come to an end. An independent and viable Palestinian state will be established alongside Israel.

   b. The Green Line will be the border between the State of Israel and the State of Palestine. Limited exchanges of territory will be possible only by mutual agreement, arrived at in free negotiations, and on the basis of 1:1.

   c. All Israeli settlers will be evacuated from the territory of the State of Palestine, and the settlements turned over to returning refugees.

   d. The border between the two states will be open to the movement of people and goods, subject to arrangements made by mutual agreement.

   e. Jerusalem will be the capital of both states. West Jerusalem will be the capital of Israel and East Jerusalem the capital of Palestine. The State of Palestine will have complete sovereignty over East Jerusalem, including the *Haram al-Sharif* (Temple Mount). The State of Israel will have complete sovereignty over West Jerusalem, including the Western Wall and the Jewish Quarter. The two states will reach agreement on the unity of the city at the municipal level.

f. Israel will recognize, in principle, the right of return of the Palestinian refugees as an inalienable human right, and assume moral responsibility for its part in the creation of the problem. A Committee of Truth and Reconciliation will establish the historic facts in an objective way. The solution of the problem will be achieved by agreement based on just, fair, and practical considerations and will include return to the territory of the State of Palestine, return of a limited and agreed number to the territory of Israel, payment of compensation, and settlement in other countries.

g. The water resources will be controlled jointly and allocated by agreement, equally and fairly.

h. A security pact between the two states will ensure the security of both and take into consideration the specific security needs of both Israel and Palestine. The agreement will be endorsed by the international community and reinforced by international guarantees.

i. Israel and Palestine will cooperate with other states in the region for the establishment of a regional community, modeled on the European Union.

j. The entire region will be made free from weapons of mass destruction.

101. The signing of the peace agreement and its honest implementation in good faith will lead to an end of the historic conflict and the reconciliation between the two peoples, based on equality, mutual respect, and the striving for maximum cooperation.

1
In the Beginning:
The Basis of Avnery's Thought

The ideas and experience that form Avnery's perspective of Israel and its place vis-à-vis the Palestinians, the region and the world, are predicated on his basic principles of post-Zionism, nationalism and humanism, colored by the events of history—including those in which he has participated. The following articles inform his thought and action.—SRP.

Uri Avnery's Speech

November 22, 2003

(Instead of my usual weekly article, this time I am posting my acceptance speech on receiving, together with Sari Nusseibeh, the Lev Kopelev prize. The award ceremony took place last week in Cologne, Germany.)

Ladies and Gentlemen,
The Ambassador of Palestine and the former Ambassador of Israel,
(I am sorry that I am unable to greet the present Israeli Ambassador, since he did not see fit to attend,)
Dear friends,

Every time I stand on German soil, I ask myself: What and where would I be now, if Adolf Hitler had never been?

Would I be standing here with Sari Nusseibeh? Would I be an Israeli at all?

I was born not far from here, in Beckum, Westphalia. My grandfather, Josef Ostermann, was the teacher of the small Jewish community there.

But my family originally came from the Rhineland. My mother once told me the name of the place, but I have forgotten it. Now there is no one left to ask.

My father, who attended the "humanist" high school where Latin was taught as the first foreign language, always maintained that we had come to Germany with Julius Caesar. However, no archaeological proof of this has yet been uncovered.

The family was steeped in German culture. My father, an enthusiastic music lover, adored Brahms and Beethoven. His favorite piece was the overture to Wagner's *Meistersinger*. No work of classic German literature was missing from our bookshelves, and I had read almost all of them before my 15th birthday.

Father knew both parts of Goethe's *Faust* by heart. When he was engaged to my mother in 1913, he stipulated that before the wedding she must learn the first part of *Faust* by heart. Mother's condition was that my father must learn to play tennis. They both fulfilled the conditions, but a day after the wedding my mother forgot every word of *Faust* and my father never played tennis again.

What caused this family, the family Ostermann, to leave Germany in 1933 forever, and to go to a far-away, foreign country, the country of the Nusseibeh family?

One word: anti-Semitism.

It is true that my father had always been a Zionist. He was nine years old when the First Zionist Congress took place. The idea excited him. As a wedding gift he received a document confirming that a tree had been planted in Palestine in his name. But he never imagined that he himself would one day go there.

(A joke current at the time: "What is a Zionist? A Jew who takes the money of a second Jew in order to send a third Jew to Palestine.")

The Zionists were then a minuscule minority in the German Jewish communities. Among our relatives it was said that my father had become a Zionist only because he had a contrary disposition. (It seems to run in the family.)

Shortly after the Nazis' rise to power, my father decided to emigrate. The immediate cause was small. My father was a court-appointed receiver of bankrupt businesses. His honesty was proverbial; he was "straight as a die." One day, during a session of the court, a young lawyer cried out: "Jews like you are not needed here any more!" My father was deeply offended, and from that moment Germany was finished for him. I still believe that a feeling of insult played a large part in the divorce between the Jews and Germany.

Where to? For a short while, Finland and the Philippines were considered. But Zionist romanticism decided the issue. We went to Palestine, and since then, the destiny of my family has been irrevocably intertwined with the destiny of the Nusseibeh family. I was then ten years old.

When my father went to police headquarters to give notice of our departure, as required by law, the police officer exclaimed: "But Mr Ostermann, what has entered your head? After all, you are a German like me!"

I tell this story frequently, in order to warn my Palestinian friends not to be tempted to consider the anti-Semites as their allies. On the surface it seems logical: the anti-Semites hate the Jews, the Jews are the majority in Israel, Israel oppresses the Palestinians, so the anti-Semites must be the friends of the Palestinians.

Nothing could be further from the truth.

Without anti-Semitism, Zionism would never have been born. True, the Zionist myth asserts that in every generation the Jews were longing for Palestine, but any such longing was limited to prayers. As a matter of fact, throughout the centuries, the Jews made not the slightest effort to gather in Palestine.

A small example: 511 years ago, half a million Jews were expelled from Christian Spain. Most of them settled somewhere in the Muslim Ottoman empire, which received them graciously. They settled down in countries like Morocco, Bulgaria, Greece, and Syria. But only a tiny handful of Rabbis settled in Palestine, then a remote corner of the Turkish Sultan's domains.

Muslims turn in prayer to Mecca, Jews turn in prayer to Jerusalem. But that has nothing to do with the Zionist idea of a Jewish state.

Modern political Zionism was clearly a reaction to the modern anti-Semitism of the national movements in Europe. It is no coincidence that the term "anti-Semitism," which was coined in Germany in 1879, was followed only a few years later by the word "Zionism," which was first used by a Vienna-born Jew, Nathan Birnbaum.[3]

It was a response to the challenge. If the new national movements in Europe, practically without exception, did not want to have anything to do with the Jews, then the Jews must constitute themselves as a nation in the European sense and found their own state.

Where? In the land of the Bible, then called Palestine.

Thus started the historic conflict between our two peoples, the people of Sari Nusseibeh and my people, a conflict that is today—in 2003—more vicious than ever.[4] It began when the Zionists wanted to realize their aim, to save the Jews from Europe, and the Palestinian Arabs wanted to realize their aim, to achieve freedom and independence in their homeland, in the same little country, without having any idea of each other.

Theodor Herzl, the founder of the modern Zionist Movement, wrote in his diary, after the First Zionist Congress in Basel in 1897: "In

Basel I founded the Jewish state." At the time he had never been to Palestine, he had no idea who lived there. A fellow activist coined the memorable phrase: "A land without a people for a people without a land."[5] For them, Palestine was empty, uninhabited.

But the grandfather of Sari Nusseibeh was living in Palestine at the time, together with another half million Arabs. They had no idea—and could have no idea—that somewhere in Switzerland, in a town they probably had never heard of, a meeting was taking place whose results would change forever their own fate and the fate of their children and grandchildren, their family, their town, their village, and their country.

Anti-Semitism set Zionism in motion, the Holocaust lent it tremendous moral power; even today it sends masses of Jews from Russia, Argentina, and France to Israel.

The Palestinians have many enemies—but none is as dangerous as anti-Semitism. If in some Arab countries an effort is made to import this foreign anti-Semitism from Europe, it is a fateful mistake.

Sari Nusseibeh and I, two Semites who speak closely related Semitic languages, must be allies in the battle against this old–new mental disease. I believe that we are.

I want to add at once: the curse of anti-Semitism must not be abused in order to choke every criticism of my state. We Israelis want to be a people like any other people, a state like every other state, to be measured by the same moral standards as others.

Yes, here, in Germany, too.

No *Sonderbehandlung*, please.[6]

The conflict has now been going on for more than a hundred years. On both sides, a fifth generation has been born into it, a generation whose whole mental world has been shaped by it. Fear, hatred, prejudices, stereotypes, and distrust fill this world.

We are standing on the edge of an abyss, and in both peoples there are leaders who command: "Forward, march!"

We are here because we want to save our peoples from this abyss, because we want to show them another way.

The state of Israel exists; nobody can throw us into the sea. The Palestinian people exist; nobody can push them out into the desert. Our Prime Minister, Ariel Sharon, wants to turn all of Palestine into a Jewish state. Muslim fundamentalists, like the Hamas and Islamic Jihad movements, want to include all of Palestine in a Muslim state. That is the direct route to catastrophe.

We both believe in peace and reconciliation between our two peoples. Not only do we believe in it, we work and struggle for it, each in his own way.

Together we have taken part in many actions. On New Year's Eve 2001, we marched together, arm in arm, through the alleys of the Old City of Jerusalem, at the head of a large group of Muslims, Christians, and Jews. But our main task is to convince our own peoples that peace and reconciliation are possible, that on both sides there is a readiness to pay the price of peace.

These are not abstract aspirations. Gush Shalom, the Israeli peace bloc to which I belong, published a peace agreement in all its details in 2001. Not long ago, Sari Nusseibeh, together with the former Israeli security service chief, Ami Ayalon, articulated the principles of a peaceful solution. Now a new group of Israeli and Palestinian politicians has worked out in Geneva the draft of a peace treaty.

The bloody confrontation that has been raging in our country for three years now is a symptom of hopelessness, frustration, and despair on both sides. Of course, there can be no symmetry between occupiers and occupied, rulers and ruled. The violence of the occupation cannot be compared with the violence of the resistance. But the hopelessness and distrust on both sides is comparable, and our task is to overcome it.

We follow the age-old wisdom: "Don't curse the darkness; light a candle." Together with our partners, the thousands of peace activists of both peoples, we have already lighted a lot of candles.

I am an optimist. I believe that the darkness of despair is slowly giving way to the twilight of hope; that it is getting lighter. In Israel, the conviction is gaining ground that the shedding of blood leads nowhere.

Thirty of our combat pilots refuse to follow immoral orders. The number of conscientious objectors among our soldiers is growing. The chief of staff, until recently an extreme hawk, has talked back to his superiors and declared that there is no military solution. The Geneva peace talks have had an impact; they show that there are indeed partners for peace. Parents of fallen soldiers protest publicly against the senseless sacrificing of their children.

A new wind is blowing. A new hope is emerging. We shall do everything possible to make this hope grow, in order to bring about a historic change.

Omelets into Eggs

November 24, 2007

I was awakened from deep sleep by the noise. There was a commotion outside, which was getting louder by the minute. The shouts of excited people. An eruption of joy.

I stuck my nose outside the door of my Haifa hotel room. I was told enthusiastically that the United Nations General Assembly had just decided to partition the country.

I went back into my room and closed the door behind me. I had no desire to join the celebrations.

November 29, 1947—a day that changed our lives forever.

At this historic moment, how could I feel lonely, alienated, and most of all—sad?

I was sad because I love all of this country—Nablus and Hebron no less than Tel-Aviv and Rosh-Pina.

I was sad because I knew that blood, much blood, would be shed.

But it was mainly a question of my political outlook.

I was 24 years old. Two years before, I and a group of friends had set up a political-ideological group that aroused intense anger in the Yishuv (the Hebrew population in Palestine). Our ideas, which provoked a very strong reaction, were regarded as a dangerous heresy.

The Young Palestine Circle (*Eretz Yisrael Hatzira* in Hebrew) published occasional issues of a magazine called *ba-Ma'avak* (In the Struggle), and was therefore generally known as "the *ba-Ma'avak* Group", advocating a revolutionary new ideology, whose main points were:

- We, the young generation that had grown up in this country, were a new nation.
- Our language and culture meant we should be called the Hebrew nation.
- Zionism gave birth to this nation, and had thereby fulfilled its mission.
- From here on, Zionism has no further role to play. It is a hindrance to the free development of the new nation, and should be dismantled, like the scaffolding after a house is built.
- The new Hebrew nation is indeed a part of the Jewish people—as the new Australian nation, for example, is a part of the Anglo-Saxon people—but has a separate identity, its own interests, and a new culture.
- The Hebrew nation belongs to the country, and is a natural ally of the Arab national movement. Both national movements are rooted in the country and its history, from the ancient Semitic civilization to the present.
- The new Hebrew nation does not belong to Europe and the

"West," but to awakening Asia and "the Semitic region"—a term we invented in order to distance ourselves from the European-colonial term "Middle East."

• The new Hebrew nation must integrate itself in the region, as a full and equal partner. Together with all the nations of the Semitic region, it strives for the liberation of the region from the colonial empires.

With this world-view, we naturally opposed the partition of the country.

Two months before the UN partition resolution, in September 1947, I published a pamphlet called "War or peace in the Semitic region," in which I proposed a completely different plan: that the Hebrew national movement and the Palestinian-Arab national movement should combine into one single national movement and establish a joint state in the whole of Palestine, based on the love of the country (patriotism, in the real sense).

This was far from the "bi-national" idea, which had important adherents in those days. I never believed in this. Two different nations, each of which clings to its own national vision, cannot live together in one state. Our vision was based on the creation of a new, joint nation, with a Hebrew and an Arab component.

We hastily translated the essence of the pamphlet into English and Arabic, and I went to distribute it to the editorial offices of the Arab newspapers in Jaffa. It was no longer the town I had known from earlier days, when my work (as a clerk in a law office) frequently took me to the government offices there. The atmosphere felt dark and ominous.

With the expected UN resolution looming, we decided to publish a special issue of *ba-Ma'avak* devoted completely to it. A student of the Haifa Technical University volunteered to supply a drawing for the front page, and that's why I found myself at that fateful moment in that small Haifa hotel.

I couldn't go back to sleep again. I got up and, in the excitement of the moment, wrote a poem that was published in that special issue. The first verse went like this:

"I swear to you, motherland, / On this bitter day of your humiliation, / Great and united / You will rise from the dust. / The cruel wound / Will burn in the hearts of your sons / Until your flags / Will wave from the sea to the desert."

One of our group composed a melody, and we sang it in the following days, as we bade farewell to our dreams.

The moment the UN resolution was adopted, it was clear that our world had changed completely, that an era had come to an end and a new epoch had begun, both in the life of the country and in the life of every one of us.

We hurriedly pasted on the walls a large poster warning of a "Semitic fratricidal war" but the war was already on. When the first bullet was fired, the possibility of creating the joint, united single country was shattered.

I am proud of my ability to adapt rapidly to extreme changes. The first time I had to do this was when Adolf Hitler came to power in Germany and my life changed abruptly and completely. I was then nine years old, and everything that had happened before was dead for me. I started a new life in Palestine. On November 29, 1947, it was happening again—to me and to all of us.

As the well-known saying has it, one can make an omelet from eggs, but not eggs from an omelet. Banal, perhaps, but how very true.

The moment the Hebrew–Arab war started, the possibility that the two nations would live together in one state expired. Wars change reality.

I joined the "Haganah battalions," the forerunner of the IDF. As a soldier in the special commando unit that was later called "Samson's Foxes," I saw the war as it was—bitter, cruel, inhuman. First we faced the Palestinian fighters, later the fighters of the wider Arab world. I passed through dozens of Arab villages, many abandoned in the storm of battle, many others whose inhabitants were driven out after being occupied.

It was an ethnic war. In the first months, no Arabs were left behind our lines, no Jews were left behind the Arab lines. Both sides committed many atrocities. At the beginning of the war, we saw the pictures of the heads of our comrades paraded on stakes through the Old City of Jerusalem. We saw the massacre committed by the Irgun and the Stern Group in Deir Yassin. We knew that if we were captured, we would be slaughtered, and the Arab fighters knew they could expect the same.

The longer the war dragged on, the more I became convinced of the reality of the Palestinian nation, with which we must make peace at the end of the war, a peace based on partnership between the two peoples.

While the war was still going on, I expressed this view in a number of articles that were published at the time in *Haaretz*. Immediately after the fighting was over, when I was still in uniform convalescing from my wounds, I started meeting with two young Arabs (both of whom were later elected to the Knesset) in order to plan a common path. I could not have imagined that 60 years later this effort would still not be over.

Nowadays, the idea appears here and there of turning the omelet back into the egg, of dismantling the State of Israel and the State-of-Palestine-to-be, and establishing a single state, as we sang at that time, "from the sea to the desert."

This is presented as a fresh new idea, but it is actually an attempt to turn the wheel back and to bring back to life an idea that is irrevocably obsolete. In human history, that just does not happen. What has been forged in blood and fire in wars and intifadas—the State of Israel and the Palestinian national movement—will not just disappear. After a war, states can achieve peace and partnership, like Germany and France, but they do not merge into one state.

I am not a nostalgic type. I look back at the ideas of my younger days, and try to analyze what has been superseded and what is left.

The ideas of the "ba-Ma'avak group" were indeed revolutionary and bold—but could they have been put into practice? Looking back, it is clear to me that the "joint state" idea was already unrealistic when we brought it up. Perhaps it would have been possible one or two generations earlier. But by the middle of the 1940s, the situation of the two peoples had changed decisively. There was no escaping from the partition of the country.

I believe that we were right in our historical approach: that we must identify with the region we are living in, cooperate with the Arab national movement, and enter into a partnership with the Palestinian nation. As long as we see ourselves as a part of Europe and/or the United States, we are not able to achieve peace. And certainly not if we consider ourselves soldiers in a crusade against the Islamic civilization and the Arab peoples.

As we said then, before the partition resolution: the Palestinian people exists. Even after 60 years, in which they have suffered catastrophes which few other peoples have ever experienced, the Palestinian people cling to their country with unparalleled fortitude. True, the dream of living together in one state is dead, and will not come to life again. But I have no doubt that after the Palestinian state comes into being, the two states will find ways to live together in close partnership. The walls will be thrown down, the fences will be dismantled, the border will be opened, and the reality of the common country will overcome all obstacles. The flags of the country—the two flags of the two states—will indeed wave side by side.

The UN resolution of November 29, 1947, was one of the most

intelligent in the annals of that organization. As one who strenuously opposed it, I recognize its wisdom.

A Nation? What Nation?

September 25, 2004

It sounds like a joke, but it is quite serious.

The government of Israel does not recognize the Israeli nation. It says that there is no such thing.

Could you imagine the French government denying the existence of the French Nation? Or the government of the United States of America not recognizing the (US) American nation? But then, Israel is the land of unlimited possibilities.

Every person in Israel is recorded in the Interior Ministry's "registry of inhabitants." The registration includes the item "nation." This entry also appears on the identity card that every person in Israel is legally obliged to carry with them at all times or risk criminal prosecution.

The Interior Ministry lists 140 recognized nations that its officers can register. This includes not only established nations ("Russian," "German," French," etc.) but also "Christian," "Muslim," "Druze," and more.[7] The "nation" of an Arab citizen of Israel, for example, may be recorded as "Arab," "Christian," or "Catholic" (but not "Palestinian"—the Interior Ministry is not yet aware of the existence of such a nation).

Most Israeli inhabitants carry, of course, identity cards saying "Nation: Jewish." This has now become a subject of debate.

A group of 38 Israelis have asked for the cancellation of their registration as "Jewish" and its replacement with "Israeli." The Interior Ministry refuses, saying that no such nation appears on its list. The group has petitioned the High Court of Justice to instruct the ministry to register them as belonging to the "Israeli" nation. This week, the case came before the court.

The 38 include some of the most eminent professors in Israel (historians, philosophers, sociologists, and the like), well-known public figures, and others (including my humble self). One of the initiators is a Druze. They are far from belonging to one political camp—indeed, they include both leftists and rightists. One of them was Benny Peled, former commander of the air force, a very right-wing person, who died after the petition was submitted.

The Supreme Court (sitting as the High Court of Justice) handled the case like a hot potato (though Justice Mishal Heshin was delighted to find in the ministry's list the "Assyrian" nation: actually a small religious community, a remnant of antiquity which still speaks an Aramaic dialect).

On the main point, the judges said that the High Court—dealing generally with administrative matters—is not equipped to rule on such a profound question. It advised the petitioners to apply to the District Court, where a wide discussion is possible and expert witnesses can be called. The petitioners accepted this advice, and so the battle will be transferred to another judicial forum that will have to devote to it many hearings.

Why does the Israeli government refuse to recognize the Israeli nation? According to the official doctrine, there exists a "Jewish" nation, and the state belongs to it. After all, it is a "Jewish state," or, in the words of one of the laws, "the state of the Jewish people."

According to the same doctrine, it is also a democratic state, and all its citizens are supposed to be equal, irrespective of their national affinity. But basically the state is "Jewish."

According to this doctrine, Jewry is both a nation and a religion. In the first years of Israel, it was still the rule that if people who declared, bona fide, that they were Jews, they were registered as such. But when the religious camp attained more power, the law was amended and from then on people were registered as Jews only if their mothers were Jewish or if they had converted to the Jewish faith and not adopted another religion. This is, of course, a purely religious definition (according to Jewish religious law, a person is Jewish if his or her mother is; the father is irrelevant in this context).

This situation has created another problem. In Israel, the orthodox rabbinate enjoys a monopoly on Jewish religious affairs. Two other Jewish religious factions that are very important in the United States, Conservative and Reform, are discriminated against in Israel and conversions conducted by them are not recognized by the government. Some years ago, the High Court decided that persons converted to Judaism in Israel by these two communities must also be registered under "Nation: Jewish." Whereupon the Interior Minister at that time, a religious politician, peremptorily decreed that all future identity cards will show, under the item "nation," only five stars. But in the Ministry's "registry of inhabitants," it still says "Nation: Jewish."

The roots of the confusion go back to the beginnings of the Zionist Movement. Until then, Jews throughout the world were a religious-ethnic community. This was abnormal in contemporary Europe, but quite normal 2000 years ago, when such communities—Hellenic, Jewish, Christian, and many more—were the norm. Each was autonomous in the Byzantine Empire and had its own laws and jurisdiction. A Jewish man in Alexandria could marry a Jewish woman in Antioch, but not his Christian neighbor. The Ottoman Empire continued this tradition, calling the communities millets (from an Arabic word for nation).

But when the modern national movements arose in Europe, and it appeared that the Jews had no place in them, the founders of the Zionist Movement decided that the Jews should constitute themselves as an independent nation and create a national state of their own. The religious-ethnic community was simply redefined as a nation, and thus a nation came into being that was also a religion, and a religion that was also a nation.

That was, of course, a fiction, but a necessary one for Zionism, which claimed Palestine for the Jewish "nation." In order to conduct a national struggle, there must be a nation.

However, two generations later, the fiction became reality. In Palestine a real nation, with a national reality and a national culture developed. Members of this nation considered themselves Jews, but Jews who are different in many respects from the other Jews in the world.

Before the creation of the State of Israel, and without a conscious decision being made, in everyday Hebrew parlance a distinction was made between "Hebrew" and "Jewish." One spoke of the "Hebrew Yishuv" (the new society in Palestine) and "Jewish religion," "Hebrew agriculture" and "Jewish tradition," "Hebrew worker" and "Jewish Diaspora," "Hebrew underground" and "Jewish Holocaust." When I was a boy, we demonstrated for Jewish immigration and a Hebrew state.

When Israel came into being, things became simpler. Every Israeli who is asked abroad about his national identity, answers automatically: "I am an Israeli." It would not enter his head to say "I am a Jew," unless specifically asked about his religion.

There is no contradiction between our being Israelis and Jews. Modern individuals are composed of different layers that do not cancel each other out. A person can be a man by gender, a vegetarian by inclination, a Jew by religion, and an Israeli by national group. A woman in Brooklyn can be Jewish and American at one and the same time— Jewish by origin and religion, belonging to the (US) American nation.

According to modern Western norms, a nation is defined by citizenship; indeed in many languages "nationality" does denote citizenship. All US citizens belong to the (US) American nation, whether they are by origin Scottish, Mexican, African, or Jewish. By religion, an American can be Catholic, Jewish, Buddhist, or Evangelical. That has no bearing on belonging to the nation, which is a political collective.

European nations, too, adapt themselves slowly to these norms. Only Fascists demand "total" conformity of race, nation, and language.

Why is this important? Contrary to the now defunct Fascist doctrine, belonging to a nation is a matter of autonomous decision. The hundreds of thousands of Russians who came to Israel legally (as close relatives of Jews), who serve in the Israeli army, and pay Israeli taxes— if they want to belong to the Israeli nation, they do indeed belong to it. Arab citizens who want to belong to the Israeli nation are indeed Israelis—without giving up their Palestinian identity and their Muslim, Christian, or Druze religion.[8]

For many people it is difficult to give up the Zionist myths with which they grew up. They try to evade any discussion on this subject— and indeed, it is hardly ever mentioned in our media. Our petition to the High Court of Justice, and soon to the District court, is designed to provoke, at long last, such debate.

Two thousand years ago, the Prophet Jonah found himself on a ship tossed by a storm. The frightened seamen, looking for someone to blame, asked him (Jonah, 1:8): "What is thy country? And of what people art thou?" To which Jonah replied: "I am Hebrew!"

In response to the same question we declare: "We are Israelis!"

Anti-Semitism: A Practical Manual

January 17, 2004

A Hungarian joke: During the June 1967 war, a Hungarian meets his friend. "Why are you looking so happy?" he asks. "I heard that the Israelis shot down six Soviet-made MiGs today," his friend replies.

The next day, the friend looks even more jubilant. "The Israelis downed another eight MiGs," he announces.

On the third day, the friend is crestfallen. "What happened? Didn't the Israelis down any MiGs today?" the man asks. "They did," the friend answers, "But today someone told me that the Israelis are Jews!"

This is the whole story in a nutshell.

The anti-Semite hates the Jews because they are Jews, irrespective of their actions. Jews may be hated because they are rich and ostentatious or because they are poor and live in squalor. Because they played a major role in the Bolshevik revolution or because some of them became incredibly rich after the collapse of the Communist regime. Because they crucified Jesus or because they infected Western culture with the "Christian morality of compassion." Because they have no fatherland or because they created the State of Israel.

That is in the nature of all kinds of racism and chauvinism: one hates someone for being a Jew, Arab, woman, Black, Indian, Muslim, Hindu. His or her personal attributes, actions, achievements are unimportant. If people belong to the abhorred race, religion, or gender, they will be hated.

The answers to all questions relating to anti-Semitism follow from this basic fact. For example:

Is everybody who criticizes Israel an anti-Semite?

Absolutely not. Somebody who criticizes Israel for certain of our actions cannot be accused of anti-Semitism for that. But somebody who hates Israel because it is a Jewish state, like the Hungarian in the joke, is an anti-Semite. It is not always easy to distinguish between the two kinds, because shrewd anti-Semites pose as *bona fide* critics of Israel's actions. But presenting all critics of Israel as anti-Semites is wrong and counterproductive; it damages the fight against anti-Semitism.

Many deeply moral persons, the cream of humanity, criticize our behavior in the occupied territories. It is stupid to accuse them of anti-Semitism.

Can a person be an anti-Zionist without being an anti-Semite?

Absolutely yes. Zionism is a political creed and must be treated like any other. One can be anti-Communist without being anti-Chinese, anti-capitalist without being anti-American, anti-globalist, anti-anything. Yet, again, it is not always easy to draw the line, because real anti-Semites often pretend just to be "anti-Zionists." They should not be helped by erasing the distinction.

Can a person be an anti-Semite and a Zionist?

Indeed, yes. The founder of modern Zionism, Theodor Herzl, tried to enlist the support of notorious Russian anti-Semites, promising to take the Jews off their hands. Before World War II, the Zionist underground organization IZL established military training camps in Poland under the auspices of anti-Semitic generals, who also wanted to get rid of the Jews. Nowadays, the Zionist extreme right receives and welcomes massive support from American fundamentalist evangelists, whom the majority of American Jews, according to a poll published this week, consider profoundly anti-Semitic. Their theology prophesies that on the eve of the second coming of Christ, all Jews must convert to Christianity or be exterminated.[9]

Can a Jew be anti-Semitic?

That sounds like an oxymoron. But history has known some instances of Jews who became ferocious Jew-haters. The Spanish Grand Inquisitor, Torquemada, was of Jewish descent. Karl Marx wrote some very nasty things about the Jews, as did Otto Weininger, an important Jewish writer in *fin-de-siecle* Vienna. Herzl, his contemporary and fellow-Viennese, wrote in his diaries some very uncomplimentary remarks about the Jews.[10]

If a person criticizes Israel more than other countries that do the same, is he an anti-Semite?

Not necessarily. True, there should be one and the same moral standard for all countries and all human beings. Russian actions in Chechnya are not better than ours in Nablus, and may be worse. The trouble is that the Jews are pictured and picture themselves as (and indeed were) a "nation of victims." Therefore, the world is shocked that yesterday's victims are today's victimizers. A higher moral standard is required from us than from other peoples. And rightly so.[11]

Has Europe become anti-Semitic again?

Not really. The number of anti-Semites in Europe has not grown; perhaps it has even fallen. What has increased is the volume of criticism of Israel's behavior towards the Palestinians, who appear as "the victims of the victims."

The situation in some suburbs of Paris, which is often cited as an example of the rise of anti-Semitism, is a quite different affair. When North African Muslims clash with North African Jews, they are transferring the Israeli–Palestinian conflict to European soil. It is also a continuation of the feud between Arabs and Jews that started in Algeria when the Jews supported the French regime and Muslims considered them collaborators of the hated colonialists.

Then why did most Europeans state in a recent poll that Israel endangers world peace more than any other country?

That has a simple explanation: Europeans see on television every day what our soldiers are doing in the occupied Palestinian territories. This confrontation is covered more intensively than any other conflict on earth (with the possible exception of Iraq, for the time being), because Israel is more "interesting," considering the long history of the Jews in Europe, and because Israel is closer to the Western media than Muslim or African countries. The Palestinian resistance, which Israelis call "terrorism," seems to many Europeans very much like the French resistance to the German occupation.[12]

What about the anti-Semitic manifestations in the Arab world?

No doubt, typically anti-Semitic indications have crept lately into Arab discourse. Suffice it to mention that the infamous *Protocols of the Elders of Zion* have been published in Arabic. That is a typically European import. The *Protocols* were invented by the secret police of Czarist Russia.[13]

Whatever inanities may be voiced by certain "experts," there was never any widespread Muslim anti-Semitism of the kind that existed in Christian Europe. In the course of his fight for power, the prophet Muhammad fought against neighboring Jewish tribes, and therefore there are some negative passages about the Jews in the *Qur'an*. But they cannot be compared to the anti-Jewish passages in the New Testament story about the crucifixion of Christ that have poisoned the Christian world and caused endless suffering. Muslim Spain was a paradise for the Jews, and there has never been a Jewish Holocaust in the Muslim world. Even pogroms were extremely rare.

Muhammad decreed that the "Peoples of the Book" (Jews and Christians) be treated tolerantly, subject to conditions that were incomparably more liberal than those in contemporary Europe. The Muslims never imposed their religion by force on Jews and Christians, as shown by the fact that almost all the Jews expelled from Catholic Spain settled in the Muslim countries and flourished there. After centuries of Muslim rule, Greeks and Serbs remained thoroughly Christian.

When peace is established between Israel and the Arab world, the poisonous fruits of anti-Semitism will most probably disappear from the Arab world (as will the poisonous fruits of Arab-hating in our society).

Aren't the utterances of the Prime Minister of Malaysia, Mahathir bin Muhammad, about the Jews controlling the world, anti-Semitic?

Yes and no. They certainly illustrate the difficulty of pinning anti-Semitism down. From a factual point of view, the man was right when he asserted that the Jews have a far bigger influence than their percentage of the world's population alone would warrant. It is true that the Jews have a large influence on the policy of the United States, the only superpower, as well as on the US and international media. One does not need the phony *Protocols* in order to face this fact and analyze its causes. But the sounds make the music, and Mahathir's music does indeed sound anti-Semitic.

So should we ignore anti-Semitism?

Definitely not. Racism is a kind of virus that exists in every nation and in every human being. Jean-Paul Sartre said that we are all racists, the difference being that some of us realize this and fight against it, while others succumb to the evil. In ordinary times, there is a small minority of blatant racists in every country, but in times of crisis their number can multiply rapidly. This is a perpetual danger, and every people must fight against the racists in their midst.

We Israelis are like all other peoples. Each of us can find a small racist within ourselves, if we search hard enough. We have in our country fanatical Arab-haters, and the historic confrontation that dominates our lives increases their power and influence. It is our duty to fight them, and leave it to the Europeans and Arabs to deal with their own racists.

Unearthing the Truth[14]

July 27, 1998

We have already become accustomed to the scene: *yeshiva* students chasing archaeologists on the hills, cops chasing the *yeshiva* students. The diggers into holy books are at war with the diggers into antiquities.

And what is this fight about? On the face of it, they are fighting over dry bones in old graves. But that is only a pretense. The real bone of contention lies buried much deeper, in the subconscious of the warring parties.

When the founding fathers of Zionism decided to go to Palestine—against the inclinations of the atheist Theodor Herzl—they pulled out the Old Testament. It contained the divine Deed of Purchase to the land. It was also a record of a magnificent national history, which is essential for any modern national movement. We are not invading someone else's country. After all, it's right here in writing.

The Hebrew Bible is an extraordinary literary work which also tells a historical tale. But first and foremost, it is a religious document. It records the covenant between The Almighty God and his people Israel. Its writers used historical and literary materials solely for the purpose of driving home the religious moral lessons. ("And he did wrong in the eyes of The Lord ..."). As far as the great Torah sages of the last century were concerned—most of who regarded the Zionist Founding

Fathers with venomous hatred—the Old Testament had a purely religious significance.

The Zionists, on the other hand, completely ignored the religious contents of the Hebrew Bible. They used its literary elements to create the new Hebrew culture and the new Hebrew language, but most of all, they used the "historical" story in order to establish their claim to the land. Generations of archaeologists swarmed the land in order to "prove" the correctness of the biblical descriptions. Numerous amateurs, from Moshe Dayan to Rehavam Ze'evi, turned archaeology into a kind of national sport. All were feeding the public "evidence" and bent the "findings" in accordance with their imagination and enthusiasm. The orthodox, who did not need proof for matters of faith, did not care.

But as the Zionist fervor declined, and as the existence of the Hebrew nation on the land became an established fact no longer in need of "proof," the bitter truth began to trickle out. All that vast effort on the part of those archaeologists did not unearth a single proof to attest to any truth in those biblical stories. No exodus from Egypt, no conquest of Canaan, no Kingdoms of Saul, David, or Solomon—none of these have left behind even a shred of evidence.

Learned professors, whose religious or nationalistic faith got the better of their scientific purity, were busy making up excuses for this astounding fact. Perhaps the Kingdom of David was not in the tenth century but instead in the ninth, perhaps all of David's and Solomon's buildings are actually buried under the Dome of the Rock, making it impossible for us to excavate there, and so on. But in recent years, a new crop of archaeologist has emerged, one no longer afraid to speak the truth. All those many centuries between the conquering of Canaan and the Kingdom of Solomon did not leave the slightest imprint on the land. And that is very strange indeed.

The result has been a kind of a draw: there is no evidence to support those biblical stories, but neither is there any evidence to disprove it. There are those who reasonably ask: "How is it possible that there is no shred of historical truth in so many magnificent stories?" After all, those fairy tales must have some historical kernel of truth! Moses, Joshua, David, and Solomon probably existed, albeit not exactly as depicted in the Bible. Perhaps the writers exaggerated a bit.

But this, too, is not true. Archeologists did, indeed, provide the evidence that all those stories were pure fiction. Researchers of antiquities in Egypt deciphered thousands of Egyptian documents that span the entire biblical period. The land of Canaan had always been most vital to the Egyptian national security, as well as to its foreign affairs, its economy, and its transportation. Throughout the different historical periods, Canaan was a permanent host to Egyptian envoys, diplomats, military commanders, spies, and merchants. All those individuals provided continuous reports on everything going on in Canaanite cities and in their environs. The pharaohs themselves also recorded in writing on stone their own victories and achievements, real and imagined.

Hence, there exists a rich body of contemporaneous documentation of events in virtually every city and at all times. And lo and behold: there is no exodus, no conquering of Canaan, no Kingdom of David, no Kingdom of Solomon. None of those ever happened or could have happened, since all the reports from the country of Canaan reveal an entirely different state of affairs in that land at the time when those events are purported to have taken place there.

Only during the period of the two Kingdoms—Israel and Judea—does the Biblical story begin to match the historical one. Everything prior to this period—from the Book of Genesis through the Book of Samuel II—is legend.

There is no escaping the conclusion—one accepted by virtually every serious scientist in the world—that the Hebrew Bible, written after the Babylonian exile by religious preachers with stunning literary skills, is not a history book. And because the archaeologists proved it, they are hated by the orthodox.

Does this detract from the greatness of the Bible? Of course not. It has always been, and still remains, a work of literary, cultural, and linguistic magnificence, surpassed by nothing else among the cultures of the world. Its stories influenced billions throughout the ages. Even if Joshua never really conquered Canaan, and King David never really ruled in Jerusalem, and neither even existed—still they have influenced our lives and our spiritual world more than any historical figures.

And as for the archaeologists—they reveal what really happened, beyond the myths. That's their job.

Israel at 50: A Pronounced Case of Split Personality[15]

July 4, 1998

When you are 50 years old, you should know already who you are. The State of Israel does not. What is it? A "Jews' state," as the founder of the Zionist Movement called the future state? A "state of the Jewish people," as defined in one of Israel's laws? A state that belongs to its citizens? Or a "Jewish and democratic state," as the official doctrine, endorsed by the Supreme Court, announces? And how can a state whose every fifth citizen is a non-Jew be Jewish and democratic at the same time? Who is a Jew? What does a "Jewish state" mean?

Such questions may sound abstract, but they have a direct bearing on our everyday life in Israel. In the beginning, most Zionists declared that "Jewish" is a purely national identity. But after a long juridical struggle, it was accepted in Israel that the only valid definition of "Jewish" was religious. Israeli law says, therefore, that a Jew is a person whose mother is Jewish, or who has converted to Judaism in a religious ceremony.

As Jews in Israel enjoy many overt and covert privileges, this definition is very important.

(When one says in Israel "I am an atheist', one is often asked in jest: "Jewish or Christian atheist?")

If Israel is a Jewish state, it seems logical that a Jew in Paris has the right to immigrate to Israel at any time and to automatically receive Israel citizenship, while a Palestinian refugee in Paris, whose family has lived in Haifa for centuries, has no right to return, much less to citizenship. (The Knesset has been able to forbid the import of pork, in direct contravention of a Basic Law. A huge part of the lands in the state belongs to a Zionist fund, whose statutes expressly forbid their sale, or even lease, to non-Jews.)

Recently it was reported that there is a secret "demographic" department in the Prime Minister's office, whose job is to encourage Jewish mothers to bear as many children as possible, while discouraging Arab mothers from doing so.

For most Israelis, this makes sense, since the aim of the Jewish state is to "ingather" as many Jews as possible. After all, that is the Zionist *raison d'etre*.

But who are we Israelis? Are we really Jews? A new kind of Jews? Jewish Israelis? Israeli Jews? Or just Israelis? I am a convinced atheist; I think of myself primarily as a human being and then as a Hebrew-speaking Israeli of Jewish descent. Simple? Well, in a recent public opinion poll Israelis were asked how they defined their identity. 34 percent answered "Jewish," 35 percent "Israeli," 30 percent "Jewish and Israeli."

Among those who defined themselves as left wing, 60 percent answered "Israeli." Among 12–18-year-olds, 44.5 percent answered "Israeli." (Practically nobody had the idea of identifying themselves primarily as human beings—in Hebrew: *Ben Adam*, child of Adam.)

Are Israelis really Jews in the accepted sense? Not long ago a Polish friend told me about one of his acquaintances in Warsaw, who had visited Israel for the first time. He told him breathlessly: "Do you know what? In Israel there are Jews too!" He meant, of course, orthodox Jews, those who wear black gowns and hats, as they have done for centuries in Eastern Europe.

This Pole had probably never before seen a Jew, but in many folklore shops in Poland you find, among other wooden figures of Polish types, Jewish musicians dressed in black gowns and hats.

This sounds like a joke, but isn't. Everybody understands that there is a huge difference between Jews and Israelis.

Only the orthodox think that religious Jews are the same all over the world, because for them religious beliefs are more important than worldly nonsense like state, nation, and other such pagan notions. For this reason, Theodor Herzl, the founder of the Zionist Movement, was cursed and damned by all the "Torah greats" of his time. Non-religious Israelis who identify themselves primarily as Jews consider themselves "new Jews" and look down with the utmost contempt upon Jews in Brooklyn and Berlin. Even a casual observer perceives that over the last generations, Jews in Palestine/Israel have become a new people. (By way of a metamorphosis, perhaps a mutation.)

The religion, too, has changed. The ultra-nationalist, messianic tribal religion of today's settler movement, which plays such a big role in Israeli politics, bears little resemblance to the humanistic Jewish religion of Western Europe.

The main link that ties Israelis to the Jews everywhere is the memory of the Holocaust and preceding persecutions. Indeed, the great orthodox philosopher Jeshayahu Leibowitz alleged that Jewish religion had died 200 years ago, and that the Holocaust was a kind of ersatz-religion, the only one that Jews around the world have in common.

There is a certain danger in this remembrance. It corresponds to a deep urge. One cannot, one should not, forget this monstrous chapter because that would be treason to the memory of the victims, our relatives, our flesh and blood. But this remembrance comes with the conviction that not only the Nazis, not only the Germans, were to blame, but all the other peoples too—all who did not raise a finger when the industrialized mass murder was in progress. This is a notion that comes naturally, nearly inevitably, to Jews. But for Israelis it is dangerous. (A few years ago entertainment groups of the Israeli army used to sing to a jolly melody the words: "All the world is against us / But we don't give a damn. / It was always that way ...")

If one grows up with the conviction that the whole non-Jewish world wants only to annihilate the Jews—indeed, that the whole of human history is nothing but a chain of anti-Jewish persecutions—and that Israelis are Jews like any other, then the logical conclusion is that we Israelis cannot make peace, that peace is a dangerous illusion, that we must be constantly on guard.

It is difficult to understand the Israeli reaction after the Oslo peace accords without grasping the important role of this conviction in our political life. Yet Israel is a new nation. Millions of people were transplanted not only from one country to another, but also from one culture to another, from one language to another, from one climate to another, from one way of life to another, from one geopolitical situation to another, often also from one social class to another. It would have been a wonder if nothing new came out of this.

Australia and the United States are based on British culture and British values, but they are, of course, new nations. Israel is Jewish as Canada is British, yet both are new nations.

This new nation, Israel, is suffering from great inner stresses. Today, 50 years after the official creation of the state, a deep rift passes through its middle.

We refer to "left" and "right' but these terms have little resemblance to the way they are understood in Europe. Generally speaking, "left" in Israel means the social and economic upper classes, the Jews of European origin ("Ashkenazim"), the better educated, the non- and anti-religious. This left is reinforced by practically all of the Arab citizens of Israel—a national minority of nearly 20 percent.

"Right" means the socially and economically underprivileged, the Jews of oriental descent (often referred to as "Sephardim"), the less educated, and the religious Jews of all shades. The different definitions actually overlap: most oriental Jews are religious or "traditional," and belong to the "lower" classes, for instance. That's why the various differences have become one great dangerous rift. The rift between the two camps is widening constantly. Some speak already about "two peoples," the left based in Tel-Aviv, the right in Jerusalem. When the left's Shimon Peres faced the right's Binyamin Netanyahu two years ago, the election results showed that each camp commands almost exactly 50 percent of the vote.

The rift runs through all the problems of Israeli society: state and religion (the "right" prevents any separation), the constitution (the religious don't want one), the laws, and the Supreme Court (too liberal for the religious), the education system (dominated by the religious), the Arab minority in Israel proper (equal rights on paper only), even the music is involved: the left's pop versus the right's oriental songs.

The peace process has fallen into this abyss. The right has condemned the "Ashkenazi" Oslo-agreement; a rightist religious fanatic murdered Yitzhak Rabin, an Ashkenazi par excellence, at a leftist mass meeting.

For the rightists, Greater Israel is vastly more important than peace. Ironically, their leader, Netanyahu, is a typical Ashkenazi son of the upper classes.

How will Israel develop over the next 50 years? Nobody knows. Only one thing is certain: it will remain an interesting country.

The Mother of All Pretexts

October 13, 2007

When I hear mention of the "clash of civilizations" I don't know whether to laugh or to cry.

To laugh, because it is such a silly notion.

To cry, because it is liable to cause untold disasters.

To cry even more, because our leaders are exploiting this slogan as a pretext for sabotaging any possibility of an Israeli–Palestinian reconciliation. It is just one more in a long line of pretexts.

Why was the Zionist Movement in need of excuses to justify the way it treated the Palestinian people?

At its birth, it was an idealistic movement. It laid great weight on its moral basis. Not just in order to convince the world, but above all in order to set its own conscience at rest.

From early childhood we learned about the pioneers, many of them sons and daughters of well-to-do and well-educated families, who left behind a comfortable life in Europe in order to start a new life in a far-away and—by the standards of the time—primitive country. Here, in a savage climate they were not used to, often hungry and sick, they performed back-breaking physical labor under a brutal sun.

For that, they needed an absolute belief in the rightness of their cause. Not only did they believe in the need to save the Jews of Europe from persecution and pogroms, but also in the creation of a society so just as never seen before, an egalitarian society that would be a model for the entire world. Leo Tolstoy was no less important for them than Theodor Herzl. The *kibbutz* and the *moshav* were symbols of the whole enterprise.[16]

But this idealistic movement aimed at settling in a country inhabited by another people. How could they bridge this contradiction between sublime ideals and the fact that their realization necessitated the expulsion of the people of the land?

The easiest way was to repress the problem altogether, ignoring its very existence: the land, we told ourselves, was empty, there was no population living here at all. That was the justification that served as a bridge over the moral abyss.

Only one of the Founding Fathers of the Zionist Movement was courageous enough to call a spade a spade. Ze'ev Jabotinsky wrote as early as 80 years ago that it was impossible to deceive the Palestinian people (whose existence he recognized) and to buy their consent to the Zionist aspirations. We are white settlers colonizing the land of the native people, he said, and there is no chance whatsoever that the natives will resign themselves to this voluntarily. They will resist violently, like all the native peoples in the European colonies. Therefore we need an "iron wall" to protect the Zionist enterprise.[17]

When Jabotinsky was told that his approach was immoral, he replied that the Jews were trying to save themselves from the disaster threatening them in Europe, and therefore their morality trumped the morality of the Arabs in Palestine.

Most Zionists were not prepared to accept this force-oriented approach. They searched fervently for a moral justification they could live with.

Thus started the long quest for justifications—with each pretext supplanting the previous one, according to the changing spiritual fashions in the world.

The first justification was precisely the one mocked by Jabotinsky: we were actually coming to benefit the Arabs. We would redeem them from their primitive living conditions, from ignorance and disease. We would teach them modern methods of agriculture and bring them advanced medicine. Everything—except employment, because we needed every job for the Jews we were bringing here, whom we were transforming from ghetto-Jews into a people of workers and tillers of the soil.

When the ungrateful Arabs went on to resist our grand project, in spite of all the benefits we were supposedly bringing them, we found a Marxist justification: it was not the Arabs who opposed us, but only the *effendis*. The rich Arabs, the great landowners, were afraid that the glowing example of the egalitarian Hebrew community would attract the exploited Arab proletariat and cause them to rise against their oppressors.

That, too, did not work for long, perhaps because the Arabs saw how the Zionists bought the land from those very same *effendis* and drove out the tenants who had been cultivating it for generations.

The rise of the Nazis in Europe brought masses of Jews to the country. The Arab public saw how the land was being withdrawn from under their feet, and started a rebellion against the British and the Jews in 1936.[18] Why, the Arabs asked, should they pay for the persecution of the Jews by the Europeans? But the Arab Revolt gave us a new justification: the Arabs support the Nazis. And indeed, the Grand Mufti of Jerusalem, Hajj Amin al-Husseini, was photographed sitting next to Hitler. Some people "discovered" that the Mufti was the real instigator of the Holocaust. (Years later it was revealed that Hitler had detested the Mufti, who had no influence whatsoever over the Nazis.)

World War II came to an end, to be followed by the 1948 war. Half of the vanquished Palestinian people became refugees. That did not trouble the Zionist conscience, because everybody knew that they ran away of their own free will. Their leaders had called upon them to leave their homes, to return later with the victorious Arab armies. True, no evidence was ever found to support this absurd claim, but it has sufficed to soothe our conscience to this day.

It may be asked: why were the refugees not allowed to come back to their homes once the war was over? Well, it was they who in 1947 rejected the UN partition plan and started the war. If because of this they lost 78 percent of their country, they have only themselves to blame.

Then came the Cold War. We were, of course, on the side of the "Free World," while the great Arab leader, Gamal Abd-el-Nasser, got his weapons from the Soviet bloc. (True, in the 1948 war the Soviet arms flowed to us, but that's not important.) It was quite clear. No use talking with the Arabs, because they support Communist tyranny.

But the Soviet bloc collapsed. "The terrorist organization called the PLO," as Menachem Begin used to call it, recognized Israel and signed the Oslo agreement. A new justification had to be found for our unwillingness to give back the occupied territories to the Palestinian people.

The salvation came from America: a professor named Samuel Huntington wrote a book about the *Clash of Civilizations*. And so we found the mother of all pretexts.[19]

The arch-enemy, according to this theory, is Islam. Western Civilization—Judeo-Christian, liberal, democratic, tolerant—is under attack from the Islamic monster: fanatical, terrorist, murderous.

Islam is murderous by nature. Actually, "Muslim" and "terrorist" are synonymous. Every Muslim is a terrorist, every terrorist a Muslim.

A skeptic might ask: How did it happen that the wonderful Western culture gave birth to the Inquisition, the pogroms, the burning of witches, the annihilation of the Native Americans, the Holocaust, the ethnic cleansings, and other atrocities without number?—but that was in the past. Now Western culture is the embodiment of freedom and progress.

Professor Huntington was not thinking about us in particular. His task was to satisfy a peculiar American craving: the US empire always needs a virtual, world-embracing enemy, a single enemy that includes all the opponents of the United States around the world. The Communists delivered the goods: the whole world was divided between Good Guys (the Americans and their supporters) and Bad Guys (the Commies). Everybody who opposed US interests was automatically a Communist—Nelson Mandela in South Africa, Salvador Allende in Chile, Fidel Castro in Cuba—while the masters of apartheid, the death squads of Augusto Pinochet and the secret police of the Shah of Iran belonged, like us, to the Free World.

When the Communist empire collapsed, America was suddenly left without a worldwide enemy. This vacuum has now been filled by the Muslims-terrorists. Not only Osama bin Laden, but also the Chechnyan freedom fighters, the angry North African youth of the Paris *banlieus*, the Iranian Revolutionary Guards, the insurgents in the Philippines.

Thus the American world-view rearranged itself: a good world (Western civilization) and a bad world (Islamic civilization). Diplomats still take care to make a distinction between "radical Islamists" and "moderate Muslims," but that is only for appearances' sake. Between ourselves, we know of course that they are all Osama bin Ladens. They are all the same.

This way, a huge part of the world, composed of manifold and very different countries, and a great religion with many different and even opposing tendencies (like Christianity, like Judaism), which has given the world unmatched scientific and cultural treasures, is thrown into one and the same pot.

This world-view is tailored for us. Indeed, the world of the clashing civilizations is, for us, the best of all possible worlds.

The struggle between Israel and the Palestinians is no longer a conflict between the Zionist Movement, which came to settle in this country, and the Palestinian people, which inhabited it. No, it has been from the very beginning a part of a worldwide struggle which does not stem from our aspirations and actions. The assault of terrorist Islam on the Western world did not start because of us. Our conscience can be entirely clean—we are among the good guys of this world.

This is now the line of argument of official Israel: the Palestinians elected Hamas, a murderous Islamic movement. (If it didn't exist, it would have to be invented—and indeed, some people assert it was created from the start by our secret service.) Hamas is terroristic, and so is Hizbullah. Perhaps Mahmoud Abbas is not a terrorist himself, but he is weak and Hamas is about to take sole control over all Palestinian territories. So we cannot talk with them. We have no partner. Actually, we cannot possibly have a partner, because we belong to Western Civilization, which Islam wants to eradicate.

In his book *Der Judenstaat*, Theodor Herzl, the official Israeli "Prophet of the State," prophesied this development, too.

This is what he wrote in 1896: "For Europe we shall constitute (in Palestine) a part of the wall against Asia, we shall serve as a vanguard of culture against barbarism."

Herzl was thinking of a metaphorical wall, but in the meantime we have put up a very real one. For many, this is not just a Separation Wall between Israel and Palestine. It is a part of the worldwide wall between the West and Islam, the front-line of the clash of civilizations. Beyond the wall there are not men, women, and children, not a conquered and oppressed Palestinian population, not choked towns and villages like Abu-Dis, a-Ram, Bil'in, and Qalqilia. No, beyond the wall there are a billion terrorists, multitudes of bloodthirsty Muslims, who have only one desire in life: to throw us into the sea, simply because we are Jews, part of Judeo-Christian Civilization.

With an official position like that—who is there to talk to? What is there to talk about? What is the point of meeting in Annapolis or anywhere else?

And what is left to us to do—to cry or to laugh?

One State: Solution or Utopia[20]

Uri Avnery's speech in a public debate with Ilan Pappe.

May 12, 2007

This is not a duel to the death of gladiators in a Roman arena.

Ilan Pappe and I are partners in the battle against the occupation. I respect his courage. We stand side by side in a joint struggle, but we advocate two sharply opposing goals.

What is the disagreement about?

We have no disagreement about the past. We agree that Zionism, which has made its mark on history and created the State of Israel, also brought a historic injustice upon the Palestinian people. The occupation is an abominable situation, and it must be ended. No debate about that.

Perhaps we also have no disagreement about the distant future. About what should happen in a hundred years. We shall touch upon that later in the evening.

But we have a sharp disagreement about the foreseeable future—the solution for the bleeding conflict during the next 20, 30, 50 years.

This is not a theoretical debate. We cannot say, as the Hebrew expression goes, "May every man live with his own faith," and may peace reign in the peace movement. Between these two alternatives there can be no compromise. We have to decide, we have to choose, because they dictate quite different strategies and different tactics—not tomorrow, but today, here and now. The difference is fateful.

For example, should we concentrate our efforts on the struggle for public opinion in Israel, or should we give up on the struggle here and concentrate on the struggle abroad?

I am an Israeli. I stand with both feet on the ground of Israeli reality. I want to change this reality radically. But I want the State of Israel to exist.

Those who oppose the existence of Israel as a state that expresses our Israeli identity deprive themselves of any possibility to act here. All their activities in Israel are doomed to failure.

A person can despair and say: "There's nothing to be done. Everything is lost. We have passed the 'point of no return.' The situation is 'irreversible.' We have nothing more to do in this country."

Everyone can despair for a moment. Perhaps each of us has despaired at one time or other. But one should not turn despair into an ideology. Despair destroys the ability to act.

I say: "There is no reason at all for despair. Nothing is lost. Nothing in life is 'irreversible,' except life itself. There is no such thing as a 'point of no return.'"

I am 83 years old. In my lifetime, I have seen the advent of the Nazis and their downfall. I have seen the Soviet Union at its zenith and watched its collapse. A day before the fall of the Berlin wall, no German believed that he would witness that moment in his lifetime. The smartest experts did not foresee it. Because in history, there are subterranean streams that nobody perceives in real time. That's why the theoretical analyses are so rarely confirmed.

Nothing is lost until the fighters raise their hands and say that all is lost. Raising hands is no solution. Neither is it moral.

In our situation, a person who despairs has three alternatives: (a) emigration, (b) inner emigration, which means staying at home and doing nothing, or (c) escape to the world of idealist solutions for the days of the Messiah.

The third alternative is the most dangerous at the moment, because the situation is critical, especially for the Palestinians. There is no time for a solution in a hundred years. We need an urgent solution, a solution that can be realized within a few years.

It has been said that Avnery is old, he sticks to old solutions, he is unable to absorb a new idea. And I wonder: a new idea?

The idea of "one joint state" was old when I was a boy. It flourished in the 30s of the last century. But it went bankrupt. The idea of the two-state solution grew in the soil of the new reality.

If I may be permitted to make a personal remark: I am not a historian. I was alive when it happened. I am an eyewitness, an ear-witness, a feeling witness. As a soldier in the 1948 war, as the editor of a news magazine for 40 years, as a Knesset member for ten years, as an activist of Gush Shalom, I have seen the events from different angles. My hand is on the public pulse.

There are three questions concerning the one-state idea:

1. Is it at all possible?
2. If it is possible—is it good?
3. Will it bring a just peace?

As to the first question, my absolutely unequivocal answer is: "No, it is not possible."

Anyone connected with the Israeli-Jewish public knows that its innermost desire is the existence of a state with a Jewish majority, a state where the Jews are masters of their fate. That desire trumps all other aims, even the desire for a state in all of *Eretz Israel*.

One can talk about one state from the Mediterranean Sea to the Jordan River, a bi-national or non-national state—in practice what it means is the dismantling of the State of Israel, the negation of all the nation building that has been carried out by five generations. That must be said clearly, without mumbling and equivocation, and that's what the public—the Jewish, and certainly the Palestinian public—quite rightly thinks it is. What we are talking about is the dismantling of the State of Israel.

We want to change many things in this state, its historical narrative, its accepted definition as a "Jewish and democratic" state. We want to put an end to the occupation outside and the discrimination inside. We want to create a new basis for the relationship between the state and its Arab-Palestinian citizens. But it is impossible to ignore the basic ethos of the huge majority of the state's citizens.

99.99 percent of the Jewish public do not want to dismantle the state. And that's quite natural.

There is an illusion that this can be changed through pressure from outside. Will outside pressure compel this people to give up the state?

I propose to you a simple test: think for a moment about your neighbors at home, at work, or at the university. Would any one of them give up the state because somebody abroad wants them to?

Because of pressure from Europe? Even pressure from the White House? No, nothing but a crushing military defeat on the battlefield will compel the Israelis to give up their state. And if that happens, our debate will become irrelevant anyhow.

The majority of the Palestinian people, too, want a state of their own. It is needed to satisfy their most basic aspirations, to restore their national pride, to heal their trauma. Even the chiefs of Hamas, with whom we have talked, want it. Anyone who thinks otherwise is laboring under an illusion. There are Palestinians who talk about one state, but for most of those, it is just a codeword for the dismantling of the State of Israel. They, too, know that it is utopian.

There are also some Palestinians who delude themselves into thinking that if they talk about one state, it will frighten the Israelis so much that they will agree to the establishment of the Palestinian state next to Israel. But the result of this Machiavellian thinking is quite the opposite: it frightens the Israelis and pushes them into the arms of the right. It arouses the fearful dog of ethnic cleansing, which is sleeping in the corner. That dog must not be forgotten for a moment.

All over the world, the tendency is going the other way: not the creation of new multi-national states, but on the contrary, the breaking up of states into national components. In Scotland, this week, victory was achieved by a party that wants to split from England. The French-speaking minority in Canada is always wavering on the brink of secession. Kosovo is about to gain independence from Serbia. The Soviet Union has broken up into its component parts, Chechnya wants to separate from Russia, Yugoslavia has broken apart, Cyprus has broken apart, the Basques want independence, Corsicans want independence, in Sri Lanka a civil war is raging, as it is in the Sudan. In Indonesia, the stitches are coming loose in a dozen different places. Belgium has endless problems.

In the entire world there is no example of two different nations deciding of their own free will to live together in one state. There is no example—except Switzerland—of a bi-national or multi-national state really functioning. (And the example of Switzerland, which has grown for centuries in a unique process, is the proverbial exception that proves the rule.)

To hope that after 120 years of conflict, into which a fifth generation has already been born, there could be a transition from total war to total peace in a joint state, giving up all aspiration to independence— that is a complete illusion.

How is this idea to be realized? The advocates of the one state never go into this in detail.

It is supposed, so it seems, to come about something like this: the Palestinians will give up their struggle for liberation and their aspiration for a national state of their own. They will announce that they want to live in a joint state with the Israelis. After the establishment of this state, they will have to fight for their civil rights. People of good-will around the world will support their struggle, as they once did in South Africa. They will impose a boycott. They will isolate the state. Millions of refugees will come back to the country. Thus the wheel will turn back and the Palestinian majority will attain power.

How much time will that take? Two generations? Three generations? Four generations?

Does anyone imagine how such a state will function in practice? The inhabitants of Bil'in will pay the same taxes as the inhabitant of Kfar-Sava? The inhabitants of Jenin will enact a constitution together with the inhabitants of Netanya? The inhabitants of Hebron and the settlers will serve in the same army and the same police force, shoulder to shoulder, and will be subject to the same laws? Is that realistic?

Some say: but that situation already exists. Israel is already governing one state from the sea to the river. One has only to change the regime. But nothing of the sort exists. What does exist are an occupying state and an occupied territory.

It is far, far easier to dismantle settlements than to compel 6 million Jewish Israelis to dismantle the state.

No, the one state will not come into being. But let's ask ourselves— if it did come into being, would that be a good thing?

My answer is: absolutely not.

Let's examine this state, not as an imaginary creature, the epitome of perfection, but as it would be in reality.

In this state, the Israelis will be dominant. They have a complete superiority in practically all spheres: quality of life, military power, technological capabilities. The average per annum income of an Israeli is 25 times (25 times!) higher than that of an average Palestinian— $20,000 as against $800. The Israelis will see to it that the Palestinians will be the hewers of wood and the drawers of water for a long, long time.

It will be an occupation by other means. A disguised occupation. It will not end the conflict, but open another phase.

Will this solution bring a just peace? Hardly.

This state will be a battlefield. Each side will try to take over as much land as possible and bring in as many persons as possible. The Jews will fight by all means to prevent the Arabs from becoming the majority and coming to power. In practice, this will be an apartheid state. If the Arabs become the majority and try to assume power, there will be a struggle that may become a civil war. A new edition of 1948.

Even an advocate of the one-state solution must admit that the struggle will go on for several generations. Much blood may flow, and the results are far from assured.

The idea is utopian. To realize it, one has to change the people, perhaps the two peoples. One has to create a new human being. That's what the Communists tried to do at the start of the Soviet Union. That's what the founders of the kibbutzim tried to do. Unfortunately, the human being has not changed.

Utopianism can bring about terrible consequences. The vision that "the wolf shall dwell with the lamb" requires the provision of a new lamb every day.

There are some who cite the model of South Africa. A beautiful and encouraging example. Unfortunately, there is hardly any similarity between the problem there and the problem here.

In South Africa, there were no two nations, each with a tradition, a language, and a religion that go back for more than a thousand years. Neither the whites not the blacks wanted a separate state of their own, nor did they ever live in two separate states. The one state had already existed for a long time, and the struggle was over power in this one state.

The bosses of South Africa were racists, who admired the Nazis and were incarcerated during World War II because of that. It was easy to boycott their state in all fields of activity. Israel, on the other hand, is accepted by the world as the state of the Holocaust survivors, and apart from small groups, nobody will boycott it. It is enough for the Israelis to point out that the first step on the way to Auschwitz was the Nazi slogan *Kauft nicht bei Juden*—Don't buy from Jews.

Furthermore, a worldwide boycott will arouse in the hearts of many Jews all over the world the deepest fears of anti-Semitism, and will push them into the arms of the extreme right.

A quite different thing is a focused boycott against specific elements of the occupation. We were the pioneers of this approach, when, more than ten years ago, we started a boycott of the products of the settlements and pulled the European Union along with us.

By the way, experts on South Africa tell me that the effects of the boycott are much overrated. The boycott was not the main factor that brought the apartheid regime down, but the international situation. The United States supported the regime as a bastion in the fight against Communism. Once the Soviet Union had collapsed, the Americans just dropped South Africa.

The relationship between the United States and Israel is immeasurably more profound and complex. It has deep ideological layers: a similar national narrative, the Christian Evangelist theology, and more.

The two-state solution is the only practical solution in the realm of reality.

It is ridiculous to assert that it has been defeated. The very opposite is true. In the most important sphere, the collective consciousness, it is winning all out.

On the morrow of the 1948 war, when we raised this flag for the first time in Israel, we were a tiny band. We could be counted on the fingers of two hands. Everybody denied that a Palestinian people even existed. In the late 1960s I tramped around Washington DC and spoke with officials at the White House, the Department of State, the National Security Council, and the US delegation to the UN; nobody there was prepared to entertain this idea.

Now there is a worldwide consensus that this is the only solution. The United States, Russia, Europe, Israeli public opinion, Palestinian public opinion, the Arab League. One has to realize the full meaning of this: the entire Arab world now supports this solution. This is extremely important for the future.

Why did this happen? After all, it is not that we are so gifted as to win over the whole world. No, it is the inner logic of this solution that conquered the globe. True, some of the new adherents of this solution only pay lip service to it. Perhaps they use it to divert attention from their real aims. People like Ariel Sharon and Ehud Olmert act as if they support this idea, while in reality their intention is to maintain the occupation forever. But this shows that even they realize that they cannot go on opposing the two-state solution openly. When the whole world recognizes that this is the only practical solution it will, in the end, be realized.

The parameters are well known, and they, too, now enjoy world-wide agreement:

1. A Palestinian state will come into being next to Israel.
2. The border between them will be based on the Green Line, perhaps with an agreed-upon and equal swap of territories.
3. Jerusalem will be the capital of the two states.
4. There will be an agreed-upon solution of the refugee problem. In practice, this means that an agreed number will return to Israel, and the rest will be rehabilitated in the State of Palestine or in their present places of domicile, with the payment of generous compensation that will turn them into welcome guests. When there

is an agreed plan that tells every refugee family what their choices are, it must be submitted to the refugees wherever they are. They must be partners in the final decision.

5. There will be an economic partnership in which the Palestinian government will be able to defend Palestinian interests, unlike the present situation. The very existence of two states will mitigate, at least to some extent, the huge difference of power between the two sides.

6. In the more distant future—a Middle Eastern union, on the model of the EU, which may also include Turkey and Iran.

The obstacles are well known, and they are big. They cannot be circumvented by patent medicine. They must be faced and overcome. Here, in Israel, we must weaken the fears and anxieties, and point out the benefits and profit that we will gain from the creation of a Palestinian state at our side.

We must bring about a change of consciousness. But we have already come a long way from the days when the entire public denied the very existence of the Palestinian people, rejected the idea of a Palestinian state, rejected the partition of Jerusalem, rejected any dialogue with the PLO, rejected an agreement with Arafat. In all these areas our stand trickled down and has been accepted in various degrees.

It is clear that this is still far from what is necessary. But that is the direction things are moving—and there are hundreds of opinion polls to show it.

Real obstacles to the two-state solution can be overcome. They are small compared to the obstacles on the way to one state. I would say the ratio is 1:1,000. It is like a boxer who fails to win against a lightweight opponent, and therefore chooses to confront a heavyweight. Or an athlete who fails in the 100-meter sprint and therefore enters the marathon. Or somebody who despairs of climbing Mont Blanc and therefore decides to climb Mount Everest.

No doubt, the one-state idea gives its adherents moral satisfaction. Somebody told me: OK, it is not realistic, but it is moral, and that is the place where I want to be. I say: that is a luxury we cannot afford. When the fate of so many human beings is in the balance, a moral stand that is not realistic is immoral. I repeat: a moral stand that is not realistic is immoral.

There are those that despair because the peace forces have not succeeded in putting an end to the occupation. We have remained a small minority. The government and the media ignore us. True. But we, too, bear a part of the responsibility for that. We have not been think-ing enough, we have not identified the reasons for the failures. When was the last time a thorough discussion of the strategies and tactics of the fight for peace took place?

We have not succeeded in connecting with the Oriental Jewish community. We have remained strangers to the Russian immigrants. We don't even have a real partnership with the Arab-Palestinian community inside Israel. We have not found the way to touch the hearts of the general public. We have not succeeded in creating a unified and efficient political force that would be able to exert an influence on the Knesset and the government. We must examine ourselves.

It is not enough to point out that the one-state solution cannot be realized. This "solution" is also very dangerous.

1. It diverts the efforts into a mistaken direction. We see this already happening. It both results from despair and produces despair. It causes people to desert the battlefield in Israel and creates the illusion that the real battlefield is abroad. That is escapism.
2. It causes the loss of irreplaceable time. Tens of years, in which terrible things can happen to the Palestinians, and also to us. Anyone who is afraid of ethnic cleansing (and rightly so) must be conscious of this danger and this urgency.
3. It divides the peace camp and deepens the gap between it and the public. It strengthens the right, because it frightens the sane public and causes it to lose sight of a sensible solution.
4. It pulls the rug from under the feet of those who fight against the occupation. If the whole country between the sea and the Jordan is to become one state anyhow, then the settlers can put their settlements anywhere they like.
5. It strengthens the argument that there is "no solution" to the conflict. If the two-state solution is wrong, and if the one-state solution is not realizable, then the right is correct in claiming that there is no solution at all—an argument that justifies every evil, from the eternal occupation to ethnic cleansing. No solution means an endless occupation.

Let us be clear: there will be no end to the occupation as long as there is no peace agreement.

As for the distant future, perhaps we shall meet at unexpected places.

When we reach the station that is called peace between two states, everyone will be free to choose what their next station should be.

Somebody will want to strive for the amalgamation of the two states into one? Go ahead. Somebody will think that the two-state solution is good forever? Why not? Somebody will think, like me, that the two states will move gradually, with mutual consent all along the way, towards a confederation or federation? Welcome.

(At our very first meeting in 1982, Yassir Arafat spoke with me about a Benelux solution, like the one that existed for some time between Belgium, the Netherlands and Luxemburg—Israel, Palestine, Jordan, and perhaps even Lebanon. He continued to talk about this until the end.)

Experience proves that the classic national state is here to stay formally, everyone under his own flag, while in practice many of its functions are being transferred to super-national structures, like the European Union.

(By the way, when the idea of uniting Europe was first aired, many people wanted to create the United States of Europe, on the American model. Charles de Gaulle warned against ignoring national feelings. He called for a "Europe des patries," a Europe based on national states. Fortunately, his view prevailed, and now life does the rest.)

Something like this, I assume, will in the end happen here, too. But for now, we must treat the immediate problem. We have before us an injured person, bleeding profusely. The bleeding has to be stopped and the wound has to be healed before we can treat the roots of the disease.

Summing up, this is my opinion:

The situation is terrible (as always), but we are progressing nevertheless.

True, on the surface the situation is depressing and shocking: the settlements are getting bigger, the wall is getting longer, the occupation is causing untold injustices every day.

Perhaps it is the advantage of age: today, at the age of 83, I am able to look at things in the perspective of a much longer time span.

Because under the surface, things are moving in the opposite direction. All the polls prove that the decisive majority of the Israeli public is resigned to the existence of the Palestinian people and is resigned to the necessity of a Palestinian state. The government recognized the PLO yesterday and will recognize Hamas tomorrow. The majority has more or less accepted that Jerusalem must become the capital of the two states. In ever widening circles, there is the beginning of a recognition of the narrative of the other nation.

There is a worldwide consensus on the two-state solution, which has been reached by way of elimination: in reality, there is no other. But in order for it to be realized, support must come from the inside, from the Israeli public. This support we must create. That is our job.

And a word of warning: we must beware of Utopias. A Utopia looks like a light at the end of the tunnel. It warms the heart. But it is a deceptive light that can induce us to enter a branch of the tunnel from which there is no exit.

We have never heard answers to the two decisive questions about the one-state solution: how will it come about and how will it function in practice? But without clear answers to these questions, this is not a plan but at best a vision.

True, 120 years of conflict have created in our people a huge accumulation of hate, prejudice, suppressed guilt feelings, stereotypes, fear (most importantly, fear), and absolute mistrust of the Arabs. These we must fight, to convince the public that peace is worthwhile and good for the future of Israel. Together with a change in the international situation and a partnership with the Palestinian people, our chances of achieving peace are good.

I, anyhow, have decided to stay alive until this happens.

2
Facts on the Ground; Devastation all Around

The most immediate issue that must be addressed is Israel's occupation and its concomitant inflammatory aspects that prevent any possibility of a solution for Palestinians and Israelis. Manifestations of the occupation that are particularly problematic in any resolution to the situation include the Separation Wall, thought by many Israelis to be a barrier to future terrorist attacks by Palestinians. The wall is perceived by Palestinians to be mainly an attempt to annex more land and water in the continuing Israeli strategy of creating "facts on the ground"—a tactic of occupation which creates a physical infrastructure which will be difficult to eradicate and can be sold to the rest of the world as unreasonable to cede.

Another important facet of the "facts on the ground" strategy is the creation of ever more "settlements." The settlements are Israeli enclaves in the heart of Palestinian territory; built quickly and well fortified, they are frequently inhabited by the most zealous religious Zionists, and are flashpoints for conflict.[21]

As Avnery points out, though, while Palestinians are suffering the bulk of ill-effects from the occupation, it takes its toll on Israelis, too, creating a climate of fear through suicide bombings that kill non-combatants, affecting the economy, and compromising the moral fiber of the nation. In other words, the occupation is not good for the occupiers either.—SRP

Dear Settler

November 25, 2000

Dear (in both senses of the word) settler,
Let's not waste time on nonsense words like "dialogue," "conciliation" and such words cherished by the feeble-minded. Let's face the fact that you don't like me and I do not like you. You believe that my friends and I are "destroyers of Israel," people who conspire to evict you from your homes and turn them over to the Arabs. I believe that you and your friends are destroyers of Israel who conspire to impose their will on the state and drag it into an eternal war that may lead to its destruction.

So let's talk about practical matters.

Up until now, you have been a success story. You wanted to create "facts on the ground," so as to prevent any possibility of giving the occupied territories back to the Palestinians.[22] You have compelled all the governments, from Eshkol to Barak, to give you a huge slice of the state's resources.[23] You have turned the army into your private militia.

The Israel Defense Forces have become the Settlement Defense Forces.

Politicians of all shades have courted you, and still do. The socialist Yigal Alon planted the first settlers in the heart of Hebron, Shimon Peres planted the first settlement, Kedumim, in the heart of the West Bank. Ehud Barak, who won the elections with the slogan "Money for education and not for settlements," has turned out to be the greatest patron of the settlers ever.[24]

You have succeeded. Not since the zealots (70 AD) have so few succeeded in imposing their will on so many. The zealots, of course, after initial successes, led to the mass suicide at Massada and to the virtual elimination of the Jewish presence from this country for 1,900 years.

I know that there are major differences between the settlements. There is Kfar Darom, a tiny, fortified, and isolated settlement, in the middle of 1.2 million Palestinians, dominating the lifeline of the Gaza strip. A thorn in the flesh.

Then there is the "Jewish settlement in Hebron," a few dozen fanatical families in the middle of 160,000 Hebronites. Living in the "Jewish part" of Hebron there are 40,000 Palestinians, who are condemned to a curfew every time one of your children overturns a stand in the market.[25]

Quite different are the "quality of life" settlements. They were not founded in order to hasten the coming of the Messiah but for people to enjoy the air and the landscape ("What a beautiful minaret in the village opposite"). They have nothing in common with the violent fanatics of Ma'aleh Amos or Yitzhar. At the present time, death overshadows their quality of life.

Ma'aleh Adumim, whose area is officially bigger than all of Tel-Aviv, was implanted by that arch-settler Teddy Kollek in order to enlarge his fiefdom. Kiryat Sefer, another big township, was established by the coalition as a bribe to the orthodox, who get luxury housing for nothing.[26]

Settlements of different kinds, settlers of all shades. Yet they all have one thing in common: every settlement is a landmine on the road to peace. You are sitting on the land reserves of the Palestinian people, on stolen land, and use the water needed by another people for their very existence. You dominate the landscape, symbols of the occupation. The planners drew up the settlement map with the aim of carving up the Palestinian territory.[27]

Therefore, it was only a question of time until the Palestinian people rose up against you. It's like an alien particle implanted in a body: the body mobilizes all its strength in order to evict it. The Palestinians see this struggle as their war of liberation, whose main aim is to get you out.

Don't kid yourself: you have no chance whatsoever of winning this war.

In the last hundred years there have been dozens of such wars, and the oppressed peoples have won them all. In each of them, the occupying army was infinitely stronger than the rebels. In every one of them, the conquered people suffered far more casualties than the occupier. But the occupiers always tired of the struggle before the occupied, because the occupied people were fighting for their lives and freedom, while the occupiers were fighting for luxury. For the Israelis, the settlements are a luxury.

Some months ago, a public opinion poll surprisingly showed that you are the most unpopular sector in Israel, even more unpopular than the orthodox. You may be less unpopular today, because you are being hit—but have no illusions, this is a very temporary popularity. It will evaporate, once the number of our casualties rises, when we relinquish all our achievements in the Arab world, when our standing throughout the world sinks, when the public becomes aware of the economic price of this struggle and when the danger of a general war in the region (a danger which we have long forgotten) appears again on the horizon.

The French fought for seven years for Algeria, which they considered "a part of France, like Provence." A million people lost their lives there. At the crucial moment, the French settlers set up a militia of their own (the OAS) and committed acts of revenge. As a result, a million French settlers of the fifth and sixth generation had to flee within a few days, once France made peace. The same happened to the British settlers in Kenya. The white settlers in South Africa avoided this fate because they surrendered in time and became citizens of the black regime.

You have missed that opportunity. What you and the soldiers are doing now is creating such rage and hatred among the Palestinians that your continued presence in the territories has become impossible. Every dead child, every demolished home, every "blockade" and "liquidation" brings the end of your settlements nearer.

I am sure that you and your friends know this in your hearts. All your behavior shows this. You are acting out of despair. I propose that you exchange the despair for hope of a solution.

Instead of dreaming up empty slogans like "Let the army win," you should start to think about your return and rehabilitation.

Your enemies will say: "We owe you nothing. Nobody compelled you to go there. We have wasted billions and billions on you. Now you can look out for yourself."

I do not subscribe to that. I, and many more like me in the peace movement, believe that the state should finance your return to Israel and your orderly absorption. After we easily absorbed a million new immigrants from the Soviet Union, we shall absorb 150,000 settlers too. It will be all the easier as most of you are working in Israel anyhow, so that only the problem of housing remains. Israel in peace, with a flourishing economy, will easily solve the problem.

I am convinced that the great majority of the settlers—all except the hard-core fanatics—will sooner or later accept this solution. Sooner rather than later, I hope. Have pity on yourself, on the soldiers. Each drop of blood spilt is a waste. Let not the settlements become an altar of Moloch, on which the children are sacrificed.

When you, too, come to this conclusion, you will find that we are your allies, more trustworthy than all those who flatter you now and who will sell you down the river tomorrow.

Settlers were compensated for the homes they lost during the "disengagement" from Gaza. Palestinians do not receive compensation for the homes Israel bulldozes for various reasons including making room for settlements, bypass roads, and the Wall, or for belonging to the family member of a suicide bomber. Sometimes Palestinian homes are bulldozed for having been built without a permit, virtually unobtainable from the Israeli occupation forces. Frequently, un-permitted houses are replacements for homes previously destroyed by the occupation forces.—SRP

May Your House be Destroyed[28]

July 20, 1998

The scene could have been taken from the theater of the absurd. A senior IDF officer was facing the camera, reacting bitterly to Israeli demonstrators calling him and his soldiers "Nazis." "How can you call us Nazis?" he asked, filled with rage. "We are only carrying out orders! Without sentiment!"

I have given much thought to these words. Obviously this officer knows only that the Nazis killed Jews. He does not know that for an entire generation, the words "We only carried out orders!" have been imprinted on the Jewish consciousness as the slogan of German war criminals. And the words "without sentiment" only makes it worse.

But the question is: what caused the demonstrators, respectable folk, professors among them, to burst out with such an extreme and objectionable expression?

Every day we hear of the demolition of "illegally built" Palestinian homes.[29] At most, there are merely a few words in a newspaper. Words. But when seen with one's own eyes, it is horrifying.

One of the most serious curses in the Arab culture is: "May your house be destroyed." Because a house is not merely a structure of stones and walls. A house is the symbol of man's dignity and of a family's security.

A house is passed on from one generation to the next. The destruction of a house is not just a dry administrative act. It is an act that rocks the very foundations of human life. I suspect that even many liberal Israelis, who do not give the matter much thought, do not perceive the heinousness of this daily act.

It is shocking to watch a bulldozer moving towards a wall and taking the first bite, then the second and the third, like an evil prehistoric monster, until the wall collapses and the roof comes crashing down in a cloud of dust. To hear the wailing of the men and women being dragged out in front of the children, to see their broken belongings scattered on the ground. Are the soldiers' hearts so hardened that they can "do the job," as the phrase goes, "without sentiment"?

When those shocked Israeli demonstrators witnessed the demolition in the refugee camp of Anatah, and heard the soldiers saying that "they were only following orders," the outburst occurred. One of the demonstrators, the erstwhile Chief Rabbi of Strasbourg, was present when the soldiers opened fire and wounded a Palestinian youth in his back (he lost a kidney). Unsurprisingly, the event did not merit a single word in the Israeli press that day or the following day.

The demolition policy currently being implemented by the occupation authorities carries the seed of the next calamity. A child whose house was demolished in front of his terrified eyes becomes a walking time-bomb. The entire Palestinian community which lives with this reality every day knows that the "peace process" is nothing but a fairy tale, and in reality the war rages on throughout the territory.

Virtually every new Palestinian house in Jerusalem is built "without a permit," since virtually no new permits are issued to Palestinians. (The very few Palestinians who do obtain permits are regarded as collaborators.) The Netanyahu–Olmert–Suissa bunch want to reduce the Palestinian population of East Jerusalem and force its residents to move elsewhere. The situation is absurd: Because the blue ID cards of East Jerusalem residents who have moved out of the overcrowded Arab parts of the city are now being confiscated, a mass flow back into the city has begun. A Palestinians pays more for a small apartment in the Old City than an Israeli for a luxury apartment in Rehavia. Contractors find it lucrative to build and rent. And so the feverish pace of Palestinian construction is reaching its peak. As the Bible said (Exodus 1:12): "But the more they afflicted them, the more they multiplied and grew."

Even before the bulldozer moves out of the area after a demolition, the task of rebuilding begins with the family and neighbors. The laborers returning from their day jobs in Israel proper join in the effort. In a matter of days a new house has replaced the demolished one, with the family ensconced in it. This process repeats itself again and again. So far, the Palestinian side is winning. The number of "illegal" homes is growing.

Outside of the annexed area of Jerusalem, demolition takes place throughout "Area C," which Netanyahu and his partners (among them some of the leaders of the Labor Party) want to annex to Israel as well. The intention is to carry out a "transfer," known by the rest of the world as "ethnic cleansing," so that the territory can be acquired by Israel free of any Arab people.

Human-rights activists from all over the world have sent letters of protest to Netanyahu. His officials respond with a standard line that contains no truth whatsoever: it is just a matter of administrative routine, Jewish homes are demolished in the same manner, and assorted other lies that would fool only a simpleton. But the number of simpletons is steadily shrinking.

Once we used to sing: "We have come to the land to build and to be built." Now we can sing: "We have come to the land to destroy and to be destroyed."

Olives, Stones, and Bullets

November 18, 2000

Suddenly I noticed that we were quite alone on the road. A wonderful road, six lanes wide, parts of it still in the building stage. Completely empty.

This is a bypass-bypass road, an invention of the occupation. First, they built the cross-Samaria road, from Kafr-Kassem to Ariel and beyond, so as to bypass the Palestinian villages. But the Palestinian village of Bidia, which, on Saturdays, has become a shopping mall for Israelis, slowly crept up to the road. In anticipation of the next intifada, Benjamin Netanyahu and Ehud Barak (each in his turn) decided on an even more sterile, bypass-the-bypass road. Again great stretches of Palestinian land were expropriated, again we demonstrated together with the Palestinian villagers (November 1998), again we were tear-gassed (one does not shoot at Israelis), again to no avail.

But now the road is empty. Only from time to time we meet groups of cars. The settlers are driving in convoys for fear of stone-throwing children. But we were lucky. Here and there we saw stones lying around on the road, remnants of previous stone-showers, but we passed unmolested.

On the previous evening we received an SOS call from the villagers of Hares asking us to please go there. This Palestinian village, near the big Ariel settlement, is cut off from the world. The army is blockading it, no one is allowed to enter or leave. The olives, the only products of the village, are going to rot on the trees, especially in the orchard border-ing the Revava settlement. Anyone trying to harvest there is in mortal danger. A 14-year-old boy was shot and killed there only three days ago, when he was alone in the orchard with his father. The villagers hope that the presence of Israelis will restrain the settlers and soldiers, allowing them harvest the olives on which their livelihood depends.

A woman from the village also called. She cried excitedly that at that moment the soldiers had opened fire on the village and on her. She begged us to come the next morning. Until darkness, she promised, there is generally no shooting.

Hares is situated on a hill, 100 meters away from the road, at a stretch where the bypass-bypass joins the bypass road. The stretch is an ideal place for throwing stones, and therefore the settlers are angry. We know the landscape well, because in March 1999 we helped a family in the next village, Kiffel-Hares, to rebuild a house demolished by the army.

It was not easy for us to decide what to do. It was clear that this was a war zone. In order to get to the place, we had to risk being stoned or shot at by Palestinians who would think that we were settlers. On the other hand, our presence would be like a red rag to the settlers. The army would consider us breakers of the occupation laws. All this in order to pick olives a few dozen yards from a settlement.

Gush Shalom activists who can turn out on a workday include youngsters in their teens and elderly people. Men and women. Was it responsible to advise them to enter a war-zone?

On the other hand, in these difficult days, in the middle of the Palestinian war of liberation, it is very important that the threads still connecting Israelis and Palestinians are not broken, as extremists on both sides would wish. It is also important to show the Palestinians that there are peace forces in Israel who want to display solidarity during their hardest hour.

These arguments won. It was decided to mobilize by phone the activists who were ready to leave their work on a working day and to take part in the action. Within two hours, 20 volunteered. And so, on Friday, we were on our way from Tel-Aviv in a minibus driven by an Arab-Israeli. From Jerusalem, another contingent, led by the "Rabbis for Human Rights" group, were also on their way.

We arrived at Hares without mishap. On the way we did not encounter any army checkpoint. Even the checkpoint which was located for years on the Green Line, near Kafr Kassem, had mysteriously disappeared.[30]

We entered the village on foot, climbing the hill, crossing a field of desolation—old olive trees cut down, ancient terraces destroyed, apparently to enable the army to shoot without hindrance.

From the direction of the mosque we heard the Friday prayers as we crossed the quiet village by foot and left it by the western entrance, on the way to the plantations. There the army stopped us with armored jeeps and heavily armed soldiers. A tough major (or perhaps lieutenant-colonel, the bullet-proof vest made it difficult to be sure) quickly filled out a prepared form, signed in advance by the C/O Central Command for all occasions, declaring the Hares plantations a "closed military area." We were requested to leave.[31]

We refused, of course. We pointed out that the settlers, who were shouting slogans and cursing us, were allowed to pass freely in their cars. Then a superior officer, a lieutenant colonel or perhaps colonel (as above) appeared. We were told that he was the brigade commander.

We argued with him. He was a sympathetic, intelligent officer, with a sense of humor, one of those who are called "regular fellows," which made what he said sound even more objectionable. Why the discrimination between the settlers and the Palestinian villagers? Well, it's because the villagers throw stones. Why punish a whole village for the deeds of a minority? "I am not sure it's a minority." It was quite clear that his heart is with the settlers, whose life, as he said, "had become hell." For him, the Palestinians were enemies, no sentiments attached.

Why does he not permit us to harvest olives? "Because you came here to provoke the settlers." We answered honestly that we had no such intention.

While this argument went on, our activists started to infiltrate into the plantations one by one. The brigade commander had to choose between several alternatives: he could call for reinforcements to get us out by force, or he could allow us to harvest olives. Wisely, he chose the latter course.

The next six hours were an experience taken straight out of an old Zionist propaganda film. We picked olives, one by one, from the trees nearest the settlement. We used our hats as containers, until buckets were brought. We climbed trees in order to get at the higher branches. Hard work, but really enjoyable. On the hill, opposite us, at a distance of some 50 meters, a cluster of angry, bearded, skull-cap-wearing settlers had gathered, but soldiers prevented them from approaching us.

When the villagers saw us working, families of the tree-owners dared to come and harvest too. Friendships developed quickly. Everything was done at a hectic speed. The Palestinians knew that they could work there only as long as we were there. They chose work methods that were damaging to the trees, hitting the branches, gathering the olives on nylon sheets spread on the ground, in order to gather as many olives as possible in a few hours.

At 3 p.m., when we were about to finish, we received a call on the mobile phone. We were asked to come as quickly as possible to the other side of the village, where a confrontation was developing with the army. The villagers wanted to use the presence of Israelis (those who had come from Jerusalem) in order to remove the road-block put up by the army to prevent them having contact with the neighboring village and the world at large. The Palestinians calculated that the army would not open fire in the presence of Israelis and foreign TV crews. Since the situation was deteriorating rapidly, we were asked to come and try to prevent a fatal clash.

We boarded the minibus and drove into the village. Along the main street, a lot of children were standing around. At some distance, children were playing (training?) throwing stones at each other. Some local youngsters volunteered to walk in front of our bus and tell the children that we were not settlers. Proceeding this way we were nearing the place of the clash when we were stopped by the village head and a very authoritative young man. The head said that the confrontation had ended and that he would show us the place. The young man said that the confrontation was still going on and that we should not go on any further. It was clear that he was the boss. He strongly suggested that we go by the way we had come. But first he gave us a short, passionate speech, in which he called Ehud Barak some highly uncomplimentary names from the animal kingdom.

The village head volunteered to show us the way, so that we could view the site of the clash from the army side, from the main road. But as we were leaving the village, we encountered an army jeep. A sergeant with Russian features stopped us with a movement of his hand generally reserved for Arabs. One of us asked him to be polite. He became very angry and told us that we could not leave the village. A blockade was in force; no one comes in, no one goes out. He doesn't give a damn whether we are Israelis or not. Orders are orders.

Only with great difficulty did we convince him to call his superior, who told him, of course, to let us pass. We reached the main road (the cross-Samaria) and had to drive behind a convoy of settlers, when suddenly we were hit by a shower of stones. At some distance we saw a group of small children. Fortunately, only the body of our bus was hit. At lightning speed police and army jeeps appeared on the scene and took up firing positions opposite the village. But the children had already disappeared.

In the meantime, we were told over the phone that the confrontation was really over, so we decided to make for home. On the way, the village head (a renovation contractor active in the Tel-Aviv area) alighted. We waited for a few minutes, to make sure that he got home safely. He started to climb the hill, but before he had gone no further than a few meters, soldiers ran after him, rifles ready to shoot. We got down from the bus and convinced the soldiers that the man was not a dangerous terrorist, but a villager who had been kind enough to show us the way. They let him return to his village. But in the meantime, police had stopped near our bus and made out a traffic-violation ticket, because it was standing on a part of the road where it was not allowed to stand. A stubborn young policewoman refused to yield, but we finally convinced the Druze policeman at the wheel to relent. After all, the bus had been standing there only because we were talking with the soldiers.

Over the phone we heard that two activists from the Jerusalem group had been arrested during the clash at the roadblock. (Neither of the two belonged to Peace Now, as was erroneously reported on the Israeli Channel 1. Peace Now had taken no part in the events of the day.)

This is how the reality of the occupation, November 2000, looks.

We returned home tired but content, as they say. The time was 4 p.m., the hour shooting usually starts.

For me it was a long day. An old friend of mine had invited me to a dinner party in Caesarea. The elite of the elite was there, financiers, doctors, senior bureaucrats, media people, artists. Wonderful food, excellent wines. I had no strength left to get into arguments. So I just sat aside, looked and wondered about what was happening at the time in Hares, some light-years away.

At midnight, on the long way home, I heard on the news that a settler woman had been slightly wounded by stones near Hares village.

Love of the Cannibals

May 14, 2000

Three people say: "I love children." One is a father. One is a pedophile who uses children for carnal satisfaction. One is a cannibal who eats them. They use the same words, but they mean quite different things.

The settlers love this country. They say so every day. They settle everywhere. But their love is like that of the cannibal, who likes the children fried.

This thought came to my mind a couple of days ago, when I was standing on a hill north of Ramallah, near the village of Dora al-Kareh. Before me there stretched a beauty spot I had not seen before, hidden from the Jerusalem–Nablus highway.

A charming, flat valley between two ridges of steep hills is divided into small plots on which vegetables grow organically. The water of local springs flows in small canals that, the locals say, date back to Roman times. The water is divided between seven *hamulahs* (extended families) according to an unchanging quota worked out 400 years ago. On the Ramallah market, these well-known vegetables fetch prices considerably higher than others.

All this beauty is now threatened with extinction. All in the name of love for the country.

The slogan is "bypass road," two innocuous words that hide a cruel reality.

On the face of it, what's wrong with a road? It helps the flow of traffic. A narrow strip of asphalt can't bother anybody. That's what people think when they hear about yet another bypass road.

The reality is quite different. Let's take, for example, this particular road. It is designed to connect two settlements: Beth-El and Ofrah. Length: 5.9 kilometers. Width: 220 (two hundred and twenty!) meters. The road itself will be 60 meters wide, with a security margin of

80 meters on each side. 370 *dunams* will be expropriated outright, another 950 *dunams* will be rendered useless.[32]

But the hidden is more important than the transparent. The road will separate three villages from a great part of their lands. In practice, these will be added to the settlements.

Some explanations may be in order.

Before the elections, Ehud Barak visited Beth-El and Ofrah and promised publicly that they will stay there forever. That was rather odd, because the recurring theme in his propaganda was "separation" ("We shall be here and they will be there …"), meaning that only big "settlement blocs" will be annexed to Israel, while the settlers in isolated spots will be evacuated or become residents of Palestine.

Beth-El and Ofrah are both isolated in the middle of the Palestinian population, far from the green line. But the leaders of the fanatical settlers live there, and Barak wants to cultivate them. How? Simple: These isolated settlements will be turned into a new "settlement bloc," to be annexed to Israel.

The "bypass road" serves this purpose. From a transportation point of view it is quite superfluous: These two settlements are already connected by existing roads. The new road will save the settlers five minutes driving time. Even if a new road has to be built, it can be much shorter. The planned road is unnecessarily long and winding.

So what's the real purpose? Well, the road is, of course, to be annexed to Israel. It follows automatically that all the land between the road and the settlements will be annexed too. The road is a knife cutting off a big slice of territory from the future State of Palestine.

The same happens now all over the West Bank. This case is different only because of the beauty of the landscape. While Barak chatters endlessly about "framework" and "permanent status" agreements, and while negotiators meet all the time, Barak conducts a resolute campaign to enlarge the "settlement blocs." The roads serve this purpose.

In this campaign of "creating facts on the ground," not only are new injustices added to old ones, but also irreparable damage is being done to the landscape of this country. It's a new crime: the murder of the land, perhaps to be called "terracide."

A Slap in the Face

August 18, 2001

A middle-aged man approaches the army checkpoint. Three bored soldiers look at him. One, probably the one in charge, who was standing two or three meters away, comes up to him and slaps his face.

A few hours later this was shown on television in Israel and all the Arab countries. It appears that the beaten man is an Egyptian television reporter, who was on his way to a press conference.

The IDFL (Israel Defense Forces Liar, an anonymous officer in charge of inventing pretexts for transgressions) provided the usual response: the man had provoked and cursed the soldiers. The soldier got some suspended penalty, probably for slapping people on camera. One may assume that he will be promoted soon.

What is so special about this incident? Only the presence of a foreign TV team, and the amazing chutzpah of the soldier who behaved like this without first making sure that no camera was present. Apart from that, it was a very normal incident. Things like that—and much worse—happen daily at dozens of checkpoints all over the occupied territories. Routine harassment, "in order to relieve the boredom," as a soldier recently explained concerning another incident.

Slaps in the face. Beatings. Compelling people to stand in line for hours in the blazing sun. Compelling people to sit for hours in their cars in the sun with the windows closed. Taking away car keys or identity cards. Puncturing tires. Detaining women in labor on the way to the hospital. Detaining children with cancer on the way to treatment. Detaining kidney patients on the way to dialysis. Stealing money and valuables. So what's so special about slapping an Egyptian journalist? After all, an Arab is an Arab.

Nevertheless, it is worthwhile examining this incident a little further. The soldier (Sergeant? Lieutenant?) did what he did, as do thousands of other soldiers at regular and sporadic checkpoints, because they believe that it is permitted, perhaps even desirable.

If that is true, it shows that the situation is grave. If it is not true, it shows that the situation is even worse.

When thousands of soldiers at the checkpoints behave like this for years, it is clear that the commanders are turning a blind eye. The immediate commander. The battalion commander. The brigade commander. The front commander. The chief of staff. The minister of defense. The prime minister. It would be enough for one of these people to issue an unequivocal order to stop the practice. It would be enough for the chief of staff to remove a brigade commander under whose command such an incident happened. Or for a brigade commander to remove a battalion chief. Or for the battalion commander to dismiss a company captain. Indeed, it would be enough to send one soldier to prison for 28 days (the penalty usually imposed on soldiers refusing to serve in the occupied territories) for the practice to stop at once.

If this does not happen, one cannot but hold the whole chain of command responsible—from the harassing soldier at the checkpoint up to the chief of staff. This means that the harassment is a policy. A policy designed to break the population, to turn their life into hell and induce them to leave the country. And also to teach the soldiers to treat the "locals" like dirt.

There is another interpretation, and it is no less grave: that there is no such policy. This means that the discipline in the army has broken down, that the command at all levels has lost control. Not an army anymore, but a lawless militia.

That would hardly be surprising, of course. One cannot employ an army for dozens of years as an oppressive, colonial police force without causing a breakdown of discipline. One cannot demand that soldiers stick to the truth in their reports when they hear every day the reports of the above-mentioned IDFL ("killed while trying to escape," "tried to run the soldiers over," "were compelled to shoot when their life was in danger," "cursed the soldiers," "tried to wrest the gun from the hands of the soldier," and similar routine untruths). One cannot expect a soldier who harasses venerable old men and respectable women in the occupied territories to behave like a quiet, courteous boy in a Haifa discotheque or to treat his wife and children decently. One cannot expect a soldier who for years has been a hero confronting women and children to be a hero against tanks and artillery on a future battlefield.

Every year, when the generals want to extract several billions more from the public treasury, they tell us that any moment now a major war may break out. Syria, Iraq, Iran, jointly or separately, are going to throw missiles at us full of bacteria or poison gas, and only a strong and sophisticated Israeli army will save us. The same army that has trained for years at the checkpoints.

There was another picture on TV the other day: Micky Levi, commander of the Jerusalem police, was seen quarreling with an Arab woman. Suddenly he struck out with his fist. It looked like a powerful blow. But the camera was located behind him and could not see where the fist landed. On her belly? Her breast? Or did he miss altogether and hit the air?

The IPL (Israel Police Liar, a younger brother of his army colleague) gave some silly explanation. But there is no better witness than one's own eyes. The district police commander, an officer with the rank of general, used his fist while arguing with a woman.

There was no public outcry. Neither in the media, nor in the Knesset, nor in the cabinet. After all, who wants to quarrel with the police?

One aspect of the occupation that is relatively new—unlike the home demoli-
tions and checkpoints—is the building of the so-called "Security/Separation/
Annexation Wall." Its construction is gobbling huge swathes of farmland,
centuries-old olive trees and houses that stand in its way inside occupied
Palestine.—SRP

The Evil Wall[33]

May 3, 2004

For a fraction of a second, I was panic-stricken.

The terrible monster coming towards me was not more than five
meters away and continued to move as if I weren't there. The giant bulldozer pushed a great heap of dirt and boulders before it. The driver,
two meters above me, seemed a part of the machine. It was clear that
nothing would stop him. I jumped aside at the last moment.

Some weeks ago, in a similar situation, the American peace activist
Rachel Corrie expected the driver to stop. He did not, and she was
crushed to death.[34]

I did not come on this occasion to demonstrate (we shall do this
today) but to look around. In the olive grove, a few meters from the
tents that were set up by the villagers of Mas'ha, together with Israeli
and international peace activists, three monsters were preparing the
ground for the Separation Wall.[35] They raised clouds of dust and a
deafening roar, so that we could hardly converse. They work every day,
even on Passover, twelve hours a day, without a break.

The whole Israeli public supports the Separation Wall. It has no
idea what it is supporting. One has to come to the place in order to
understand all the implications of the project.

First of all, it has to be said unequivocally: this wall has nothing to
do with security.

It is being sold to the Israeli public as a "security fence." The army
calls it an "obstacle." The public, which of course yearns for security,
is buying the goods eagerly.

At long last something is being done!

And indeed, the idea looks quite simple. Even the most unsophisti-
cated person can grasp it. It seems almost self-evident: a Palestinian
who wants to blow himself up in Israel has first of all to cross the pre-
1967 border, the so-called Green Line. If a wall or fence is built along
the Green Line, the terrorists will not be able to come. No more
attacks, no more suicide bombers.

But logic says that if this had indeed been a security-wall, it would
have been built directly along the Green Line. All Israelis (except the

settlers) would be on one side of it (the western one) and all the Palestinians on the other. The line should be as straight and as short as possible, because it will need inspecting, patrolling, and defending. The shorter it is, the easier and cheaper it will be to defend it. That is the logic of security.

But in reality, except for short sections, the wall is not being built on the Green Line, nor in a straight line. On the contrary, it meanders like a river, twisting and turning, approaching the Green Line and receding from it.

Not by accident. The bed of a river is dictated by nature. The water has to obey gravity. But the design of the wall has no connection with nature. The bulldozers are quite indifferent to nature; they cut through it remorselessly. What then determines this design?

Standing near it, the answer is clearly visible. The sole consideration that dictates its path is the settlements.[36] The wall twists like a snake according to a simple principle: most of the settlements must remain on the western side of the wall, so as eventually to be absorbed into Israel.

Standing on a hill that will be crossed by the wall, I saw down below, on the western side, Elkana, a large settlement. On the eastern side, only a few dozen meters away, there is the Palestinian village of Mas'ha. The village itself stands on the eastern side, but almost all its lands lie on the western side. The wall will cut the village off from 98 percent of its lands—olive groves and fields that stretch up to the Green Line some seven kilometers away, near Kafr Kassem.

Mas'ha is a big village—like its neighbor Bidia, where thousands of Israelis used to come every Saturday to shop. Mas'ha, too, was once a blooming village. It has a big industrial zone, now completely deserted.

One can reach the village only on foot, climbing steep tracks. At the beginning of the intifada, the Israeli army blocked the main road with two piles of earth and rocks. No vehicle can pass.

"First they came to destroy our livelihood," the village chief, Anwar Amar, says bitterly. "Now they come again to take away our land."

Indeed, the foul smell of "transfer" hovers over the wall. Its location leaves whole Palestinian villages on the western side—trapped between the wall and the Green Line. The inhabitants will not be able to move, to find a livelihood, to breathe. Other villages, like Mas'ha, will remain on the eastern side of the wall, but their land, on which their livelihood depends, will be on the western side. There are places, like the town of Qalqilia, which will be almost completely surrounded by a loop of the wall, leaving only a small opening to the West Bank. One of the purposes of the wall is, without a doubt, to make the lives of the inhabitants hell, in order to convince them by and by to go away. It is a kind of "creeping transfer."

Like the terrifying bulldozer pushing before it rocks and lumps of earth, so the occupation pushes before it the Palestinian population— always eastwards, always out.

Historians can see this as a continuous process that started 120 years ago and has not stopped for a moment. It began with the eviction of the *felaheen* from land that was purchased from absentee landowners and continued with the *Nakba* of 1948,[37] the massive land expropriations from Arabs in Israel after that war, the expulsions during the 1967 war, the creeping eviction by means of settlements and bypass roads throughout the years of the occupation, and now the expulsion caused by the wall. The Hebrew bulldozer rolls in front. Not by chance, Ariel Sharon's nickname is "the bulldozer."[38]

The wall of Mas'ha and Kalkiliya, which continues to the Gilboa mountains, is not the only one. To the east of it, a second wall is already being planned. It will embrace the Ariel and Kadumim settlements and penetrate 20 kilometers into Palestinian territory, almost reaching the central axis of the West Bank, the Ramallah–Nablus road.

However, even this is not the whole picture. Sharon is now planning the "Eastern Wall" that will cut off the West Bank from the Jordan Valley.[39] When it is finished, the whole West Bank will become an island surrounded by Israeli territory, cut off on all sides.

Also, the southern West Bank (Hebron and Bethlehem) will be cut off from the northern West Bank (Ramallah, Nablus, Jenin), which will also be divided into several enclaves.

This map is very reminiscent of the map of apartheid South Africa. The racist government set up several black "homelands," nicknamed Bantustans, ostensibly self-governing territories whose black leaders were appointed by the white government. Each Bantustan was completely surrounded by the territory of the racist state, cut off from the rest of the world.

This is exactly what Sharon has in mind when he speaks about a "Palestinian state." It will consist of several enclaves, each one surrounded by Israeli territory, without an external border with Jordan or Egypt. Sharon has been working on this plan for decades, setting up dozens of settlements according to its map.

The wall will serve this purpose. It has nothing to do with security; it certainly will not bring peace. It will only bring more hatred and bloodshed. The very idea that an obstacle of cement or wire could stop the hatred is ludicrous.

The work continues now from early morning to late evening. Sharon talks about the roadmap while creating "facts on the ground."

But this wall also has a deeper meaning. It is no accident that it is so hugely popular in Israel, from Sharon to Mitzna and Beilin. It satisfies an inner need.

In his book *Der Judenstaat*, (1896) the founding document of Zionism, Theodor Herzl wrote the following sentences: "For Europe, we shall be there (in Palestine) a section of the wall against Asia. We shall do pioneer service for culture against barbarism."

This idea, that we are the outpost of Europe and need a high wall between us and Asiatic barbarism—i.e. the Arabs—is thus embedded in the original vision. Perhaps it has even deeper roots. When the Jews began to congregate in ghettos, before this was decreed from the outside, they surrounded themselves with a wall, in order to separate themselves from a hostile environment. Wall and separation, as guarantees of security, are deeply imprinted in the Jewish collective unconscious.

But we, the new Hebrew society in this country, did not want to be a new Jewish ghetto. We did not seek separation, but the opposite—to be open to the region. Not "a villa in the jungle," as Ehud Barak put it, not a European outpost against Asiatic barbarism, as seen by Herzl, but an open society that lives in peace and prospers in partnership with the nations of this region.

This evil wall is not only an instrument for dispossessing the Palestinians, not only an instrument of terrorism masquerading as a defense against terrorism, not only an instrument of the settlers disguised as a security measure. It is, most of all, an obstacle facing Israel, a wall blocking our way to a future of peace, security, and prosperity.

Not all the issues comprise facts on the ground; some of the issues are facts of the person: imprisonment, assassination, and exile.—SRP

Blood on Our Hands

April 14, 2007

At this moment, negotiations on a prisoner exchange are in full swing.[40] The term "negotiations" is really inappropriate. "Haggling" seems more fitting. One could also use an uglier expression: "trafficking in human beings."

The planned deal concerns living people. They are being treated like goods, for which the officials of the two sides are bargaining as if they were a piece of land or a load of fruit.

In their own eyes, and in the eyes of their spouses, parents, and children, they are not goods. They are life itself.

Immediately after the signing of the Oslo agreement in 1993, Gush Shalom publicly called on Prime Minister Yitzhak Rabin to free all the Palestinian prisoners.

The logic was simple: they are in reality prisoners of war. They did what they did in the service of their people, exactly like our own soldiers. The people who sent them were the chiefs of the Palestinian Liberation Organization (PLO) with whom we have just signed a far-reaching agreement. Is there any sense in signing an agreement with the commanders, while their subordinates continue to languish in our jails?

When one makes peace, prisoners of war are expected to be released. In our case, this would not only be a sign of humanity, but also of wisdom. These prisoners come from all the towns and villages. Sending them home would release an outburst of joy all over the occupied Palestinian territories. There is hardly a Palestinian family that does not have a relative in prison.

If the agreement is not to remain just a piece of paper, we said, but be imbued with content and spirit, there is no wiser act than this.

Unfortunately, Rabin did not listen to us. He had many positive traits, but he was a rather closed person, devoid of imagination. He was himself a prisoner of narrow "security" concepts. For him, the prisoners were goods to be traded for something. True, before the founding of Israel he himself had been held in detention by the British for some time, but, like many others, he was incapable of applying the lessons of his own experience to the Palestinians.

We considered this a fateful matter as far as the peace efforts were concerned. Together with the unforgettable Faisal Husseini, the adored leader of the Palestinian population of East Jerusalem, we organized a demonstration opposite the Jneid prison in Nablus. It was the largest joint Israeli–Palestinian demonstration ever. More than 110,000 people took part.

In vain. The prisoners were not released.

Fourteen years later, nothing has changed. Prisoners have been released after completing their sentences, others have taken their place. Every night, Israeli soldiers capture a dozen or so new "wanted" Palestinians.

At any one time, there are some 10,000 Palestinian prisoners, male and female, from minors to old people.

All our governments have treated them as goods. And goods are not given away for nothing. Goods have a price. Many times it was proposed to release some prisoners as a "gesture" to Mahmoud Abbas, in order to strengthen him vis-à-vis Hamas. All these suggestions were rejected by Ariel Sharon and Ehud Olmert.

Now, the security services oppose the prisoner exchange deal for the release of the soldier Gilad Shalit.[41] And not because the price— 1,400 in exchange for 1—is exorbitant. On the contrary, for many Israelis it seems quite natural that one Israeli soldier is worth 1,400 "terrorists."[42] But the security services raise much weightier arguments: if prisoners are released for a "kidnapped" soldier, it will encourage the "terrorists" to capture more soldiers.

At least some of the released prisoners will return to their organizations and activities, and that will result in more bloodshed. Israeli soldiers will be obliged to risk their lives in order to arrest them again.

And there is something else lurking in the background: some of the families of Israelis killed in attacks, who are organized in a very vociferous lobby connected with the extreme right, will raise hell. How could this pitiful government, devoid of any public standing, withstand such pressure?

For each of these arguments, there is a counter-argument.

Not releasing the prisoners leaves the "terrorists" with a permanent motivation to "kidnap" soldiers. After all, nothing else seems to convince us to release prisoners. In these circumstances, such actions will always enjoy huge popularity with the Palestinian public, which includes many thousands of families that are waiting for the return of their loved ones.

From a military point of view, there is another strong argument: "Soldiers are not left in the field." This is held as a sacred maxim, a mainstay of army morale. Every soldier must know that if he or she is captured, the Israeli army will do everything, but everything, to get him free. If this belief is undermined, will soldiers be as ready to take risks in battle?

Furthermore, experience shows that a high proportion of released Palestinian prisoners do not return to the cycle of violence. After years in detention, all they want is to live in peace and devote their time to their children. They exercise a moderating influence on their surroundings.

And as for the thirst for revenge of the families of "terror victims"—woe to a government that gives in to such emotions, which, of course, exist on both sides.

The political argument goes both ways. There is pressure from the "terror victims," but there is even stronger pressure from the family of the captured soldier.

In Judaism, there is a commandment called "ransom of prisoners." It arose from the reality of a persecuted community dispersed across the world. Every Jew is obliged to make any sacrifice and pay any price for the release of another Jew from prison. If Turkish pirates captured a

Jew from England, the Jews of Istanbul paid the ransom for his release. In today's Israel, this obligation still holds.

Public meetings and demonstrations are now being held for the release of Gilad Shalit. The organizers do not say openly that the aim is to push the government to accept the exchange deal. But, since there is no other way to get him back alive, that is the message in practice.

One cannot envy the members of the government who find themselves in this situation. Caught between two bad options, the natural tendency of a politician like Olmert is not to decide at all and postpone everything. But this is a third bad option, and one that carries a heavy political price.

The strongest emotional argument voiced by the opponents of the deal is that the Palestinians are demanding the release of prisoners with "blood on their hands." In our society, the words "Jewish blood"—two words beloved by the right—are enough to silence even many on the left.

But that is a stupid argument. It is also mendacious.

In the terminology of the security service, this definition applies not only to a person who has personally taken part in an attack in which Israelis were killed, but also to anyone who thought about the action, gave the order, organized it, and helped to carry it out—prepared the weapons, conveyed the attacker to the scene, or assisted in other ways.

According to this definition, every soldier and officer of the Israeli army has "blood on his hands," along with many politicians.

Somebody who has killed or wounded Israelis—is he different from us, the Israeli soldiers past and present? When I was a soldier in the 1948 war, in which tens of thousands of civilians, fighters, and soldiers on both sides perished, I was a machine-gunner in the Samson's Foxes commando unit. I fired thousands of bullets, if not tens of thousands. It was mostly at night, and I could not see whether I hit anybody, and if so—whom. Do I have blood on my hands?

The official argument is that the prisoners are not soldiers, and therefore they are not prisoners of war, but common criminals, murderers and their accomplices.

That is not an original argument. All colonial regimes in history have said the same. No foreign ruler, fighting an uprising of the oppressed people, has ever recognized its enemies as legitimate fighters. The French did not recognize the Algerian freedom fighters, the Americans do not recognize the Iraqi and Afghan freedom fighters (they are all terrorists, who can be tortured and held in abominable detention centers), the South African apartheid regime treated Nelson Mandela and his comrades as criminals, as the British did Mahatma Gandhi and the fighters of the Hebrew underground in Palestine. In Ireland, they hanged the members of the Irish underground, who left behind moving songs ("Shoot me like an Irish soldier / Do not hang me like a dog; / For I fought for Ireland's freedom / On that dark September morn ...").

The fiction that freedom fighters are common criminals is necessary for the legitimization of a colonial regime, and makes it easier for a soldier to shoot people. It is, of course, twisted. Common criminals act in their own interest. Freedom fighters or "terrorists," like most soldiers, believe that they are serving their people or cause.

One paradox of the situation is that the Israeli government is negotiating with people who themselves have served time in Israeli prisons. When our leaders speak about the need to strengthen the "moderate" Palestinian elements, they mainly mean these.

That is a feature of the Palestinian situation, which I doubt exists in other occupied countries. People who have spent five, ten and even 20 years in Israeli prisons, and who have every reason in the world to hate our guts, are quite open to contact with Israelis.

Since I know some of them, and some have become close friends, I have wondered many times about this.

At international conferences I have met Irish activists. After several pints of Guinness they have told me that they know no greater joy in life than killing Englishmen. I was reminded of the song of our poet Nathan Alterman, who prayed to God "Give me hatred gray like a sack" (for the Nazis). After hundreds of years of oppression, that's how they felt.

Of course, my Palestinian friends hate the Israeli occupation. But they do not hate all Israelis, just for being Israelis. In prison, most of them have learned good Hebrew and listened to Israeli radio, read Israeli newspapers, and watched Israeli TV. They know that there are all kinds of Israelis, just as there are all kinds of Palestinians. Israeli democracy, which allows members of the Knesset to vilify their prime minister, has made a deep impression on them. When the Israeli government showed a readiness to negotiate with Palestinians, the best partners were to be found among these ex-prisoners.

That is also true for the prisoners that are to be released now. If Marwan Barghouti is released, he will be a natural partner in any peace effort.[43]

I shall be very happy when both he and Gilad Shalit are free.

Children of Death

June 14, 2003

A week after the ship of peace was solemnly launched on its perilous voyage from Aqaba harbor, it was hit by a torpedo. It is not yet clear whether it is wrecked or can continue on its way in spite of the damage.

The story of its voyage so far: an Israeli helicopter gunship tried to kill Abd-al-Aziz al-Rantisi, one of the leaders of the political wing of Hamas. He miraculously survived. Immediately afterwards, the gunships killed other Hamas leaders. Clearly, this was the beginning of a campaign to kill the leaders of all the wings of Hamas—military, political, social, educational, and religious.

Such a campaign is, of course, the outcome of long preparations, which take weeks and months. It was evidently planned even before the Aqaba summit conference convened, but postponed by Sharon in order to afford President Bush his moments of photographic glory on the shore of the Red Sea. Immediately after the president and his entourage went home, radiant with success, the machinery of death went into action.

In establishing intent, all courts around the world act upon a simple principle: a person who carries out an action with predictable results is held to have intended that result. That is true for this campaign, too.

The killing of the Hamas leaders (together with their wives, children, and casual bystanders) is intended to attain the following results: (a) acts of revenge by Hamas, i.e. suicide bombings, (b) the failure of the Palestinian Authority's efforts to secure the agreement of Hamas to a ceasefire, (c) the destruction of Abu Mazen's political standing right from the start, (d) the demolition of the Roadmap, (e) compensation for the settlers after the removal of some sham "outposts."

All five objectives have been achieved. Blood and fire cover the country, the media on both sides are busy with funerals and mutual incitement, the efforts to establish a *hudnah* (truce) have stopped, Sharon called Abu Mazen a chicken without feathers, the Roadmap is tottering, Bush has mildly reproached Sharon while directing his wrath at Hamas.

The "dismantling" of the phony settlement-outposts, a joke to start with, has been stopped. Construction activity in the settlements is in full swing, and so is the building of the "fence" that is establishing a new border deep inside the West Bank. (Both Bush and Blair have demanded that it be stopped, a boost to the campaign we started months ago). The closures and blockades have been tightened. The situation in the occupied Palestinian territories is back to what it was before, as if the entire performance in Aqaba had never taken place.

The decision to kill Rantisi was, therefore, a decisive point in the history of Israel. And the first question must be: who was it that took this decision?

It is easy to say who did not take it.

Not the government, which has become a choir of flatterers and yes-men. Sharon treats them with contempt. He would not dream of consulting them.

Not the Knesset, which has reached an unprecedented low. It now openly includes representatives of the underworld, a murderer who has asked for (and received) a pardon, and some small politicians who look as if they had been picked at random from the street. The Speaker is known as an entertaining character.

And not the public at large, of course. All public opinion polls show that the public wanted the Roadmap to succeed. All believed that Sharon was serious about seeking peace. On the left, too, there were many simpletons who lauded Sharon for changing his spots. Nobody asked the public if it wants to start a new round of violence.

Indeed, the latest poll indicates that 67 percent of the public did not support the attempt on Rantisi's life after it happened. But Sharon knew that the public would accept his decisions and follow him like the sheep on his ranch.

So, who took the decision?

That is no secret. The decision was taken by five generals:

- The prime minister, Ariel Sharon, a retired two-star general.
- The minister of defense, Sha'ul Mofaz, a retired three-star general.
- The chief of staff, Moshe Ya'alon, a serving three-star general.
- The Mossad chief, Me'ir Dagan, a former one-star general.
- The security service chief, Avi Dichter, with a rank equivalent to a three-star general.

This military quintet is now making decisions about the fate of Israel, perhaps for generations, perhaps forever. In Latin America they would be called a junta (military committee).

We have spoken more than once about the special status of generals—in and out of uniform—in our state. It has no equivalent in the Western world. In no democratic country does a general now serve as prime minister. In no democratic country does a professional soldier serve as minister of defense, certainly not one who was wearing a general's uniform right on the eve of his ministerial appointment. In no democratic country does the chief of staff attend all cabinet meetings, where he serves as the highest authority in all "security" matters—which, in Israel, include practically all matters of national policy.

The rule of the generals is based on an extensive infrastructure. Israeli generals leave the army, as a rule, in their early 40s. If they do not join the top leadership of a political party (Likud, Labor, and the National Religious Party are at present led by generals, and Meretz is practically led by a colonel), or manage to get elected as a mayor, their comrades help them to settle down as directors of large government corporations, universities, or public utilities.

The hundreds of ex-generals who hold most of the key posts in government and society are not only a group of veterans sharing common memories. The partnership goes much deeper. Dozens of years of service in the regular army form a certain outlook on life, a political world-view, ways of thinking and even language. In all the years of Israel, there have been no more than three or four exceptions to this rule.

On the face of it, there are right-wing and left-wing generals, but that is an optical illusion. This week that was particularly obvious: after the assassination attempt on Rantisi and the Hamas revenge attack, dozens of generals appeared in the media. (An Israeli general, however stupid he may be, automatically becomes a sought-after commentator in the media.) For the sake of "balance," generals-of-the-right and generals-of-the-left were brought on screen, and lo and behold, they all said more or less the same thing, even using the same terminology.

More than in the "commentaries" themselves, this found expression in two Hebrew words: *Ben Mavet* ("son of death," meaning a person who must be killed).

As if by order, this week these two detestable words entered the public discourse. There was hardly a general, politician or correspondent who did not roll them on his tongue with obvious relish. They had never been heard before in the media. Now, suddenly, everybody has started to use them. Rantisi was a "son of death." Sheikh Yassin was a "son of death." The other Hamas leaders were "children of death." Perhaps even Yassir Arafat himself.

The expression appears in the Bible, II Samuel, XII. King David has committed a heinous crime, deliberately arranging for his most loyal officer, Uriah the Hittite, to be killed in battle, so he can have his wife, Bath-sheba, for himself. The prophet Nathan denounces him for this deed, telling him the story of the rich man who slaughtered the only sheep of a poor man. David gets very angry and tells the prophet: "As the Lord liveth, the man that hath done this thing is a son of death!" To which Nathan replies: "Thou art the man!"

Ironically, the Bible applied the term to the greatest leader of the people of Israel, who had committed an abominable crime. Now it is used by the leaders of the State of Israel against Palestinians.

But this is not the most important point. It is more significant that the prime minister and his small group of generals introduce these two words, and all the people repeat them like a giant flock of parrots, without thinking, without protesting. This is rather frightening in itself, but when these words reflect a disastrous national decision and the public accepts it without question, that is even more frightening.

It is not yet clear whether Sharon has succeeded in scuttling the boat of the peace initiative. Perhaps President Bush will after all show some resolution and save the initiative, in which he has invested his personal prestige. But in the meantime the dance of death continues, and the blood flows—quite literally—in the streets of Israel and Palestine.

... To the Shores of Tripoli

May 26, 2007

The bloody battles that have erupted around the Nahr al-Bared refugee camp near Tripoli in Lebanon remind us that the refugee problem has not disappeared.[44] On the contrary, 60 years after the *Nakba*, the Palestinian catastrophe of 1948, it is again the center of attention throughout the world.

This is an open wound. Anyone who imagines that a solution to the Israel–Arab conflict is possible without healing this wound is living with delusion.

From Tripoli to Sderot, from Riyadh to Jerusalem, the Palestinian refugee problem continues to cast its shadow across the whole region. This week, the media were again full of photos of Israeli and Palestinian refugees fleeing from their homes and of mothers mourning the deaths of their loved ones in Hebrew and Arabic—as if nothing had changed since 1948.

Ordinary Israelis shrug their shoulders when confronted with the suffering of the Palestinian refugees and dismisses it with five words: "They brought it on themselves."

Learned professors and market vendors repeat that the Palestinians caused their own downfall when, in 1947, they rejected the Partition Plan of the United Nations and started a war to annihilate the Jewish community in the country.

That is a deeply rooted myth, one of the basic myths of Israeli consciousness. But it is far from reflecting what really happened.

First of all, because at that time there did not even exist a Palestinian national leadership which could take a decision.

In the Arab Revolt of 1935 to 1939 ("the troubles" in Israeli parlance), the Grand Mufti, Hajj Amin al-Husseini, then the leader of the Palestinian Arabs, had most of the prominent Palestinians who did not accept his authority killed. He then fled the country and the remaining Palestinian leaders were exiled by the British to a remote island.

When the hour of destiny struck and the UN adopted the partition resolution, there was no Palestinian leadership capable of deciding one way or the other. Instead, the leaders of the neighboring Arab states decided to send their armies into the country once the British Mandate had come to an end.

True, the masses of the Palestinian people opposed the partition plan. They believed that all of Palestine was their patrimony, and that the Jews, almost all of whom had recently arrived, did not have any right to it. The more so, since the UN plan gave the Jews, then only a third of the population, 55 percent of the country. Even in this territory, the Arabs constituted 40 percent of the inhabitants.

(In fairness it should be mentioned that the territory allotted to the Jews included the Negev—a huge desert that was desolate then and has mostly remained so to this day.)

The Jewish side did indeed accept the UN decision—but only in appearance. In secret meetings, David Ben-Gurion did not hide his intention to take the first opportunity to enlarge the territory allotted to the Jewish state and to ensure that there was an overwhelming Jewish majority in it. The war of 1948, which was started by the Arab side, created an opportunity to realize both aims: Israel grew from 55 percent to 78 percent of the country, and this territory was emptied of most of its Arab inhabitants. Many of them fled the terrors of war, many others were driven out by us. Almost none were allowed to return after the war.

In the course of the war, some 750,000 Palestinians became refugees. Natural increase doubles their number every 18 years, so they are now approaching 5 million.

That is an immense human tragedy, a humanitarian issue, and a political problem. For long periods it seemed that the problem would disappear by itself with the passing of time, but it has repeatedly reared its head again.

Many parties have exploited the problem for their own ends. Various Arab regimes have at times tried to hitch their wagon to it.

The fate of the refugees varies from country to country. Jordan has accorded them citizenship, yet has kept many of them in miserable camps. The Lebanese have not given the refugees any civil rights at all, and have committed several massacres. Almost all Palestinian leaders demand the implementation of UN Resolution 194, which was adopted 59 years ago and which promised the refugees a return to their homes as peaceful citizens.

Few noticed that the right of return has served successive Israeli governments as a pretext to reject all peace initiatives. The return of 5 million refugees would mean the end of Israel as a state with a solid Jewish majority and turn it into a bi-national state—something that arouses the adamant opposition of at least 99.99 percent of the Israeli-Jewish public.

This has to be realized if one is to understand the way Israelis view peace. Ordinary Israelis, even decent people who sincerely desire peace, tell themselves: the Arabs will never give up the right of return, therefore there is no chance for peace, and it isn't worthwhile even to start doing anything about it.

Thus, paradoxically, the refugee problem has turned into an instrument for those Israelis who oppose any peace based on compromise. They rely on the fact that almost no Arab leader would dare to give up the right of return openly. In private conversations, many Arab leaders recognize that the return is impossible, but they dare not say so openly. To do so would mean political suicide—just as announcing a readiness to take back refugees would be suicidal for an Israeli politician.

In spite of this, a subterranean shift has taken place in recent years on the Arab side. There have been hints that Israel's demographic problem cannot be ignored. Here and there, creative solutions have been proposed. (Once, in a public meeting of Gush Shalom, a Palestinian representative said: "Today, the Arab minority constitutes 20 percent of Israel's citizens. So let us agree that for every 80 new Jewish immigrants coming to the country, 20 Palestinian refugees will be allowed to return. In such a way, the present proportion would be maintained." The public reacted enthusiastically.)

Now, a revolutionary development has taken place. The Arab League has offered Israel a peace plan: all 22 Arab states would recognize Israel and establish diplomatic and economic relations with it, in return for Israel's withdrawal from the occupied territories and the establishment of a Palestinian state.

The offer did not ignore the refugee problem. It mentioned UN Resolution 194, but added a qualification of fundamental importance: that the solution would be reached "by agreement" between the two parties. In other words, Israel would have the right of veto over refugees returning to Israeli territory.

This put the Israeli government in a difficult position. If the Israeli public understood that the entire Arab world was offering a comprehensive peace agreement without the actual realization of the right of return, they might accept it gladly. Therefore, everything was done to obscure the decisive words. The guided (and misguided) Israeli media emphasized the plan's mention of Resolution 194 and played down the talk of an "agreed upon" solution.

The government treated the Arab offer with manifest disdain, but nevertheless tried to derive advantage from it. Ehud Olmert announced his readiness to talk with an Arab delegation—provided that it did not consist of Egypt and Jordan alone. This way, Olmert and Tzipi Livni hope to attain an important political achievement without paying for it: to compel Saudi Arabia and other states to enter into relations with Israel. Since there are "no free lunches," the Arabs refused. Nothing came out of the whole affair.

If someone had offered Israel this Arab League peace plan on June 4, 1967, a day before the Six-Day War, we would have thought that the Messiah had arrived. Now, our government considers this offer nothing but a clever trick: the Arabs are indeed ready to relinquish the return of the refugees, but want to compel us to give up the occupied territories and to dismantle the settlements.

In a historical perspective, the Arab League is correcting an error it made 40 years ago, which had far-reaching consequences. Soon after the Six-Day War, on September 1, 1967, the heads of the Arab states assembled in Khartoum and decided upon the "Three No's"— No peace with Israel, No recognition of Israel, No negotiations with Israel.

One can understand why such a misguided resolution was adopted. The Arab countries had just suffered a humiliating military defeat. They wanted to prove to their peoples and the world that they had not gone down on their knees. They wanted to keep their national dignity. But for the government of Israel, it was a present from heaven.

The resolution freed it from any need to conduct negotiations which might have compelled it to return the territories it had just conquered. It gave the green light for the founding of settlements, an enterprise that continues unhindered to this very day, removing the land from under the feet of the Palestinians. And, of course, it swept the refugee problem from the table.

The new Arab League proposal could repair the damage done to the Palestinian cause at Khartoum. The entire Arab world has now adopted a realistic resolution. From now on, the task is to get the Israeli public to grasp the full meaning of this proposal, and especially its significance concerning the return of the refugees. This task rests on the shoulders of the Israeli peace forces, but also of the Arab leadership.

To achieve this goal, the refugee problem must be transferred to the realm of reality. It must undergo a process of de-mystification.

At present, an Israeli sees only a nightmare: 5 million refugees are waiting to flood Israel. They will demand the return of their lands, on which Israeli towns and villages are now located, and their homes, which were demolished long ago or in which Israelis are now living. Israel, as a state with a Hebrew majority, will disappear.

This fear must be neutralized, and this wound must be healed. On the psychological level, we must recognize our responsibility for that part of the problem which was actually caused by us. A "Committee for Truth and Reconciliation" could, perhaps, determine the dimensions of this part. For this we must sincerely apologize, as other nations have apologized for injustices committed by them.

On the practical level, the real problem of 5 million human beings must be solved. All of them will have a right to generous compensation, which will enable them to start a new life any way they wish. Those who want to stay where they are, with the consent of the local government, will have the ability to rebuild the life of their families. Those who want to live in the future State of Palestine, perhaps in the areas cleared of settlements, must receive the necessary international assistance. I, personally, believe that it would be good for us to receive back a certain agreed-upon number of refugees in Israel proper, as a symbolic contribution to the end to the tragedy.

That is neither a dream nor a nightmare. We have already mastered more difficult tasks. It would be much easier and cheaper than to continue a war that has no military solution and no end.

Sixty years ago, a deep wound was opened. Since than it has not healed. It infects our life and endangers our future. It is high time to heal it. That is the lesson of Tripoli in the north and Sderot in the south.

The Right of Return[45]

January 14, 2001

We Israelis need a bogeyman to frighten ourselves, one frightening enough to pump adrenaline into our national bloodstream. Otherwise, it seems, we cannot function.

Once it was the Palestinian charter. Very few Palestinians ever read it, even fewer remembered what it said, but we compelled the Palestinians to abolish its paragraphs in a solemn ceremony. Who remembers it today? But since this bogeyman was laid to rest, there is a need for a replacement.

The new bogeyman is the "right of return." Not as a practical problem, to be dealt with in rational terms, but as a hair-raising monster: now the Palestinians' sinister design has been revealed! They want to eliminate Israel by this terrible ploy! They want to throw us into the sea!

The right of return has again widened the abyss, which seemed to have been narrowed to a rift. We are frightened again. The end of our state! The end of the vision of generations! A second Holocaust!

It seems that the abyss is unbridgeable. The Arabs demand that each and every Palestinian refugee return to his home and land in Israel. The Israelis staunchly object to the return of even one single refugee. On both sides, everything or nothing. There goes the peace.

In the following lines I shall try to show that the bogeyman is indeed a bogeyman; that even this painful problem can be resolved; that a fair compromise can even lead to a historic conciliation.

The roots of the conflict

The refugee problem arouses such deep emotions because it touches the root of the conflict between to two peoples.

The conflict stems from the historic clash between two great national movements. One of these, Zionism, sought to establish a state for the Jews, so that, for the first time in thousands of years, they could be masters of their own fate. In the furthering of this aim, Zionism completely ignored the population living in the country. It envisioned a homogenous national state, according to the European model of the late nineteenth century, without non-Jews, or with at least as few non-Jews as possible.

The Palestinian national movement expressed the struggle of the native Arabs for national freedom and independence. It vehemently opposed the penetration of their homeland by another people. As Ze'ev Jabotinsky, the militant Zionist leader, wrote at the time, any other people would have reacted in the same way.

Without understanding this aspect of the conflict, the events leading to the creation of the refugee problem cannot be understood.

Ethnic cleansing

In the war of 1948, the historic clash came to a head.

On the eve of the war some 1,200,000 Arabs and some 635,000 Jews lived in Palestine. During the course of the war, started by the Arab side to prevent the partition of the country, more than half of the Palestinian people, around 750,000 persons were uprooted. Some were driven out by the conquering Israeli army; others fled when the battle reached their homes, as civilians do in every war.

The 1948 war was an ethnic struggle, much like the one in Bosnia. In wars of this kind, every side tries to set up an ethnic state by conquering as much territory as it can without incorporating the opposing population. In fairness to the historical facts, it should be mentioned that the Arab side behaved in the same way, and in the few territories it conquered (the old city of Jerusalem, the Etzion bloc) no Jews remained in their homes.

Immediately after the war, the new State of Israel declined to allow the refugees to come back to the territories it had conquered. The Ben-Gurion government eradicated about 450 abandoned Arab villages and put up Jewish settlements on their sites. The new Jewish immigrants—many from Arab countries—were put into the abandoned houses in the Arab towns. Thus the refugee problem was created.

Resolution 194

While the war was still going on, the General Assembly of the United Nations adopted Resolution 194 of November 11, 1948. It stated that the refugees were entitled to choose between compensation and return to "their homes." Israel's refusal to abide by this resolution may have led it to miss the opportunity—if it existed—of achieving peace with the Arab world as early as 1949.

In the 1967 war, some events repeated themselves. Hundreds of thousands of Palestinians were driven out, by force or intimidation, from areas near the Jordan river (the huge Jericho refugee camps) and near the Green Line (the Tulkarem, Kalkiliya, and Latrun areas).

According to official UN statistics, the number of refugees is up to 3.7 million by now, a number that is reasonable in view of the very high rate of natural growth. They are mostly dispersed among the countries bordering Israel, including the West Bank and the Gaza strip.

Apocalypse now

On the Israeli side, the refugee problem aroused deep-rooted fears, stemming from the first days after the 1948 war. The number of Jews in the new state had not yet reached a million. The idea that 750,000 Palestinians would return to Israeli territory and submerge it like a deluge aroused panic.

This apocalyptic vision has become a fixation in the Israeli national psyche. Even today, when the demographic facts are quite different, it hovers over every discussion of this issue. In this respect, there is no difference between the "left" and the "right." It is enough to merely mention the refugee problem for writers like Amos Oz to react like Ariel Sharon, and for a "new historian" like Benny Morris to voice opinions similar to those of an adherent to the very same old myths that he himself helped to debunk.[46]

No wonder that raising the issue now is shaking many of the Israeli "peace camp" to the roots of their soul. "We thought that the problem had gone away," many of them exclaim angrily, accusing the Palestinians of fraud, as if they had suddenly sprung earth-shattering demands, whereas until now they had presented only "simple" problems, like the establishment of a Palestinian state, borders, and settlements.

This attests to an abysmal lack of understanding. The right of return expresses the very core of the Palestinian national ethos. It is anchored in the memories of the *Nakba*, the Palestinian catastrophe of 1948, and the feeling that a historic injustice was committed against the Palestinian people. Ignoring this feeling of injustice makes it impossible to understand the Palestinian struggle, past and present.

Everyone who really tried to bring about peace and conciliation between the two peoples knew all the time that the refugee problem was only dormant, like a sleeping lion that could wake up at any minute. The hope was that this moment could be postponed until after the other problems could be resolved, and both sides could start healing this wound in a more congenial atmosphere. The hope was that after a good measure of mutual trust could be created, a rational approach would be possible. The Oslo Declaration of Principles of 1993 did not ignore the problem, but postponed it to the "final status" negotiations.

The man who upset the cart was Ehud Barak. He kicked the sleeping lion in the ribs. In a typical mixture of arrogance, ignorance, recklessness, and contempt for the Arabs, he was convinced that he could induce the Palestinians to give up the right of return. Therefore he demanded that the Palestinians sign a new declaration of principles, in which they would announce the "end of the conflict."

The moment these five words—"the end of the conflict"—were uttered in the negotiations, the right of return landed on the negotiating table with a bang. It should have been foreseen that no Palestinian leader could possibly sign the "end of the conflict" without a solution to the refugee problem.

Now there is no way to avoid a courageous confrontation of this problem.

A "truth commission"

The refugee problem is multi-layered; some layers are ideological and concerned with basic principles, others are practical. Let's address the ideological first.

Israel must acknowledge its historic responsibility for the creation of the problem. In order to facilitate the healing of the wound, such acknowledgement must be explicit.

It must be acknowledged that the creation of the refugee problem was an outcome of the realization of the Zionist endeavor to achieve a Jewish national renaissance in this country. It must also be acknowledged that at least some of the refugees were driven from their home by force after the battle was already over, and that their return to their homes was denied.

I can imagine a dramatic event: the president or prime minister of Israel solemnly apologizes to the Palestinians for the injustice inflicted upon them in the realization of the Zionist aims; at the same time he emphasizes that these aims were mainly directed towards national liberation and saving millions from the Jewish tragedy in Europe.

I would go further and propose the setting up of a "truth committee," composed of Israeli, Palestinian, and international historians, in order to investigate the events of 1948 and 1967 and submit a comprehensive and agreed report that can become part of both Israeli and Palestinian school curriculum.

The right of return

The right of return is a basic human right and cannot be denied in our time.

A short time ago, the international community fought a war against Serbia in order to implement the right of the Kosovars to return to their homes. It should be mentioned that Germany gave up the right of evicted Germans to return to their homes in East Prussia, Poland, and the Sudetenland, but this was the result of the deeply felt guilt of the German people for the horrible crimes of the Nazis. The often-heard phrase "but the Arabs started the war" is irrelevant in this context.

I propose that the State of Israel recognize the right of return in principle, pointing out that the implementation of the principle will come about by way of negotiation and agreement.

Palestinian citizenship

After the ideological aspect is satisfied, it becomes possible to address the practical aspect of the problem.

The solution of the refugee problem will coincide with the establishment of the State of Palestine. Therefore, the first step can be the granting of Palestinian citizenship to every Palestinian refugee, wherever he or she may be, if the State of Palestine so decides.

For the refugees, this step will be of utmost importance, not only for symbolic, but also for very practical reasons. Many Palestinians who have no citizenship are denied the privilege of crossing borders altogether; for all others the crossing of borders entails suffering, humiliation, and harassment.

The granting of citizenship will completely change the situation and status of the refugees in places like Lebanon, where refugees are exposed to danger.

Free choice

A basic element of the right of return is the right of every single refugee to choose freely between return and compensation.

This is a personal right. While the recognition in principle is a collective right, its implementation in practice is a choice for the individual Palestinians. In order to be able to make their decisions, they must know all the rights accruing to them: what sums will be paid to those choosing not to return and what possibilities are open to those who wish to return.

Every refugee has the right to compensation for properties left behind when he or she was uprooted, as well as for the loss of opportunities and other injuries. Without making any comparison between the Holocaust and the *Nakba*, one can learn from the German method of compensating their Jewish victims. This will enable all the refugees to decide what is good for them and their families.

The compensations, which undoubtedly will entail great sums, must be paid by an international fund, to which all the wealthier economies must contribute. The Palestinians can rightfully demand this from the member states of the United Nations who voted for the partition of Palestine in 1947 and did not lift a finger to prevent the tragedy of the refugees.

Israelis must not delude themselves that only others will pay. The Israeli "custodian of absentee property" holds huge properties—buildings, lands, movable property—left behind by the refugees, and it is his duty to register and administer them.

Return to Palestine

The historic compromise between Israel and Palestine is based on the principle of "two states for two peoples." The State of Palestine is designed to embody the historic personality of the Palestinian-Arab people and the State of Israel is designed to embody the historic personality of the Israeli-Jewish people, with the Arab citizens of Israel, who constitute a fifth of all Israeli citizens, being full partners in the state.

It is clear that the return of millions of Palestinian refugees to the State of Israel would completely change the character of the state, contrary to the intentions of its founders and most of its citizens. It would abolish the principle of two states for two peoples, on which the demand for a Palestinian state is based.

All this leads to the conclusion that most of the refugees who opt for return will find their place in the State of Palestine. As Palestinian citizens they will be able to build their lives there, subject to the laws and decisions of their government.

To absorb a large number of returnees and provide them with housing and employment, the State of Palestine must receive appropriate compensation from the international fund and Israel. Also, Israel must transfer the settlements intact to the Palestinian government, after the return of the settlers to Israeli territory. When deciding upon the just and equitable division of water and other resources between Israel and Palestine, this large-scale absorption must also be taken into account.

If the border between Palestine and Israel is opened to the free movement of people and goods, according to the principles of peaceful co-existence between good neighbors, the former refugees, as Palestinian citizens, will be able to visit the places where there forefathers lived.

Return to Israel

In order to make the healing of the psychological wounds and a historic conciliation possible, there is no way to avoid the return of an appropriate number of refugees to the State of Israel. The exact number must be decided upon by a negotiation between Israel and Palestine.

This part of the plan will arouse the strongest opposition in Israel. As a matter of fact, not a single Israeli politician or thinker has dared to propose it. The extreme opposition exists both on the right and the left of the Israeli spectrum.

However, such a limited return is the natural fulfillment of the recognition in principle of the right of return and the acceptance of responsibility for the events of the past. As we shall see immediately, the opposition to it is irrational and an expression of old fears that have no basis in reality.

The government of Israel recently offered to take back a few thousands of refugees (3,000 were mentioned) annually in the framework of "family reunification." This reflects a mistaken attitude. Instead, it is the open return, in the framework of the right of return, which is necessary as a symbolic act of conciliation. The number mentioned is, of course, ridiculous.

Nobody claims that Israel, which has just successfully absorbed a million new immigrants from the former Soviet Union, is economically unable to absorb a reasonable number of refugees. The argument is clearly ideological and demographic: that the return of any number of refugees will change the national-demographic nature of the state.

If the irrationality of the argument needs proof, one need only mention that the extreme right in Israel demands the annexation of the Arab neighborhoods of East Jerusalem and is quite ready to grant Israeli citizenship to the quarter of a million Arabs living there. The right wing also demands the annexation of big "settlement blocs," which include many Arab villages, without being unduly worried by the increase in the number of Arab citizens of Israel.

It is also worthwhile to remember that in 1949 the government of David Ben-Gurion and Moshe Sharett offered to take back 100,000 refugees. Whatever the motives that inspired that offer, and even if this was merely a diplomatic maneuver, the offer is an important precedent. In proportion to the Jewish population in Israel at that time, this number is equivalent to 800,000 today. In proportion to the number of refugees at that time, the number would be half a million now.

The decisive question is: How many can be brought back? Minimalists may speak about 100,000, maximalists about half a million. I myself have proposed an annual quota of 50,000 for ten years. But this is a subject for negotiations, which must be conducted in a spirit of goodwill with the intent of putting a successful end to this painful issue, always remembering that it concerns the fate of living human beings who deserve rehabilitation after tens of years of suffering.

At present 1.1 million Palestinian-Arab citizens live in Israel. An increase of that number to 1.3 or even 1.5 million will not fundamentally change the demographic picture, especially when Israel is absorbing more than 50,000 new Jewish immigrants every year.

Yet this concept arouses deep fears in Israel. Even the historian Benny Morris, who played such an important role in exposing the expulsion of 1948, is ready only for "perhaps a trickle of refugees being allowed to return to Israel—a few thousand, no more."

I am aware that the offer far from satisfies the Palestinian demands. But I am convinced that the great majority of Palestinians know that there is a price that both sides have to pay in order to leave behind the painful past and prepare for the building of their future in the two states.

When will it happen?

If this solution is adopted, in the framework of a comprehensive peace between Israel and Palestine that will bring with it peace between Israel and the entire Arab world, it can be implemented in a few years.

The first stage will be, of course, the achievement of an agreement between the two parties. Hopefully, this will not be a process of bitter haggling, but a negotiation in good faith, with both sides realizing that an agreed resolution will not only put an end to a great human tragedy but will also open the way for real peace.

The second stage will be the process of choosing. An international agency will have to make certain that every refugee family thoroughly knows its rights and the options available to it. The agency must also make sure that every family can choose freely, without pressure. There must also be an orderly process of registering properties and submitting claims.

Nobody can know at this moment how many refugees will choose each of the options. One can assume that many will prefer to remain where they are, especially if they have married locally or established businesses and put down roots. The compensation will improve their situation considerably.

Others will prefer to live in the Palestinian state, where they will feel at home within their nation and their culture. Others may wish to return to Israeli territory, where they are close to the homes of their families, even if they cannot return to destroyed homes and non-existent villages. Others again may be disinclined to live in a state with a different national and cultural background, after seeing the reality there with their own eyes. A real choice will be possible only when all the facts are clear, and even then not a few might change their minds repeatedly.

Once the great national issue, the symbol of the Palestinian sense of injustice, becomes a personal issue of hundreds of thousands of individual families, each one of them will reach an individual decision.

At the same time the international agency must come into being. Experience shows that this will not be easy and that countries that promise generous contributions for such an effort do not always fulfil their promises.

The third stage will be the implementation, which will certainly take several years.

Clearly the fear of many Israelis, that a catastrophe on the scale of a natural disaster will suddenly engulf them, is without basis. The solution of the problem will be a prolonged, controlled, reasonable, and logical process.

Historic conciliation

I believe that this plan can achieve a moral, just, practical, and agreed-upon solution.

Both sides will accept it, in the end, because there is no other. There can be no peace without the solution of the refugee question, and the only solution is one that both sides can live with.

Perhaps it will all be to the good. When both sides start on the path to the solution, it may facilitate the conciliation between them. When they sit together to find creative solutions, all kinds of interesting ideas may turn up. For example, why not rebuild two or three Palestinian villages which were destroyed after 1948, and whose sites are still vacant? Many things that seem impossible today may appear on the table once the atmosphere between the parties changes.

Perhaps then the ancient saying of the Psalmist will apply to the refugees: "The stone which the builders rejected has become the head stone of the corner."

Reform Now

June 22, 2002

To: the President of the United States.
From: the National Security Advisor.
Top Secret.

I hereby submit to you, Mr President, the report of the secret task force for reforming Israel, parallel to the task force working on the reform of the Palestinian Authority.

The faults of the Israeli system are known to all: an autocratic one-man rule by a leader surrounded by cronies and yes-men; a leader who is a chronic liar, whose every word is untrustworthy; corruption that penetrates every echelon of government; democratic institutions which serve only as window-dressing; the lack of a constitution; the absence of a real opposition; a multi-party system that is just a pretense; media that are fully mobilized in the service of the government.

This system is unable to move towards peace. Since you, Mr President, have determined that peace is in the basic national interest of the United States, we must use our power in order to bring about a thorough reform.

The following are some of the findings of the task force:

One-man rule: In theory, Israel is governed by a democratic leadership with decentralized authorities and a system of checks and balances. In fact, the situation is quite different.

By a sophisticated labyrinth of make-belief institutions—government, cabinet, inner cabinet, "kitchen," "kitchenette"—a situation has been created that allows Mr Sharon to decide and execute anything he wants.

In practice, Mr Sharon acts through a small group of family members and cronies who have been devoted to him for decades, but who have never been elected. (Conspicuous among them are his son Omri and Messrs Weisglas and Genger.) Members of the official cabinet have no influence whatsoever. Messrs Peres and Ben-Eliezer, for example, serve only as rubber-stamps.

Corruption: The existing Israeli system is based on general, systematic, and institutionalized corruption.

Large chunks of the national budget are transferred—both openly and secretly—as bribes to religious and other parties who keep Mr Sharon in power, and parts of these go into the pockets of their functionaries. These huge sums are stolen from the general public at a time of growing unemployment and lack of funds for the infrastructure, when there is not even money to assure a decent living to invalids, the elderly, the unemployed, and handicapped children, or decent hospitalization for the sick, not to mention decent living conditions for prisoners, who are kept in barbarous conditions.

Election campaigns are tainted by general corruption. Leading candidates secretly and illegally receive huge amounts of money from local and foreign interest groups, which expect, of course, to be repaid many times over once their candidate comes to power. Every campaign is followed by a long train of criminal indictments that are but the tip of the iceberg.

The Prime Minister himself, who is the owner of the biggest private farm in Israel, is involved in directing agricultural policy, including the price of water and the regulation of agricultural imports,

Much as in the Palestinian Authority, almost all the leading positions in the government and private services and corporations are handed out to cronies of the Prime Minister and members of the central committee (numbering thousands) of the governing party, most of them without elementary qualifications or talent. All the previous governments did the same. Every ministry is, of course, staffed and stuffed with cronies of the minister, and so are local authorities and other bodies. In this way, a huge parasitical apparatus has been created at the expense of ordinary taxpayers.

In addition, taxpayers have to carry the burden of a large sector of people called *haredim* (God-fearing) who do not work or pay taxes (nor do they serve in the army, thereby increasing the compulsory service and reserve duties of all the others). Many settlers are also flourishing at the expense of the general public.

The gap between rich and poor in Israel is bigger than in any Western country, a fact that turns Israel into a Third World country.

Mendacity: Mr Sharon is a certified liar. Even at the beginning of his career, the then Prime Minister, Mr Ben-Gurion, defined him as a habitual liar. On January 29, 1960, Mr Ben-Gurion wrote about him in his diary: "If he would wean himself from the habit of not speaking the truth ... he would be an exemplary military leader." Two years earlier, when Mr Sharon was promoted to the rank of Colonel, Mr Ben-Gurion asked him: "Have you stopped saying the untruth?"

The mendacity is not a personal trait of Mr Sharon only, but a method deeply imbedded in the Israeli leadership. A predecessor of Mr Sharon, former Prime Minister Shamir, has publicly declared that lying for the state is a virtue.

One could cite innumerable instances of this official trait. Mr Sharon's immediate predecessor, Mr Barak, for example, spread a mendacious account of the Camp David summit conference (Summer 2000), in order to put the blame for the failure on Mr Arafat. Since then, all the Israeli media repeat this legend daily, in spite of the fact that most leading commentators know the truth.[47]

The same goes for the Oslo agreements. The Israeli leadership, with the help of the media, hides the fact that most of the violations have come from the Israeli side (they did not implement the third troop deployment, did not open the four agreed "safe passages" between Gaza and the West Bank, have embezzled the tax and customs money collected for the Palestinian Authority, and refused to negotiate in good faith about Jerusalem, settlements, and refugees, as stipulated in the agreements, among other violations).

It will be remembered that even Mr Rabin announced that "there are no sacred dates," thereby relieving himself of the duty to fulfill any obligation at the agreed time.

It should be mentioned that at the time when the Israeli government has pretended to stop settlement activity, this activity is in fact continuing at a frantic pace, as discovered by our satellites.

This, Mr President, is a summary of the report. The task force proposes suspending our economic and military aid to Israel until a thorough reform has been undertaken, and appointing a team of monitors to oversee the results. Israel, like the Palestinians, should also be forced to adopt a constitution.

Yours respectfully,
The Advisor.

At Midnight, a Knock on the Door

April 19, 2003

It was an almost unbelievable news story: in order to trim the national budget, the Ministry of Education had decided to dismiss hundreds of teachers. A private company got the job of delivering the bitter news to the dismissed teachers. Two days before Passover—one of the highpoints of the Jewish calendar, both for religious and secular Jews, when families sit together around the table for the joyous Seder ceremony—the messengers of the company spread out to do their job. They knocked on the doors at midnight and delivered the notices.

Even the Israeli public, which does not get excited any more about anything, was shocked for a moment. How could such a thing happen? Couldn't they have waited until after the feast? What brutality!

For me, it was much more than a mistake of some government office. This is a symbolic act, which reflects all that is wrong in today's Israel.

First of all, the cruelty. It wasn't deliberate, of course. The Minister of Education did not tell the private contractor: hand them the notice in as painful a way as possible. The contractors, too, did not sit down and decide: let's do it just before Passover and knock on their doors in the middle of the night, like Stalin's secret police or our undercover soldiers in Nablus.

No, nobody decided. Nobody thought about it. And that is really the most shocking part: the total insensitivity.

Even three or four years ago, this would not have been possible. Somebody would have intervened in time and shouted: "What are you doing? Are you crazy?"

The Jews always defined themselves as "the compassionate sons of the compassionate." They believed that compassion is a Jewish invention and quoted the old texts (such as the Sabbath injunction in the Ten Commandments, ordering Jews to relieve their slaves and draft animals every seventh day). Nietzsche, who abhorred pity, accused Judaism of creating a morality of pity.

The new Hebrew society that was created in this country was

always proud of its "mutual responsibility," the fact that nobody went hungry in our society, that the incapacitated, sick, old, and unemployed were protected by the whole of society. Once, when I was asked what being a Jew meant to me in my childhood, I mentioned compassion, together with seeking justice, hating violence, striving for peace, and loving education.

Not any more. After two years of the al-Aqsa Intifada, the senses of Israeli society have become almost completely blunted. The terrible things that happen daily in the occupied territories pass without mention. "Closures" and curfews that last for months, hunger and thirst, sick people dying for lack of treatment, the demolition of homes, and the uprooting of groves—these are "small change," routine matters. Men, women, and children shot by snipers in their homes and on the streets? Who cares? A young American woman crushed to death by a giant bulldozer while trying to prevent the demolition of a Palestinian home? So what. She deserved it, anyway. A stone-throwing Palestinian boy shot dead by a tank? Three lines in the paper. Maybe not even that.

The callousness has spread from the occupied territories into Israel itself. Photos in the paper show people rummaging in garbage bins? Well, that's how it is. Government offices send hungry poor people to get a free meal at private charities? Who cares?

The new Minister of the Treasury, Binyamin Netanyahu, a man who receives $50,000 for a single lecture in the United States, has submitted an economic plan that hurts the poorest of the poor. It reduces monthly old-age allowances (to less than $300), child allowances, unemployment payments, subsidies for homes for retarded children and the elderly, and the education and health budgets.

Does the public revolt? Do masses of students take to the streets? Do the media explode in anger? Does the opposition in the Knesset (if there is such an animal) shake heaven and earth? Not at all. The Trade Union Federation (Histadrut), representing the strongest and richest workers' committees, threatens a general strike. What else? Here and there a politician issues a statement, hoping to get into the headlines. Here and there a handful of people of conscience protest. Here and there a columnist writes an indignant article. And that's that. So the poor will be a little poorer and the rich a little richer. Big deal.

When Netanyahu himself is asked about the plan, he resorts to the well-established Israeli line: there is no alternative. The Israeli economy is sinking. It's all the fault of Arafat. The intifada has destroyed our economy.

And that is a new thing altogether, with far-reaching implications.

This needs an explanation: for more than five decades, Israeli society has enjoyed the sweet illusion that there is no connection at all between our policy towards the Arabs and our economic situation. This is a cornerstone of our national consciousness.

During my ten years in the Knesset, I made at least a hundred speeches on this one point. In economic debates I pointed to the security policy and the occupation. In debates about security policy, I raised questions about the economic price.

Each one of these speeches aroused a furious and impatient reaction from all parts of the House. In security debates they shouted at me: "What has that to do with the economy? We are now speaking about terrorism!" In economic debates they shouted: "We are discussing the economy, so what are you dragging your Palestinians into this for!" (Just once in all those years, a deputy minister of the Treasury took me aside in the corridor and said: "You are the only one who made sense." Not being an economist, I was flattered.)

This ignoring of the price of the war and the occupation has had curious results: the poorest people, the unemployed, and the inhabitants of the run-down so-called "development towns" have always voted Likud. In the last elections, they voted solidly for Sharon. They had only two demands: to screw the Arabs and to put an end to the economic crisis. They saw no contradiction between the two.

But for some months now, there has been a change in public consciousness. In order to counter the accusation that the government's economic policy has caused the depression, the Sharon people have had to admit that the intifada is the main cause, even if the worldwide crisis added to it. The intifada dealt a terrible blow to tourism, one of the most important sectors of our economy. Foreign investments, which are essential to economic growth, have all but stopped. The giant army necessary for the fight against the intifada, together with the settlers, devours a huge proportion of our GNP (many times more, per capita, than in the United States).

Some people believe that if the depression deepens, the "weak strata" (as the poor are called in Israel) will one day rise against the Sharon government, the masses will pour onto the streets and topple it. That may be too optimistic. But at least one can dream about the night when, at midnight, the people knock on the door of the government and hand it a notice of dismissal.

3
All Process, No Peace

As is well documented in his earlier books, particularly *My Friend, the Enemy*, Avnery spent many years practicing a kind of ad hoc shuttle diplomacy between his own Israeli government and representatives of the PLO, entirely on his own at considerable personal risk. Although it is difficult to measure precisely the influence he had, it can nonetheless definitively be stated that Avnery's contacts with Yassir Arafat, both directly and through PLO spokespeople Said Hammami and Issam Sartawi,[48] contributed to PLO recognition of Israel and the eventual signing of the Oslo Declaration of Principles in September, 1993, based at least in part on the 1967 UN Resolution 242, the so-called "land for peace" resolution.

Despite its many faults and ultimate failure, the Oslo Declaration of Principles was a breakthrough in Palestinian–Israeli relations, signaling, for the first time, a publicly aired willingness on each side of the issue to formally recognize the other. Since that time myriad plans have come and gone, leading to claims that the process of peace, rather than peace itself, was the goal.[49] After September 2000, when then Israeli Defense Minister Ariel Sharon, accompanied by 1,000 armed troops, entered the Haram al-Sharif, otherwise known as the Temple Mount, site of the al-Aqsa Mosque, tolling the final death knell for the Oslo agreement and igniting the second, or al-Aqsa Intifada, peace plans have proliferated without bearing much fruit.

Not all the plans that have been proposed since Oslo are represented in Avnery's works. Some were extremist schemes that were never taken seriously by the vast majority of interested parties; others were flashes in the pan, fading as soon as they appeared as incidents on the ground moved quickly. Moreover, not all the plans were actually put forth as such. Ariel Sharon's "unilateral disengagement" from Gaza was certainly unilateral if not really disengagement, and it was never a formal plan proposed for negotiation toward final status.

One idea that has been articulated time and again, though never negotiated by any involved parties as a viable alternative, is what is commonly called the one-state solution. Avnery has written quite extensively about the idea, including sentiments on both sides of the issue. Though he has, at times, lauded the general idea as part of a distant dream in a borderless world, and continues to call for a Semitic confederation with close cooperation, Avnery resides firmly in the camp calling for two independent states of Palestine and Israel. His discussion of these options is included in Chapter 1: "In the beginning."—SRP

Oslo Revisited

August 11, 2007

On these hot, sticky days of the Israeli summer, it is pleasant to feel the coolness of Oslo, even if the visit is only virtual.

Fourteen years after the signing of the Oslo agreement, it is again the subject of debate: was it a historical mistake?

In the past, only the right said so. They talked about "Oslo criminals," as the Nazis used to rail against "November criminals" (those who signed the November 1918 armistice between the defeated Germany and the victorious Allies).

Now, the debate is also agitating the left. With the wisdom of hindsight, some leftists argue that the Oslo agreement is to blame for the dismal political situation of the Palestinians, the near collapse of the Palestinian Authority, and the split between Gaza and the West Bank. The slogan "Oslo is dead" can be heard on all sides.

What truth is there in this?

On the morrow of the agreement, Gush Shalom held a public debate in a large Tel-Aviv hall. Opinions were divided. Some said that it was a bad agreement and should not be supported in any way. Others saw it as a historic breakthrough.

I supported the agreement. I told the audience:

> True, it is a bad agreement. No one looking only at the written paragraphs could stand up for it. But for me, it is not the written paragraphs that are important. What is important is the spirit of the agreement. After decades of mutual denial, Israel and the Palestinian people have recognized each other. That is a historic step, from which there is no going back. It is happening now in the minds of millions on both sides. It creates a dynamism for peace that will overcome, in the end, all the obstacles embedded in the agreement.

This view was accepted by most of those present and has since determined the direction of the peace camp. Now I am asking myself: Was I right?

Yassir Arafat said of Oslo: "This is the best agreement that could be achieved in the worst situation." He meant the balance of power, with Israel's huge advantage over the Palestinians.

For the sake of fair disclosure: I may have contributed in a small way to the shaping of his attitude. At my meetings with him in Tunis, I advocated again and again a pragmatic approach. Learn from the

Zionists, I told him. They never said "No." At every stage they agreed to accept what was offered to them, and immediately went on to strive for more. The Palestinians, on the contrary, always said "No" and lost.

Some time before the agreement was signed, I had an especially interesting meeting in Tunis. I did not yet know what was happening in Oslo, but ideas for a possible agreement were in the air. The meeting took place in Arafat's office, with Arafat, Mahmoud Abbas, Yassir Abed-Rabbo, and two or three others.

It was a kind of brainstorming session. We covered all the subjects under discussion: a Palestinian state, borders, Jerusalem, the settlements, security, and so on. Ideas were bandied about and considered. I was asked: "What can Rabin offer?" I asked in return: "What can you accept?" In the end we reached a kind of consensus that came very close to the Oslo agreement that was signed a few weeks later.

I remember, for example, what was said about Jerusalem. Some of those present insisted that they should not agree to any postponement. I said: "If we postpone the solution to the end of the negotiations, will you be in a better or worse situation then than now? Surely you will then be better situated to achieve what you want?"

The Oslo Agreement (officially the Declaration of Principles) was based, from the Palestinian point of view, on this assumption. It was supposed to give the Palestinians a minimal state-like basis, which would evolve gradually until the sovereign State of Palestine would be established.

The trouble was that this final aim was not spelled out in the agreement. That was its fatal defect.

The long-term Palestinian aim was perfectly clear. It had been fixed by Arafat long before: the State of Palestine in all the occupied territories, a return to the borders existing before the 1967 war (with the possibility of minor swaps of territory here and there), East Jerusalem (including the Islamic and Christian shrines) as the capital of Palestine, dismantling of the settlements on Palestinian territory, a solution of the refugee problem in agreement with Israel. This aim has not been and will not be changed. Any Palestinian leader who accepted less would be branded by his people as a traitor.

But the Israeli aim was not fixed at all, and has remained open to this day. That is why the implementation of practically every part of the agreement has aroused such controversy, always resolved by the immense Israeli superiority of power. Gradually, the agreement gave up its soul, leaving behind only dead letters.

The main hope—that the dynamism of peace would dominate the process—was not realized.

Immediately after the signing of the agreement, we implored

Yitzhak Rabin to rush ahead, create facts, realize its explicit and implicit meaning. For example, release all the prisoners at once, stop all settlement activity, open wide the passage between Gaza and the West Bank, start serious negotiations immediately in order to achieve the final agreement even before the date set for its completion (1999). And, more than anything else, infuse all contacts between Israel and the Palestinians with a new spirit, to conduct them "on the eye-to-eye level," with mutual respect.

Rabin did not follow this path. He was, by nature, a slow, cautious person, devoid of dramatic flair (unlike Menachem Begin, for example).

I compared him at the time to a victorious general who has succeeded in breaking through the enemy's front, and then, instead of throwing all his forces into the breach, remains fixed to the spot, allowing his opponents to regroup their forces and form a new front. After gaining victory over the "Greater Israel" camp and routing the settlers, he allowed them to start a counter-offensive, which reached its climax in his murder.

Oslo was meant to be a historic turning point. It should have put an end to the Israeli–Palestinian conflict, which is a clash between an irresistible force (Zionism) and an immovable object (the Palestinians). This did not happen. The Zionist attack goes on, and the Palestinian resistance becomes more extreme.

It is impossible to know what would have happened if Yigal Amir had not pulled the trigger. In Rabin's days, too, settlements were being built at a hectic pace and there was no serious attempt at starting serious negotiations. But relations between Rabin and Arafat were gradually getting closer, mutual trust was being established and the process might have gathered momentum. So Rabin was murdered, and a decade later Arafat was murdered, too.

But the problem of the Oslo agreement goes far beyond the personal fate of its creators.

Lacking a clear and agreed-upon aim, the Oslo agreement gave rise to a situation that has almost no precedent. That was not understood at the time, nor is it clearly understood today.

Usually, when a national liberation movement reaches its goal, the change takes place in one move. On a certain day, the French ruled Algeria; on the morrow it was taken over by the freedom fighters. The governance of South Africa was transferred from the white minority to the black majority in one sweep.

In Palestine, an entirely different situation was created: a Palestinian Authority with state-like trappings was indeed set up, but the occupation did not end. This situation was much more dangerous than perceived initially.

There was a sharp contradiction between the "state in the making" and the continuation of the liberation struggle. One of its expressions was the new class of authority-owners, who enjoyed the fruits of government and began to smell of corruption, while the mass of ordinary people continued to suffer from the miseries of the occupation. The need to go on with the struggle clashed with the need to strengthen the Authority as a quasi-state.

Arafat succeeded with great difficulty in balancing the two contrary needs. For example, it was demanded that the financial dealings of the Authority be transparent, while the financing of the continued resistance had necessarily to remain opaque. It was necessary to reconcile the Old Guard, which ruled the Authority, with the Young Turks, who were leading the armed struggle organizations. With the death of Arafat, the unifying authority disappeared, and all the internal contradictions burst into the open.

The Palestinians might conclude from this that the very creation of the Palestinian Authority was a mistake. That it was wrong to stop, or even to limit, the armed struggle against the occupation. There are those who say that the Palestinians should not have signed any agreement with Israel (still less giving up in advance 78 percent of Mandatory Palestine), or, at least, that they should have restricted it to an interim agreement signed by minor officials, instead of encouraging the illusion that a historic peace agreement had been achieved.

On both sides there are voices asserting that not only the Oslo agreement, but the whole concept of the "two-state solution" has died. Hamas predicts that the Palestinian Authority is about to turn into an agency of collaborators, some sort of subcontractor for safeguarding the security of Israel and fighting the Palestinian resistance organizations. According to a current Palestinian joke, the 'two-state solution" means the Hamas state in Gaza and the Fatah state in the West Bank.

There are, of course, weighty counter-arguments. "Palestine" is now recognized by the United Nations and most international organizations. There exists an official worldwide consensus in favor of the establishment of the Palestinian state, and even those who really oppose it are compelled to render it lip service in public.

More importantly: Israeli public opinion is moving slowly but consistently towards this solution. The concept of "the whole of *Eretz Israel*" is finally dead. There exists a national consensus about an exchange of territories that would make possible the annexation of the "settlement blocs" to Israel and the dismantling of all the other settlements. The real debate is no longer between the annexation of the entire West Bank and its partial annexation, but between partial annexation (the areas west of the wall as well as the Jordan valley) and the return of almost all the occupied territories.

That is still far from the national consensus that is necessary for making peace—but it is even further from the consensus that existed before Oslo, when a large part of the public denied the very existence of the Palestinian people, not to mention the need for a Palestinian state. This public opinion, together with international pressures, is what now compels Ehud Olmert at least to pretend that he is going to negotiate about the establishment of the Palestinian state.

It is still too early to judge Oslo, for better or for worse. Oslo does not belong to the past. It belongs to the present. What future it may have depends on us.

The Peace Criminal[50]

July 21, 2001

Everybody knows who is a war criminal. For example, somebody who kills prisoners of war or massacres a civilian population (or allows others to do this) is one.

The time has come to define who is a peace criminal: somebody who kills peace and thereby makes war inevitable. Golda Meir, for example, in the early 1970s, killed the chances for peace with Egypt and caused the Yom Kippur war, in which 2,000 Israelis and countless others died.

Ehud Barak is a peace criminal. He brought about the failure of the Camp David summit and its consequences, primarily the present intifada, in which hundreds have already died. This might well lead to a general war, in which thousands will perish.

If there were an International Court for Peace Crimes, Ehud Barak would be indicted on two counts:

Count 1: The accused pressured Arafat and Clinton into agreeing to the summit and brought about its failure by presenting to it an ultimatum of unacceptable proposals.

Count 2: The accused spread the lie that he had offered Arafat "everything he asked for" and that Arafat rejected it. By spreading this lie, the accused destroyed the Israeli peace camp which believed him, brought the extreme right to power, prepared the ground for a "national unity" based on the lie, and almost obliterated any real opposition.

At the Barak trial, evidence will be produced to show that he proposed at Camp David the formal annexation of 10 percent of the West Bank area ("settlement blocs") and informal annexation of another 10 percent (Jordan valley etc.), with the rest of the territory cut up into enclaves and cut off from the neighboring countries (Egypt and Jordan); that he pretended to "give up" East Jerusalem but without giving the Palestinians full sovereignty there, and especially not over the compound of the mosques ("Temple Mount"); that he did not agree to any compromise on the refugees; and that he demanded that the Palestinians declare this to be "the end of the conflict."

Until now, Barak's blind admirers have fervently denied these facts. But this week a witness appeared who could decide the outcome of the trial. He is a neutral and objective eye-witness, whose integrity cannot be doubted by any judge: Robert Malley, personal assistant to President Clinton on the Middle East, who took part in all the Camp David deliberations.[51] He will testify to the following facts, among others:

Before the summit, Barak reneged on his promise to transfer to the Palestinian Authority the village of Abu Dis and two other villages near Jerusalem, in spite of the fact that Clinton personally conveyed this promise to Arafat. Also, Barak refused to honor Israel's obligations under the previous agreements: the third withdrawal from most of the West Bank areas, the release of Palestinian prisoners etc. Because of this, Clinton was furious with Barak on several occasions.

Before the summit, Barak continued to enlarge the settlements and build bypass roads at a furious pace, thus destroying any vestige of Palestinian trust in his intentions.

Before and during the summit, the Palestinians not only gave up 78 percent of Mandatory Palestine, but also agreed to the annexation to Israel of "settlement blocs" and the Jewish neighborhoods built in occupied East Jerusalem. They also agreed to the principle that the right of return should be implemented without prejudicing the demographic and security interests of Israel. No other Arab government has ever agreed to similar concessions.

In exchange for the settlement blocs, Barak offered the Palestinians areas amounting to one-ninth of the territory to be annexed, a ratio of 1:9, without specifying where.

During the course of the summit, Barak did not submit any proposal in writing or specify the details of his oral proposals, and, most importantly, did not disclose either to Arafat or even to Clinton his ideas for a final settlement. In return, Arafat, too, did not submit any proposals, so that in practice there was no negotiation at all.

Clinton agreed with Arafat that Barak is "politically inept, frustrating, and devoid of personal warmth," but believed, in spite of this, that Barak wanted peace. Arafat believed that Barak did not want peace; he only wanted to convince the world that the Palestinians don't want peace. As a matter of fact, since the summit Barak's main boast has been that he "unmasked Arafat."

Clinton broke his word to Arafat. Before the summit, he promised that if it fails, he would not blame the Palestinians. Only on this condition did Arafat agree to come to the conference, which took place without proper preparation. After the failure, Clinton put the sole blame on Arafat, in order to help Barak in his reelection campaign.

*   *   *

When Barak's admirers were compelled to admit that the story about "the generous Camp David offers" is a legend, they fell back upon another line: "True, at Camp David no reasonable offers were made, but later, at the Taba meeting in January 2001, much more generous offers were made. These met all Palestinian demands, but were nevertheless rejected by them. At Taba the Israeli negotiators also submitted a map that reduced further the areas that Barak wanted to annex."

Here are some of the responses to this line:

If Barak really wanted to make much more "generous" offers, why did he not make them at Camp David, even when he realized that the summit was about to break down?

The failure of the summit caused the outbreak of the intifada, as we (and, it now appears, the Americans, too) prophesied. From that moment on, the political reality on the Palestinian side changed completely, hundreds were killed, and it became much more difficult for Arafat to convince his public to halt the uprising without achieving an important political concession in advance.

The Taba proposals were never put on paper, and until this very moment it is not clear what was proposed, or who proposed what and on whose authority. Barak, of course, repudiated everything the next day.

In the meantime, the election campaign had started in Israel and all the polls showed that Barak was about to be defeated by a landslide. How could Arafat make sweeping concessions to a man who, almost certainly, would lose power within two months? Especially since Barak did not reveal the proposals to his own public?

Arafat did not reject the Taba proposals, but declares even now that they must serve as a basis for any future negotiations, while Barak himself proclaims that the Taba proposals are null and void.

At the end of the trial, the question will remain: Did the accused, Barak, sincerely intend to reach a peace agreement, and did only a mixture of arrogance, ignorance, and political stupidity prevent him from achieving it (as Clinton believes, according to Malley), or did he, from the beginning, not have any such intention, but only intended to convince the world that he wanted peace while Arafat wants to throw the people of Israel into the sea?

It's up to the judges to decide that.

How to Torpedo the Saudis[52]

March 2, 2002

If, in May 1967, an Arab prince had proposed that the whole Arab world would recognize Israel and establish normal relations with it, in return for Israel's recognition of the Green Line border, we would have believed that the days of the Messiah had arrived. Masses of people would have run into the street, singing and dancing, as they did on November 29, 1947, when the United Nations called for the establishment of a Jewish and an Arab state in Palestine.

But then disaster struck: we conquered the West Bank and the Gaza Strip, the Labor and Likud governments filled them up with settlements, and today this offer sounds to many like a malicious anti-Semitic plot.

The leaders of Israel tell us: Don't worry. Just as we survived Pharaoh, so we shall survive Emir Abdullah.[53]

So what will happen?

In Israel, every international initiative designed to put an end to the conflict passes through three stages: (a) denial, (b) misrepresentation, (c) liquidation. That's how the Sharon–Peres government will deal with this one, too. It can draw on 53 years of experience, during which both Labor and Likud governments have succeeded in scuttling every peace plan put forward.

We must not suspect, God forbid, that the successive Israeli governments were opposed to peace. Not at all. Every one of them wanted peace. They all longed for peace. "Provided peace gives us the whole country, at least up to the Jordan River, and lets us cover all of it with Jewish settlements." Until now, all peace plans have fallen short of that.

PHASE A is designed to belittle the offer. "There is nothing new there," the political sources would assert. "It is offered solely for tactical purposes. It is a political gimmick." If the offer comes from an Arab:

"He says it to the international community, but not to his own people."
In short, "It's not serious."

One proven method is to concentrate on one word and argue that
it shows the dishonesty of the whole offer. For example, before the
October 1973 war, President Anwar Sadat of Egypt made a far-reaching peace offer. Golda Meir rejected it out of hand. Her Arabists (there
are always intellectual whores around to do the dirty job) discovered
that Sadat spoke of "salaam" but not of "*sulh*," which "proves" that
he does not mean real peace. More than 2,000 Israel soldiers and tens
of thousands of Egyptians paid with their lives for this word. After that,
a salaam treaty was signed.

Such methods are already being applied now to the Saudi offer.
First it was said that Crown Prince Abdullah had spoken about his
initiative only with an American journalist, but not addressed his own
people.[54] When it transpired that it was widely published in all Saudi
papers, both at home and in London, another argument was put
forward: the prince has made his offer only because Saudis had become
unpopular in the United States after the Twin Towers outrage. (As if
this matters.) In short, Abdullah has not become a real Zionist.

This point was widely discussed in the Israeli media. Commentators
commented, scholars showed their scholarly prowess. But not one (not
one!) of them discussed the actual content of the offer.

PHASE B is designed to outsmart the offer. We do not reject the offer.
Of course not! We're longing for peace! So we welcome the "positive
trend" of the offer and kick the ball out of the field.

The best method is to ask for a meeting with the Arab leader who
proposed the offer, "to clarify the issues." That sounds logical.
Americans think that, if two people have a quarrel, they should meet
and discuss the matter, in order to end it. What can be more reasonable
than that?

But a conflict between nations does not resemble a quarrel between
two people. Every Arab peace offer rests on a two-part premise: You
give back the occupied territories, and you get recognition and
"normalization." Normalization includes, of course, meetings of the
leaders. When the Israeli government demands a meeting with Arab
leaders "to clarify details," it actually tries to get the reward (normalization) without delivering the goods (withdrawal from the occupied
territories). A beautiful trick indeed. If the Arab leaders refuse to meet,
well, it only shows that their peace offer is a sham, doesn't it?

Many peace offers have fallen into this trap. Ben-Gurion offered to
meet with Muhammad Naguib, the Egyptian ruler after the 1952

revolution. Several Prime Ministers asked to meet Hafez al-Assad. Only
Sadat outsmarted the smart ones and turned the tables on them. He
came to Jerusalem on his own initiative.

When the General Assembly of the United Nations adopted
Resolution 242, the Israeli government did not accept it. Only much
later, when there was no way out, it accepted it "according to the Israeli
interpretation." This concentrated on the article "the" that is missing
in the English version (which demands withdrawal from "occupied
territories" instead of from "the occupied territories"), contrary to the
French version, in which the article duly appears. (The Soviets were
caught napping, because there is no article in the Russian language.)

The preferred method is to kill the spirit of the offer slowly, to talk
about it endlessly, to interpret it this way and that way, to drag negotiations on and on, to put forward conditions that the other side cannot
accept, until the initiative yields in silence. That's what happened to the
Conciliation Committee in Lausanne, that is what happened to most of
the European and American peace plans.[55]

PHASE C: If phases A and B have not worked, the liquidation stage
arrives. Nowadays it is called "targeted prevention" or, simply,
"ascertained killing" by the army.

Against the original UN mediator, the Swedish Count Folke
Bernadotte, "targeted prevention" was applied literally: he was shot
and killed. The killers were "dissidents," but Ben-Gurion did not shed
any tears.

Usually, Israeli governments use two deadly torpedoes in their
arsenal: the US Congress and the US media. William Rogers, President
Nixon's secretary of state, for example, proposed a peace plan that
included the withdrawal of Israel to the pre-1967 border, with "insubstantial changes." Israel released its torpedoes and sunk Rogers together
with his plan. His job was taken over by the Jewish megalomaniac Henry
Kissinger, and that was the end of peace plans.

Can the Saudi initiative be sunk in the same way? If the Saudis stay
their course, it will not be easy to intercept it. This time the target is not
a small frigate, not even a destroyer, but a mighty aircraft carrier. A
great effort will be needed to torpedo it.

But Shimon Peres and his foreign office are experts at this kind of
job; they have been at it for decades. Ariel Sharon will push them. The
pitiful Labor party, under the leadership of a small-time copy of
Sharon, will join the chorus. Faced with the terrible threat of having to
end the occupation, the Israeli media will rally behind the government.

Nobody revolts, nobody cries out. In Israel, real public discourse died long ago. The national instinct of survival has become blunted. Thirty-five years of occupation and settlement have eroded the nation's ability to reason, leaving instead a mixture of arrogance and folly.

A great, perhaps unique, opportunity may be missed. Hundreds, thousands, tens of thousands may pay for it with their lives. They will not dance in the streets any more.

A Roadmap to Nowhere
Or: *Much Ado About Nothing*

May 4, 2003

This could have been an important document, **IF**:

IF All the parties really wanted to achieve a fair compromise.
IF Sharon and Co. were really prepared to give back the occupied territories and dismantle the settlements.
IF The Americans were willing to exert serious pressure on Israel.
IF There was a president in Washington like Dwight Eisenhower, who did not give a damn about Jewish votes and donations.
IF George Bush were convinced that the Roadmap served his interests, instead of being a bone to throw to his British poodle.
IF Tony Blair thought that it served his interests, instead of being a crumb to throw to his domestic rivals.
IF The United Nations had any real power.
IF Europe had any real power.
IF Russia had any real power.
IF My grandmother had wheels.

All these IFs belong to an imaginary world. Therefore, nothing will come from all the talking about this document. The embryo is dead in the womb of its mother, the Quartet.

In spite of this, let's try to treat the matter in all seriousness. Is this a good document? Could it be helpful, if all the IFs were realistic?

In order to answer this seriously, one has to distinguish between the declared objectives and the road that is supposed to lead to them.

The objectives are very positive. They are identical with the aims of the Israeli peace movement: an end to the occupation, the establishment of the independent State of Palestine side-by-side with the State of Israel, Israeli–Palestinian and Israeli–Syrian peace, the integration of Israel in the region.

In this respect, the Roadmap goes further than the Oslo agreement. In the Oslo "Declaration of Principles" there was a giant hole: it did not spell out what was to come after the long interim stages. Without a clear final aim, the interim stages had no clear purpose. Therefore the Oslo process died with Yitzhak Rabin.

The Roadmap confirms that there now exists a worldwide consensus about these objectives. This fact will remain even if nothing comes out of it. Those of us who remember that only 35 years ago there were hardly a handful of people in the world who believed in this vision can draw profound satisfaction from this Roadmap. It shows that we have won the struggle for world public opinion.

But let's not exaggerate: in this document, too, there is a gaping hole in the definition of the aims. It does not say what the borders of the future Palestinian state should be, either explicitly or implicitly. The Green Line is not even mentioned. That by itself is enough to invalidate the whole structure. Ariel Sharon talks about a Palestinian state in 40 percent of the "territories"—equivalent to less than 9 percent of Palestine under the British Mandate. Does anyone believe that this will bring peace?

When we pass from poetry to prose, from the mountaintop of the aims to the road that is supposed to get us there, the warning signs become more and more frequent. This is a perilous road with many curves and obstacles. Even a very brave athlete would shudder at the thought of having to run this course.

The road is divided into phases. In every phase the parties must fulfill certain obligations. At the end of each phase the Quartet must decide whether the obligations have been completely fulfilled, before entering the next one. At the end, the hoped-for peace will come, God willing.

Even if all the parties were imbued with goodwill, it would be extremely difficult. When David Lloyd-George, as British Prime Minister, decided to end the British occupation of Ireland, he observed that one cannot cross an abyss in two jumps. The initiators of the Roadmap propose, in effect, to cross the Israeli–Palestinian abyss in many small hops.

First question: who is this "Quartet" that has to decide at every point whether the two parties have fulfilled their obligations, and a new phase can be entered?

At first glance, there is a balance between the four players: the United Nations, the United States, Europe, and Russia. It is rather like a commercial arbitration: each side appoints one arbitrator, and the two arbitrators together choose a third one. Judgment is reached by majority decision and is binding on both parties.

This could work. The United States are close to Israel; Europe and Russia are acceptable to the Palestinians. The UN representative would have the casting vote.

Not at all. According to the document, the Quartet must take all decisions unanimously. The Americans have a veto, which means that Sharon has a veto. Without his agreement, nothing can be decided. Need more be said?

Second question: When will it end?

Well, there is no clear-cut timetable for passing from one phase to the next. The document vaguely mentions several vague dates, but they are difficult to take seriously. The first phase should have started in October 2002, and come to a close in May 2003. In the real world, the Map will be shown to the Israelis and the Palestinians for the first time in May, and only then will the serious haggling begin. Nobody can foresee when the implementation of the first phase will actually begin. And in the meantime ...

It should be remembered: in the Oslo agreements many dates were fixed, and almost all of them were missed (generally by the Israeli side). As the good Rabin declared: "There are no sacred dates."

Third question: Is there any kind of balance between the obligations on the two parties? The answer must be "no."

In the first phase, the Palestinians must stop the armed intifada, establish close security cooperation with the Israelis, and recognize Israel's right to exist in peace and security. They must also appoint an "empowered" Prime Minister (meaning, in effect, the neutralization of the elected president, Yassir Arafat) and start the drafting of a constitution that will meet with the approval of the Quartet.[56]

What must Israel do at the same time? It must enable Palestinian officials (note: officials; this does not apply to the rest of the population) to move from place to place, improve the humanitarian situation, stop attacks on civilians and the demolition of homes, and pay the Palestinians the money due to them. Also, it will dismantle "settlement outposts" erected since Sharon came to power, in violation of the government's guidelines. Who will decide to whom this applies? There is also no mention of freezing settlement activity in this phase.

Does anyone believe that Prime Minister Abu Mazen could put an end to Hamas and (Islamic) Jihad attacks without any political *quid pro quo* at all, and while the settlements keep expanding?

After this phase, the Palestinians must reform their institutions and create a constitution "based on strong parliamentary democracy" (they will not be allowed to have an American presidential system, for fear of Arafat retaining some powers). Only then, "as comprehensive security performance moves forward," will the Israeli army "withdraw progressively from areas occupied since September 28, 2000." Not immediately, not in one withdrawal, but bit by bit, "progressively." Not from Areas B and C, but only from Area A. They will be where they were before the present intifada.

(There is an old Jewish joke about a family that complains about being crowded together in one room. The rabbi advises them to bring in a goat, too. Later, when the family complains that life has become intolerable, the rabbi tells them to take the goat out again. Suddenly they feel that they have a lot of space. This time the Israeli army is told to remove the goat, but the Palestinians are told to remove father and mother.)

After all this, the next phase will start; the Palestinians will adopt their constitution and hold free elections, the Egyptians and Jordanians will send their ambassadors back to Israel, and the Israeli government will, at last, freeze settlement activity.

The next phase will focus on the "possible" creation of an independent Palestinian state with "provisional borders." So, long after all attacks have been stopped, there will be an "option" of creating a Palestinian state in Area A, a tiny part of what used to be Palestine. According to the Roadmap, this should happen by the end of 2003, but it is clear that, if at all, this will come about much later. It is also stated that "further action on settlements" will be a part of the process. What does this mean? Not the dismantling of a single settlement, not even the most remote and isolated one.

After all this comes about, the Quartet will decide (again unanimously—only with the agreement of the Americans) that the time has come for negotiations aimed at a "permanent status agreement," hopefully in 2005, including discussion of items such as borders, Jerusalem, refugees, and settlements. If Sharon or his successor want it, there will be an agreement. If not, then not.

The truth is, in this whole document there is not one word that Sharon could not accept. After all, with the help of Bush he can torpedo any step at any time.

To sum up: *Much Ado about Nothing*. As evidenced by the fact that neither Sharon nor the settlers are upset.

To Aqaba and Back[57]

July 6, 2003

First thoughts after the Aqaba meeting:

Solo performance. If there had been a printed program, it would have looked something like this:

"Peace in the Holy Land" by George W. Bush.
Director: George Bush.
Principal actor: W. B. George.
Music: G. W. Bush.
Mise en scene: Bush W. George.
Speeches: G.W.B.

What makes George run? Why this sudden enthusiasm for personal intervention in the Israeli–Palestinian conflict?

There is a purely political aspect: in Afghanistan, anarchy reigns. In Iraq, all the high-sounding plans about a "democratic Iraqi government" have been shelved. In the United States, ugly news-stories are circulating, insinuating that the administration deliberately deceived the public about the existence of Iraqi weapons of mass destruction.

Bush needs an uncontested achievement in the Middle East. What could be more beautiful on television than the picture of the President of the United States standing between the Prime Ministers of Israel and Palestine with a background of blue sea and soaring palms, bringing peace to the two suffering peoples?

For this purpose, Bush has set in motion a brutal steamroller that crushes all opposition, Palestinian or Israeli. Bush practically dictated all four speeches himself.

This is not a one-day stand. It will go on until the American election in November 2004. Bush wants to be reelected, and this time with a real majority. Therefore, we shall probably be living for a year and a half in the shadow of the Bush initiative, enforced by Colin Powell and Condoleezza Rice. Both Israelis and Palestinians will have to conduct their business within this framework.

And please remember: Bush is no Clinton. Clinton was an attractive, sympathetic, very intelligent, idealistic, and devoted president. He really wanted to solve the problem. But he suffered from a certain lack of seriousness and moral fiber. Bush, on the other hand is not sophisticated. If anything he is rather primitive. But he has a brutal willpower that does not suffer contradiction. When he wants something, he unleashes the power of the United States to attain it.

Now he wants a conspicuous achievement in the Israeli–Palestinian arena, an achievement that will look good on television and be clear to every American voter. Anyone who gets in his way will be crushed.

It is impossible to know how long this pressure will last. Some may hope that it will go on till the final agreement. Others may count in weeks. But in our desperate situation, every week is important.

The aircraft carrier changes course. Bush's personal calculations must be seen, of course, against the national background.

Immediately after the Twin Towers outrage, I wrote in this column that this traumatic event would compel the United States to change its policy towards the Israeli–Palestinian conflict. Such an atrocity would have been impossible without the huge accumulation of fury and hatred directed against the United States in the Arab—and, indeed, the entire Muslim—world. This has many causes, but the first and foremost among them is American support for Sharon's brutality in the Palestinian territories, seen daily by millions of Arabs and other Muslims on Aljazeera television.

I predicted then that the United States would act quickly to change that policy. I made my prediction—and nothing happened. I had to admit (at least to myself) that I was wrong, that American logic doesn't work this way.

And now it is happening, after all. Two years late the United States is indeed changing course. I did not take the time factor into account. A speedboat like Israel can turn around in weeks, an aircraft carrier like the United States needs years.

It is said that the American public is not interested in foreign affairs: that in elections only domestic issues matter. That is true in normal times, such as the days of George Bush Sr. But the events of 9/11 have brought the Middle East into every American living room, much like the Japanese attack on Pearl Harbor. It has now become a domestic matter.

The leopard's spots. Has Sharon changed his skin?

It may seem like that. He has spoken about the "occupation" (and denied it immediately). He is going to remove outposts (but only make-believe outposts). He talks about a "Palestinian state" (But not about the "State of Palestine"). So what has happened? Has he got old? Desperate? Wise?

None of these. As a son of the soil, he is sensitive to changes in the weather. He notices the new winds blowing from Washington. The smiling George W., his great buddy, adopts a rough tone in private conversations. He dictates instead of discussing. He issues ultimatums. What is to be done?

Sharon behaves like the Jew who was threatened with death if he did not teach the Polish nobleman's beloved horse to read and write. Pleading that the job is difficult, the Jew asked for three years. "By then, either the horse or the nobleman will be dead," he comforted his despairing wife.

Sharon accepted the Bush ultimatum, but only in appearance. He is trying to win time, at least until after the American elections. Perhaps Bush will not be re-elected, perhaps he will have other things to worry about by then. In the meantime, Sharon will do the inescapable minimum, postpone everything that can be postponed, cheat as much as he can, change what can be changed. His principal assistant, Dov Weissglass, is a grand master of this kind of thing.

Sharon's final objective has not changed, and in Aqaba he has said nothing to contradict it. If the Arabs cannot be removed from the country, they must be confined to isolated enclaves, which will be connected artificially by strips of land to create "contiguity." He is ready to call this a "Palestinian state." It will consist of 42 percent of the occupied territories, which themselves constitute 22 percent of Palestine before 1948. The main settlement blocs will remain as they are and eventually be annexed to Israel. No mention of Jerusalem or the refugees.

As we have said many times: don't listen to what Sharon says, look at what he is doing with his hands. Will he freeze the settlements, as demanded by the Roadmap? Will he really stop building in Ma'aleh Adumim, where hundreds of new houses are now planned? Will he stop building the Separation Wall, whose purpose is to cut off large chunks of the West Bank? Will he immediately remove the 60 settlement outposts that have been built since he came to power? Will the IDF get out of Area A and cease the closures and blockades of Palestinian towns and villages?

Anything else would be a sham.

The good and the bad. On the Palestinian side, something interesting has happened. Without anyone planning it, a game of "good cop, bad cop" has developed.

The Americans and Israelis have swallowed the fairy tale of the "bad Arafat," that was invented by Ehud Barak in order to cover up his monumental failure. So as not to have to talk with the evil Arafat, they have proclaimed that Abu Mazen is the incarnation of everything good and beautiful.

The result: in order to strengthen his standing vis-à-vis Arafat, they are obliged to give Abu Mazen things they refused to give Arafat. The Palestinian public gives qualified support to Abu Mazen and waits to see what he can get from Bush and Sharon. Abu-Mazen cannot move without Arafat, but the results do not bind Arafat, who can always assert that he was not a partner to the deal. An ideal situation for him.

From the Israeli point of view, this is idiotic. If we are negotiating and ready to pay the price, wouldn't it be better to do it with the person who can deliver the goods?

A huge achievement. If the armed intifada ends, who can be said to have gained from the 32 months of bloody struggle?

The objective answer: it is a draw.

The Palestinians have suffered terribly. Their infrastructure has been destroyed, their dignity trampled on. Some 2,000 men, women, and children have been killed, tens of thousands injured, 10,000 put in prison. Their homes have been demolished, their trees uprooted, their livelihood destroyed. But their resistance has not been broken. It is as strong on the last day as on the first.

The Israelis have suffered much less, but they too have suffered a lot. Some 800 Israelis killed, hundreds wounded. Fear stalks the streets, the malls, and the buses. Private watchmen, 100,000 of them, are everywhere. The intifada has cost us some $20 billion, the economy is in a deep crisis, there is no tourism and no foreign investment, the quality of life has gone down, the welfare state is collapsing, social tensions are increasing. But the IDF continues to deal blows to the Palestinian population and the settlement drive is in full swing.

The draw has created a mood of hopelessness on both sides. Both have come to the conclusion that there is no military solution.

But when there is a draw between two sides, one of which is a thousand times stronger than the other, it is a fantastic achievement for the weaker.

What has been achieved? What came out of Aqaba? What does the Roadmap present?

The easy answer is: nothing substantial, only words, words, words.

But words, too, are important.

The Oslo agreement was disabled at birth because it did not spell out the final destination: the State of Palestine side-by-side with the State of Israel. The Roadmap clearly defines this aim, confirmed by the whole world and with the agreement of the most rightist government Israel ever had. This is a big step forward, a point of no return.

The spokesman of the settlers has asserted that this is a "reward to the terrorists." And, indeed, this is an achievement of the intifada. Without it, the Palestinians would have got nothing.

The appearance of an inspection team (American, for now) is also very important. We have demanded this for years. The era of deceit is drawing to an end.

The removal of outposts is important, too. Sure, it concerns only a few, which are by themselves unimportant. But to quote again from one of the settlers: Even the removal of one single outpost breaks a national taboo. It proves that settlements can be removed; it creates a pattern, a precedent.

The Roadmap does not say where the permanent borders between Israel and Palestine will be. That will be the issue for the next battle.

But we are moving forward. Perhaps only a small step. Perhaps a bigger one than it seems. But even in the most pessimistic view, this is a move in the right direction, towards the end of the occupation, towards peace.

Pray for the Roadmap. This is the traditional "Prayer for the Road" for Jews who set out on a voyage (my translation):

> May it please you, our God and our fathers' God,
> To show us the way to peace,
> And to guide our steps towards this peace,
> And to direct our traveling in peace,
> That we may complete out journey to life, joy, and peace,
> And be safeguarded from all enemies and dangers along the way,
> And from all the disasters native to this world ...

With Whom, About What?

October 19, 2003

The Beilin–Abed-Rabbo agreement is the latest hit on the Middle Eastern market.[58]

This week I made a short visit to Germany, where a book of mine has come out, and was asked about the agreement at every event. At my meetings with President Johannes Rau and Foreign Minister Joschka Fischer, too, the subject came up at once. I used the opportunity to argue for support of this initiative by all possible means.

To avoid misunderstanding, I pointed out that I have no connections with this initiative. The Israeli participants belong to the left wing of the Labor and Meretz parties, and I do not belong to this circle. But I give this initiative all my blessings—all the more so because it continues a process that we ourselves started two years ago.

In August 2001, Gush Shalom published the draft of an Israeli–Palestinian peace agreement. It consisted of 14 paragraphs that included detailed proposals for the solution of all the problems of the conflict. It was an Israeli initiative, but we acted in close consultation with Palestinian colleagues.

The main object of the initiative was educational. The al-Aqsa Intifada was in full swing, Ehud Barak's myth ("There is no one to talk with!") had captured the public, most of the peace camp had collapsed, hopelessness and impotence reigned supreme.

We wanted to light a candle in the darkness. To prove to the public that there is a solution, that there is somebody to talk to and something to talk about. And, most importantly, to tell the people what the price of peace is, and that it is worthwhile to pay it.

We saw ourselves as an icebreaker, a compact and autonomous vessel that opens the way for much bigger ships to follow.

We published the draft treaty as a full-page ad in *Ha'aretz* (August 10, 2001). It did not cause much of a stir. As usual all the Israeli media boycotted it, and even abroad it attracted only limited attention. But we hoped that we had opened a path, and that others would use it in due course.

The first who did so were Sari Nusseibeh and Ami Ayalon, the former the president of an Arab university and the scion of an important Jerusalem family, the latter a former commander of the Israeli navy and a former chief of the security service. They presented a small number of basic principles for a peace accord, launched a big publicity campaign and called for mass signatures on both sides. Up to now, some 65,000 Palestinians and 85,000 Israelis have signed.[59]

Now comes the initiative of a group of important Israeli and Palestinian personalities. Like our initiative at the time, it takes the form of a detailed draft peace agreement. In their content, too, the two documents are quite similar. It can be said that 90 percent of the proposals are the same. And no wonder—after endless plans, endless rounds of negotiations, and endless talks, all the problems lie on the table and everyone knows what the parameters of a possible compromise are.

Both drafts are based on the principle of "two states for two peoples," with their capitals in Jerusalem, a border based on the Green Line, removal of the settlers from the Palestinian territories, and a practical solution of the refugee problem.

The differences are mainly due to Beilin–Abed-Rabbo's desire to sweeten the pill for the Israelis as much as possible. For example, we proposed to cure the historical wound through Israel's acceptance of its responsibility for the creation of at least part of the refugee problem and its recognition of the principle of the right of return. We believe that such a declaration is necessary for the cleaning of the wound.

The new initiative deliberately ignores the painful question of principle and deals only with the practical solution. Beilin says that the Palestinians have "given up" the right of return *de jure*, too—a statement the Palestinians will it find difficult to swallow.

Like us, the initiators propose in practice to allow a limited number of Palestinians to return to Israel, but they propose a sophisticated key: a number equivalent to the average number of refugees allowed in by other nations. We have proposed a quite simple method: to allow back a fixed quota (say 50,000) every year for ten years.

On the question of Jerusalem, too, the new draft tries to sweeten the pill. They avoid saying clearly that the Palestinians will be "sovereign" over their part of the city and the Temple Mount. All the paragraphs about Jerusalem are a bit clumsy, in an attempt, it seems, to make them more palatable to the Israeli public.

The document imposes several limitations on Palestinian sovereignty that may impair the feeling of equality. Also, without seeing the detailed maps, it is hard to say how much Beilin wants to swap. It seems that there is a certain disparity between their maps and ours.

But these differences are not really important. The people who drafted this document knew that they were preparing only a sample agreement. It will be presented to the public in order to show that peace is possible, that it poses no existential danger to Israel, that there is a partner on the other side, and that there is something to talk about. Even the refugee problem, which frightens so many Israelis out of their wits, stops being so threatening when one tackles it in real terms. It becomes a practical problem with practical solutions.

The reactions of the leaderships of the two sides is illuminating. Ariel Sharon has attacked the document furiously, as if it constituted high treason and stuck a knife into the back of the nation. That's no wonder, considering that there is no greater danger to Sharon and his grand design than the danger of peace. Ehud Barak, the man most to blame for the collapse of the Israeli peace camp, has also raged against the initiative. "The starling visits the raven," as the Hebrew saying goes.

Yassir Arafat, on the other hand, has blessed the initiative. He cannot accept it formally, because a real peace treaty must be negotiated between governments. No national leader can take official responsibility for terms when the leader of the other side does not. But it can safely be said that the agreement is acceptable to him—all the more so since he took part in its formulation behind the scenes. There is, of course, no symmetry: the Israeli doves are in opposition, while their Palestinian counterparts are in power.

Throughout the world, the document was well received by all who wish for an end to the conflict. The great hope is that this initiative, like the "revolt of the pilots," represents the end of the era of despair.

The first task of Beilin and his colleagues is to raise the Labor and

Meretz parties from their ruins (the Labor party chairman, the birthday darling, has not joined the initiative!) and to set up a strong and combative opposition in the spirit of the document.

To quote Winston Churchill: This is not the beginning of the end, but it is, perhaps, the end of the beginning.

Sharon's Speech: Decoded Version[60]

December 22, 2003

He read out the written text of his speech, word for word, without raising his eyes from the page.

It was vital for him to stick to the exact wording, since it was an encoded text. It is impossible to decipher it without breaking the code. And it is impossible to break the code without knowing Ariel Sharon very well indeed.

So it is no surprise that the flood of interpretations in Israel and abroad was ridiculous. The commentators just did not understand what they had heard. That's why they wrote things like "He did not say anything new," "He has no plan," "He is marking time," "He is old and tired." And the usual Washington reaction: "A positive step, but ..."

Nonsense. In his speech, Sharon outlined a whole, detailed—and extremely dangerous—plan. Those who did not understand—Israelis, Palestinians and foreign diplomats—will be unable to react effectively.

Here is the deciphered text of Sharon's "Herzliyah speech":

The name of the game is *hitnatkut* ("cutting ourselves off"). Meaning: most of the West Bank area will become de facto a part of Israel, and the rest we shall leave to the Palestinians, who will be enclosed in isolated enclaves. From these enclaves, the settlements will be removed.

Stage One: In order to do this, we need time—about half a year. We are talking about a large-scale and complicated military operation. The army will have to occupy and fortify new lines, while "relocating" dozens of isolated settlements. This will require detailed planning, which has not yet even started. The necessary forces and instruments will have to be prepared. Half a year is the minimum.

During this period we shall not be idle. On the contrary, we shall finish the Separation Fence, and it will play a major part in the new deployment. We shall develop the "settlement blocs," to which we shall transfer the settlers who will be relocated.

The execution of the plan in half a year is perfectly timed. At exactly that time the American election campaign will reach its climax. No

American politician will dare to utter a word against Israel. The Democrats need the Jewish votes and money. The Republicans also need the votes and the money of the 60 million Christian fundamentalists who support the most extreme elements in Israel.

While we quietly prepare the big operation, we shall continue to flatter President Bush and praise his idiotic Roadmap, without, of course, fulfilling any of our obligations under it. But we shall blame the Palestinians for violating it.

At the same time we shall pretend to seek negotiations with the Palestinians. We shall try to meet with Abu Ala as many times as possible and play the game to the end.[61] When we are ready to go, we shall terminate the contacts, declare the Roadmap dead and state sorrowfully that all our efforts to start peace negotiations have failed because of Arafat.

Stage two: By then, the Separation Wall will be ready. The Palestinian territories (Areas A and B under Oslo) will be surrounded on all sides. In practice there will be about a dozen isolated pockets. In order to fulfill our promise about Palestinian "contiguity" we shall connect the enclaves by special roads, bridges and tunnels, which we shall be able to cut at a moment's notice.[62]

The army will withdraw gradually to the separation barrier and re-deploy in the territories that will be annexed to Israel. These include, *inter alia*, the settlement blocs of Karney Shomron, Elkana, Ariel, and Kedumim; the Modi'in Road and the territory south of it up to the Green Line; all the Greater Jerusalem area already annexed in 1967; the new neighborhoods around Jerusalem up to Maaleh Adumim and perhaps further; the Jewish settlement in Hebron and Kiryat Arba and the settlements in the Hebron area; all the Dead Sea shore; all the Jordan valley, including about 15 kilometers of the banks. Altogether, more than half the West Bank.

These areas will not be annexed officially, but we shall annex them as rapidly as possible in practice. We shall fill them with settlements (also using the settlers from the "relocated" settlements), industrial parks, roads, public institutions, and army installations, so that they will become indistinguishable from parts of Israel proper.

At the same time, we shall evacuate the settlements beyond the barrier, including those in the Gaza Strip (with or without the Katif bloc).

In line with the American proposal, we shall call the Palestinian enclaves "a Palestinian state with temporary borders." That will give the Palestinians the illusion that they will be able to negotiate the "permanent" borders. But, of course, the "separation fence" will be the final border.

The terror will not stop completely, but the Palestinian enclaves will be at our mercy and we shall be able to cut each of them off at any time, prevent movement from one to another and make life in them intolerable. It will not be worthwhile for them to conduct violent acts.

Officially, the Palestinians will have free access to the border crossings to Egypt and Jordan, but in practice we shall maintain an effective military presence, enabling us to stop movement there at any time.

At first the world will scream, but faced with a *fait accompli* they will quieten down. Even if Bush remains in the White House, he will be paralyzed until after the elections at the end of 2004. If a Democrat is elected president, he will need some months to settle down. By then everything will be finished, and we shall be able to generously agree to some minor adjustments.

This is the Plan. Can it be realized?

It is quite possible that Sharon will convince Israeli public opinion. The great majority of the public is united around two points: (a) the longing for peace and security, and (b) the distrust of Arabs and the unwillingness to deal with them. (Some weeks ago, a satirical supplement published a slogan: "YES to peace, NO to Palestinians.")

Sharon's plan promises both. It promises peace and security, and it is entirely "unilateral." No negotiations with Palestinians are required; it does not depend on the will of the Arabs, who can be ignored entirely.

In this respect, Sharon's plan has a great advantage over the Geneva Initiative (Accord), which is entirely based on the assumption that "there is a partner" and that we must negotiate with the Palestinians and make peace with them. Long years of brainwashing, led by Ehud Barak and most of the other leaders of the "Zionist left," have convinced the Israeli public that there is no partner, that the Arabs are cheating, that Arafat has broken every single agreement he has signed, and so on. The Sharon plan conforms to all these myths, while the Geneva Initiative clashes with them.

But beneath the road to the implementation of the Sharon Plan there lie two big landmines: the settlers and the Palestinians.

The inhabitants of the settlements that are supposed to be "relocated" include some of the most extreme elements of the settlement movement. There is no chance that these will go away peacefully. They will have to be removed by force.

That will require a huge military effort. While many moderate settlers will remove themselves voluntarily if given fat compensation, many others will resist. According to an informed estimate, some 5,000 soldiers and policemen will be needed to remove just one small "outpost," Migron, near Ramallah, which Sharon was supposed to have removed long ago according to the Roadmap. When dozens of bigger and more established settlements have to be removed, it will need a giant, quasi war-like operation, requiring a general call up of reserves, with all the political implications.

The army cannot just leave these territories with the settlements remaining behind. As long as the settlements are there, the army will be there. In other words, the implementation of the plan will not be quick and tidy, like the last night in south Lebanon, but a process of many months, perhaps years.

While the deployment in the areas that will be de facto annexed to Israel will be quick and effective, the transfer of the territories that will be turned over to the Palestinians will be very slow.

It is a complete illusion to believe that all this time the Palestinians will quietly look on. They will see the execution of a plan that they believe, quite rightly, to be a device for the destruction of the national aims of the Palestinian people. Clearly there will be no place in the Palestinian enclaves for returning refugees (not to mention any return of refugees to Israel itself). To call this structure a "Palestinian state" is a joke in bad taste.

If Sharon succeeds in executing his plan, a new chapter in the 100-year-old Israeli–Palestinian conflict will be opened. The Palestinians will be crowded into territories that will constitute about 10 percent of the original territory of Palestine before 1948. They will have no chance of enlarging this territory. On the contrary: they will be afraid of Sharon and his successors trying to remove them from what is left, completing the ethnic cleansing of *Eretz Israel*.

Therefore, the Palestinians will fight against this plan, and their struggle will intensify the more it progresses. All possible means will be employed: firing missiles and mortar shells over the separation barrier, sending suicide bombers into Israel, and so on. Probably, the violent fight will spill over into many other countries around the world, both on the ground and in the air. There will be no peace, no security.

In the end, the basic factors will be decisive: the endurance of the two peoples, their readiness to continue the bloody fight, with all its economic and social implications, as well as the willingness of the world to look on passively.

The idea of "unilateral peace" is strikingly original. "Peace without the other side" is a contradiction in terms. Learned people will call it an oxymoron, a Greek term meaning, literally, a sharp folly.

Eventually, the fate of this plan will be the same as the fate of all the other grandiose plans put forward by Sharon in his long career. One need only think of the Lebanon war and its price.[63]

Sharm-al-Sheikh, We Have Come Back Again ...

February 12, 2005

Nobody called it the "Ophira Conference." Not even the papers of the extreme right. Who today even remembers the name Ophira, which was given to Sharm-al-Sheikh during the Israeli occupation, as a first step to its annexation?

Who wants to remember the famous saying of Moshe Dayan that "Sharm-al-Sheikh is more important than peace"? A few years later, the same Dayan took part in the peace negotiations with Egypt and gave Sharm-al-Sheikh back. But in the meantime, some 2,500 young Israelis and who knows how many thousands of Egyptians paid with their lives for that statement in the Yom Kippur war.

While the conference went on, I could not clear my head of a song that was haunting me: "Sharm-al-Sheikh, we have come back again ..." It was sung with gusto in the days of the stupid euphoria after the Six-Day war. It reminded people at the time that we had already conquered the place during the 1956 Sinai war but were compelled by the Eisenhower–Bulganin ultimatum to withdraw. So here we were again.

I was there in 1956. A beautiful gulf ("Sharm-al-Sheikh means "the bay of the old man"), a few small houses, and a distinctive mosque. Before our army withdrew, a few months later, it blew up the mosque in a fit of pique.

Now, 22 years after leaving Ophira for the last time (nobody sang then "Sharm-al-Sheikh, we have left you again ...") all of us are treating the place as an Egyptian resort, as Egyptian as Cairo and Alexandria. The past has been erased. The occupation has been wiped from our collective memory.

That is the first optimistic lesson from the conference. One can withdraw. One can put an end to occupation. One can even forget that it ever took place.

The spirits of two people who were not there hovered over the proceedings.

One of them was George W. Bush. Neither he nor any other American sat at the large round table. But all the four who were sitting there knew that they are completely dependent on him. Husni Mubarak (of Egypt) relies on the $2 billion he gets every year from the United States, under the auspices of a Congress dominated by the pro-Israeli lobby. King Abdullah of Jordan gets much less, but his regime, too, depends on US support.

Ariel Sharon is the Siamese twin of Bush and cannot move without him. It is barely conceivable that he would do anything, big or small, that would upset Bush. Abu Mazen, for his part, is playing *va banque* in the hope that Bush will help the Palestinians to cast off the occupation and establish their state.[64]

So why did the Americans not come to Sharm? Because they are not ready to risk taking part in a process that might fail. They will come when success is assured. And today it is not.

The second absentee was Yassir Arafat.

The conference would not have taken place without his mysterious death. It deprived Sharon of the pretext to put peace in "formalin," as described by Dov Weissglas, his closest advisor, who sat next to him throughout the conference.[65] No Arafat, no pretext. Israeli propaganda, which worked so hard to portray Arafat as a devil, will have to toil hard to do the same to Abu Mazen.

Abu Mazen succeeded in slipping the name of Arafat into his speech, but only in an indirect way. But he—like every Palestinian—knows that it was the 45 years of Arafat's work that laid the foundations on which Abu Mazen is now building his new strategy. Without the First Intifada there would have been no Oslo, and without the Second Intifada there would have been no Sharm-al-Sheikh conference. Only the violent Palestinian resistance, which the Israeli army has not been able to put down, has brought Sharon to the round table.

The Israeli army knows by now that it cannot stamp out the insurgency by military means. The Palestinians have recovered their self-respect, much like the Egyptians after Yom Kippur. Many of them also believe that in his second term of office, Bush will impose withdrawal on Israel.

Incidentally, the demonization of Arafat has by no means stopped since his death. On the contrary, it goes on with great fervor. The left and the right in Israel, in heart-warming unity, declare in almost every article and TV talk show that Arafat was the great obstacle to peace. Not the occupation. Not the settlements. Not the policy of Netanyahu–Barak–Sharon. Only Arafat. Fact: Arafat died and hopla—there is a conference.

The game played by Condoleezza Rice was especially amusing. She visited the Mukata'ah, where every stone shouts the name of Arafat.

She did not lay a wreath on his grave—a minimal gesture of courtesy that would have won the hearts of the Palestinians. However, as a diplomatic compromise, she agreed to have her handshake with Abu Mazen photographed under the picture of Arafat.

Arafat smiled his canny smile. He surely understood.

So what was achieved at this conference?

Easier to say what was not.

The Oslo agreement failed because it did not spell out the final aim that was to be achieved after the tortuous interim stages. Arafat and Abu Mazen had a clear objective: a Palestinian state in all of the occupied territories with East Jerusalem as its capital, a return to the Green Line border (with minimal adjustments), dismantling of the settlements, and a practical solution to the refugee problem. The Israelis did not have the courage to define this inevitable solution, and many still dreamed about a Greater Israel.

That was a recipe for failure. And the very next day the quarrelling about every single paragraph began.

At Sharm-al-Sheikh the resolution of the conflict was not mentioned at all. Abu Mazen succeeded in slipping in some words, but Sharon did not react. This omission is very significant. It must be emphasized: Sharon did not utter a single word that does not conform with his plan of annexing 58 percent of the West Bank and enclosing the Palestinians in small enclaves in the rest of the territories.

The same goes for the timetable. In Oslo dates were indeed fixed, but the Israeli party had no intention of keeping to them. "There are no sacred dates," Yitzhak Rabin famously declared after signing the timetable.

That was a fatal mistake. Quite literally—it killed Rabin. The postponement of the solution allowed the opponents of peace the time to regain their strength, to regroup and mount the counter-attack that culminated in the assassination of Rabin. In vain did we quote to Rabin the dictum of Lloyd-George: "You cannot cross an abyss in two jumps."

Abu Mazen said at Sharm-al-Sheikh that this was the first step on a long road. A long road is a dangerous road. All along it the saboteurs of peace, Israelis and Palestinians, are lurking.

Moreover, one of the basic conditions for a real peace process—and perhaps the most important one—is the truthful representation of reality. If one listened to all the speeches, one could get the impression that the root problem is "Palestinian terrorism," and that if this stops, everything will be alright. In the following sequence: (a) The

Palestinians end their "violence," (b) Israel stops military actions, (c) security cooperation is established and (d) God and/or Allah will take care of the rest.

Pessimists will say nothing came of the conference. The ceasefire is fragile. In the best case, Sharon will fulfill his promise of withdrawing from the Gaza Strip and dismantling a few settlements. Then the trouble will start anew.

Optimists will say this is a good beginning. The cessation of "Palestinian terrorism" will create a new atmosphere in Israel. The first dismantling of the settlements will create a crucial confrontation. The settlers and the nationalist-messianic right will be defeated. People will realize that life can be different. The dynamics of the process will carry Sharon along and he will not be able to stop it, even if he wants to.

Who is right?

Voices From Prison[66]

May 13, 2006

Prison serves an important function in the annals of every revolutionary movement. It serves as a college for activists, center for the crystallization of ideas, rallying point for leaders, platform for dialog between the various factions.

For the Palestinian liberation movement, prison plays all these roles and many more. During the 39 years of occupation, hundreds of thousands of young Palestinians have passed through Israeli prisons. At any given time, an average of 10,000 Palestinians are held in prison. This, the liveliest and most active section of the Palestinian people, is in continuous ferment. People from every class, every town and village, every political and military faction are to be found there.

Prisoners have ample time. They have an opportunity to learn, to think, to organize seminars, to concentrate full-time on the problems of their people, to exchange views, to work out solutions.

In order to prevent an explosion, the Israeli prison authorities allow these prisoners a large measure of communal life and self-government. This is a wise policy. In practice, the prisons resemble camps for prisoners of war. Clashes between the prisoners and the prison authorities are comparatively rare.

One of the results is that, in prison, the inmates learn Hebrew. They watch Israeli TV, listen to Israeli radio, become acquainted with the Israeli way of life. They do not become Zionists, by any means, but come to know Israeli reality and even to appreciate some of its components. Israeli democracy, for example. "What we liked most," an ex-prisoner once told me, "was to see the Knesset debates on TV. When we saw Knesset members shouting at the Prime Minister and cursing members of the government, we really got excited. Where do you have such a thing in the Arab world?"

This found its expression when Yassir Arafat and his people came back to Palestine. The ongoing controversy between the returnees from Tunisia and the "people from within" was not only a result of a generation gap, but also of a difference of outlook. Arafat and his people have never lived in a democratic country. When they thought about the future Palestinian state, they had before their eyes the systems of Jordan, Egypt, Tunisia, and Lebanon. They were surprised when the young people, led by the ex-prisoners, pointed towards the Israeli model.

Not by accident, almost all my Palestinian friends are ex-prisoners, people who have spent a long time in prison, sometimes 10 and even 20 years. I always wonder at the absence of bitterness in their mind. Most of them believe that peace with Israel is possible and necessary. Therefore, while many of them were critical of Arafat's way of governing, they wholeheartedly supported his peace policy.

By the way, the outlook of the ex-prisoners reflects somewhat positively on the prison authorities. Many of the prisoners had undergone torture in the interrogation stage, when they were held by the Shin-Bet, but after they reached prison their treatment there has not left many mental scars.

All this comes as an introduction to the central event of this week: the agreement achieved in prison between the representatives of all the Palestinian factions.

This is a document of very great importance for the Palestinians, because of both the identity of its authors and its content.

At this time, many leaders of the various Palestinian factions are in prison, from Marwan Barghouti, the leader of Fatah in the West Bank, to Sheikh Abd-al-Khaliq al-Natshe, a Hamas leader. With them there are the leaders of Islamic Jihad, the Popular Front, and the Democratic Front. They spend their time there in a permanent discussion, while keeping constant contact with the leaders of their organizations outside and the activists inside. God knows how they do it.

When the leaders of the prisoners speak with one voice, what they say carries a greater moral weight than the statements of any Palestinian institution, including the presidency, the parliament, and the government.

This is the background against which this fascinating document should be examined.

In general, it follows the policy of Yassir Arafat: the two-state solution, a Palestinian state in all the territory occupied in 1967 with East Jerusalem as its capital, the release of all Palestinian prisoners. This means, of course, the recognition of Israel in practice.

For the Israeli public, the most problematical part concerns, as usual, the refugee problem. No Palestinian leader can give up the right of return, and this document, too, raises this demand. But in practice, the Palestinians acknowledge the fact that this problem can be solved only in agreement with Israel. That means that return to Israel must necessarily be limited in numbers, and the greater part of the solution lies in a return to the Palestinian state and payment of compensation. There is a difference between the recognition of the right of return in principle, as a basic human right, and the exercise of this right in the real world.

An important part of the document concerns putting the Palestinian house in order. The body that is supposed to represent the whole Palestinian people, inside and outside the country, is the PLO. That is also the body that has signed all the agreements with Israel. But the PLO is now far from reflecting the domestic Palestinian political reality. Hamas, which came into being at the beginning of the First Intifada, is not represented at all. The same goes for Islamic Jihad. The document demands that both be represented in the PLO—a reasonable and wise demand. It also calls for new elections to the all-Palestinian parliament—the Palestinian National Council—and for a National Unity Government.[67]

The prison agreement can help Hamas to cope with the new reality, and that is probably one of the main motives of its authors.

The sweeping victory of Hamas in the Palestinian parliamentary elections was a surprise not only for Israel and the world, but also for Hamas itself. The movement was completely unprepared to assume the responsibilities of power. The new situation creates a severe contradiction between the ideology of Hamas and the requirements of a governing party. As Ariel Sharon said: "What you see from here you don't see from there."

This contradiction finds its expression in the declarations of different leaders of Hamas. This is not duplicity, but rather an expression of different reactions to a new reality. The point of view of Khaled Mashaal in Damascus is necessarily quite different from the point of view of Ismail Haniyeh, the new Prime Minister in Gaza. Political and military leaders also often see things differently.

That is a natural confusion, and probably more time will pass before a consensus is achieved and a joint position defined. No wonder, therefore, that leaders are voicing opinions that contradict each other. One is seen on Israeli TV declaring with much pathos that "we demand not only Jerusalem, but also Haifa, Besan, and Tiberias," while another asserts that the movement "will not recognize Israel until it returns to the 1967 borders"—a "no" that implies a "yes."

The prison agreement is designed to help in creating the new consensus, which should enable Hamas to conduct a policy based on a compromise between the ideology and theology of the movement and the requirements of the Palestinian people.

The possible line: the PLO, led by Mahmoud Abbas, will conduct negotiations with Israel and present the agreement (if there is one) for ratification by a Palestinian referendum. Hamas will undertake in advance to accept the result. At the same time, Hamas will declare a *hudna* (armistice) for many years, allowing an end to violence from both sides.

That is possible. The question is whether the Israeli government wants it. At the moment, it does not look like it.

It openly calls for the defining of the "permanent borders" of Israel unilaterally, with the annexation of large areas of territory. Such a policy necessitates a situation of "no partner." This means that the government will reject anything that might create a credible partner, one who would also be accepted by the world.

During the show trial of Marwan Barghouti, we—my colleagues and I—stood outside the hall, carrying posters that said: "Send Barghouti to the negotiation table and not to prison!" But the appearance of this document suggests that sending him to prison was perhaps the biggest favor the Israeli government could have done him and the Palestinian people.

"The Tumult and the Shouting Dies ..."

December 1, 2007

> "The tumult and the shouting dies, / The captains and the kings depart ..." Rudyard Kipling wrote in his unforgettable poem "Lest We Forget" ("Recessional")

King George departed even before the tumult had died. His helicopter carried him away over the horizon, just as his trusty steed carries the cowboy into the sunset at the end of the movie. At that moment, the speeches in the assembly hall were still going ahead at full blast.

This summed up the whole event. The final statement announced that the United States will supervise the negotiations, acting as a referee of the implementation and as a judge throughout. Everything depends on her. If she wants it—much will happen. If she does not want it—nothing will happen.

That bodes ill. There is no indication that George Bush will really intervene to achieve anything, apart from nice photos. Some people believe that the whole show was put on to make poor Condoleezza Rice feel good, after all her efforts as Secretary of State had come to nought.

Even if Bush wanted to, could he do anything? Is he capable of putting pressure on Israel, in the face of vigorous opposition from the pro-Israel lobby, and especially from the Christian-Evangelist public, to which he himself belongs?

A friend told me that during the conference he watched the televised proceedings with the sound turned off, just observing the body language of the principal actors. That way he noticed an interesting detail: Bush and Olmert touched each other many times, but there was almost no physical contact between Bush and Mahmoud Abbas. More than that: during all the joint events, the distance between Bush and Olmert was smaller than the distance between Bush and Abbas. Several times Bush and Olmert walked ahead together, with Abbas trailing behind.

That's the whole story.

Sherlock Holmes said in one of his cases that the solution could be found in "the curious incident of the dog in the night-time." When it was pointed out to him that the dog did nothing, he explained: "That was the curious incident."

Anyone who wants to understand what has (or has not) happened at Annapolis will find the answer in this fact: the dog did not bark. The settlers and their friends were keeping quiet, did not panic, did not get excited, did not distribute posters of Olmert in SS uniform (as they had done with Rabin after Oslo). All in all, they contented themselves with the obligatory prayer at the Western Wall and a smallish demonstration near the Prime Minister's residence.

This means that they were not worried. They knew that nothing would come out of it, that there would be no agreement on the dismantling of even one measly settlement outpost. And on the forecast of the settlers' leaders one can rely in such matters. If there had been the slightest danger that peace would result from this conference, they would have mobilized their followers en masse.

The Hamas movement, on the other hand, did organize mass demonstrations in Gaza and the West Bank towns. The Hamas leaders were very worried indeed.

Not because they were afraid that peace would be concluded at the meeting. They were apprehensive of another danger: that the only real aim of the meeting was to prepare the ground for an Israeli invasion of the Gaza Strip.

Ami Ayalon, a former admiral who once posed as a man of peace, and who is now a Labor member of the cabinet, appeared during the conference on Israeli TV to say so quite openly: he was in favor of the conference because it legitimizes this operation.

The line of thought goes like this: In order to fulfill his obligation under the Roadmap, Abbas must "destroy the terrorist infrastructure" in the West Bank and the Gaza Strip. "Terrorism" means Hamas. Since Abbas is unable to conquer the Gaza Strip himself, the Israeli army will do it for him.

True, it may be costly. In the last few months, a lot of arms have been flowing into Gaza through the tunnels under the border with Egypt. Many people on both sides will lose their lives. But "What can you do? There is no alternative."

It may be that in retrospect, the main (if not the only) outcome of Annapolis will be this: the conquest of the Gaza Strip in order to "strengthen Abbas."

Hamas, in any case, is worried. And not without reason.

In preparation for such a confrontation, the Hamas leaders have become even more shrill in their opposition to the meeting, to which they were not invited. They denounced Abbas as a collaborator and a traitor, reiterating that Hamas would never recognize Israel nor accept a peace agreement with it.

I can picture in my mind a conference of the opponents of the proposed peace process, a kind of anti-Annapolis. Not the routine meeting planned by Mahmoud Ahmadinejad in Tehran, to which only Muslims will be invited, but a joint meeting of all extremists on both sides. Khalid Mashal and Ismail Hanieh will sit opposite Avigdor Liberman, Effi Eytam, and Benny Elon, and deliberate together how to frustrate the "two-state solution."

If I were invited to moderate this conference, I would start like this:

Gentlemen (ladies will not be present, of course), let us begin by summing up the points on which there is agreement, and only afterwards deal with the points in dispute.

So: all of you agree that the land between the Mediterranean Sea and the Jordan River will become one state (general agreement). You, Palestinian gentlemen, agree that the Jews will enjoy full equality (agreement on the Palestinian side of the table). And you, Israeli gentlemen, agree that Arabs will enjoy full equality (agreement on the Israeli side of the table). And, of course, you do agree that there will be full freedom of religion for all (general agreement).

If this is the situation, gentlemen, then the only remaining disagreement concerns the name—whether to call the state Palestine or Israel. Is it worthwhile to quarrel and spill blood about that? Let's agree on a neutral name, something like Isrestine or Palael.

Back to the White House: if the three leaders agreed there in secret deliberations that the Israeli army will invade the Gaza Strip, that is very bad news.

It would have been better to get Hamas involved—if not directly, then indirectly. The absence of Hamas left a yawning gap at the conference. What is the sense in convening 40 representatives from all over the world, and leaving more than half the Palestinian people without representation?

The more so since the boycott of Hamas has pushed the organization further into a corner, causing it to oppose the meeting even more vociferously and incite the Palestinian street against it.

Hamas is not only the armed body that now dominates the Gaza Strip. It is first of all the political movement that won the majority of the votes of the Palestinian people in democratic elections—not only in the Gaza Strip, but in the West Bank, too. That will not change if Israel conquers the Strip tomorrow. On the contrary: such a move may stigmatize Abbas as a collaborator in a war against his own people, and actually strengthen the roots of Hamas in the Palestinian public.

Olmert said that first of all the "terrorist infrastructure" must be eliminated, and only then can there be progress towards peace. This totally misrepresents the nature of a "terrorist infrastructure"—regrettable from a person whose father (like Tzipi Livni's father) was a senior Irgun "terrorist." It also shows that peace does not head the list of his aspirations—because that statement constitutes a deadly landmine on the way to an agreement. It is putting the cart before the horse.

The logical sequence is the other way round: first of all we have to reach a peace agreement that is acceptable to the majority of the Palestinians. That means (a) laying the foundations for a State of Palestine whose border will run along the Green Line (with limited swaps of territory) and whose capital will be East Jerusalem, (b) calling upon the Palestinian people to ratify this agreement in a referendum, and (c) calling upon the military wing of Hamas to lay down their arms or be absorbed into the regular forces of the new state, similarly to what happened in Israel, and join the political system in the new state.

If there were an assurance that this is the way things will go, there is still a reasonable chance of convincing Hamas not to obstruct the process and to allow Abbas to manage it—as Hamas has agreed in the past.

Why? Because Hamas, like any other serious political movement, is dependent on popular support. At this point, with the occupation getting worse from day to day and all the routes to peace seemingly blocked, the Palestinian masses are convinced that the method of armed resistance, as practiced by Hamas, is the only one that offers them any hope. If the masses become convinced that the political path of Abbas is bearing fruit and is leading to the end of the occupation, Hamas will be compelled to change course.

Unfortunately, the Annapolis conference did nothing to encourage such hopes. The Palestinian public, like the Israeli one, treated it with a mixture of distrust and disdain. It looks like an empty show run by a lame duck American president, whose only remaining pleasure is to be photographed as the leader of the world. And if Bush gets the UN resolution he wants to hide behind—another resolution that nobody will take seriously—it will not change anything.

Especially if it is true, as reported in the Israeli press, that the Israeli government is planning a huge expansion of the settlements, and if the army chiefs start another bloody war, this time in Gaza.

Did this spectacle, then, have no positive side at all? Will it be forgotten tomorrow, as dozens of other meetings in the past have been forgotten, so only people with an exceptional memory are aware they ever happened?

I am not sure that this is so.

True, it was only a waterfall of words. But in the lives of nations, words too have their value.

Almost the whole of humanity was represented at this conference: China, India, Russia, Europe. Almost all Arab governments lent their support. And in this company, it was solemnly resolved that peace must be established between Israel and an independent and viable State of Palestine. True, the terms were not spelled out, but they were hovering over the conference. All the participants knew what they were.

The representatives of the Israeli mainstream joined—at least *pro forma*—this consensus. Perhaps they did so tongue in cheek, perhaps only as a ploy, perhaps as an act of deceit. But as our sages said ages ago: he who accepts the Torah not because of itself will in the end accept it for itself. Meaning: if people accept an idea from tactical calculation they will be compelled to defend it, and in the end will convince themselves. Even Olmert has already declared on his way home: "Without the two-state solution, the State of Israel is finished."

In connection with this, competition between cabinet members is already developing, and that is a good sign. Tzipi Livni has set up more than a dozen committees of experts, each one charged with dealing with a particular aspect of peace, from the division of water to the allocation of television channels. (For those with a good memory: this is happening 50 years after I proposed the setting up of exactly such an apparatus, which I called the "White General Staff," as opposed to the "Khaki General Staff").

True, the Annapolis conference was no more than a small step, taken under duress. But it was a tiny step in the right direction.

The consciousness of a large body of people changes only in a long and slow process, at an almost geological pace. This cannot be detected with the naked eye. But, as Galileo Galilei murmured to himself: "And yet it does move!"

4
Squaring the Circle
Palestinian and Israeli Resistance

Resistance to Israeli policies takes many forms and is practiced by both Palestinians and Israelis. An international resistance presence has also taken root in the Palestinian territories. Religiously based groups like the American Friends Service Committee (AFSC) and Christian Peacemaker Teams (CPT) have been active for some time in the region, while strictly secular organizations are becoming more common, most notably the International Solidarity Movement (ISM) co-founded by Palestinian-American Huwaida Arraf and Jewish-American Adam Shapiro. Other solidarity groups practice a kind of resistance to Israeli policy from their various nations around the world through education efforts, financial support, and development projects.

Gush Shalom, the Israeli peace organization co-founded by Avnery, posts many ISM reports. However Avnery has not devoted specific essays to the international resistance movement to change Israeli policy, other than one article below on the British academic boycott movement. Moreover, most of Avnery's articles that address Palestinian non-violent resistance, concentrate on joint Palestinian–Israeli demonstrations rather than such topics as the tax resistors and general strikes of the First Intifada, however small or seemingly insignificant. Nonetheless, the following selections present both violent and non-violent resistance in context of the devastating situation in Palestine and Israel.—SRP

All Kinds of Terrorists

November 3, 2001

President Bush has declared a "war on terrorism." Indeed?

Osama bin Laden is undoubtedly a terrorist. Killing 4,800 civilians at the World Trade Center was a terrorist outrage. But the United States would have declared war on bin Laden even if he had been satisfied with killing American soldiers in Saudi Arabia or blowing up oil installations across the Middle East. It is not the methods of bin Laden that have caused this war, but his aim: to get rid of the United States and its satellites, the Arab kings and presidents, throughout the Middle East.

In order to pursue its war, the United States has set up a worldwide coalition. Everyone joining it has been issued an American permit to call their enemies "terrorists": Putin in Chechnya, China in its Muslim regions, India in Kashmir, Sharon in the occupied territories—all are now fighting against "terrorists." Everyone and his bin Laden.

Many years ago I coined a definition I am quite proud of: "The difference between freedom fighters and terrorists is that the freedom fighters are on my side and the terrorists are on the other side." I am glad that this definition has been adopted by my biggers and betters.

Since the New York atrocity, it has become fashionable to talk about "terrorism." As a result, it has lost all precise meaning.

"Terror" means extreme fear. The root of the word is the Latin "terrere"—to frighten or be frightened. The modern term was first used to describe the regime of terror instituted by the Jacobins, one of the factions of the French Revolution, to destroy their opponents by beheading them with the guillotine during the years 1793–94. In the end, their leader, Robespierre, suffered the same fate.

Since then, the term has acquired a more general use. Terrorism is a method of attaining political goals by frightening the civilian population. It does not apply to the frightening of soldiers. The Japanese who attacked the American fleet in Pearl Harbor were not terrorists. Neither were the Jews who attacked the soldiers of the British occupation regime in Palestine.

Clausewitz said that war is the continuation of politics by other means.[68] That is true for terrorism, too. Terrorism is always an instrument for the attainment of political aims. Since these may be rightist or leftist, revolutionary or reactionary, religious or secularist, the term "international terrorism" is nonsense. Each terrorist body has its own specific agenda.

There is hardly a liberation movement that has not used terrorism. Algerian women put bombs in the cafes of the French settlers (some of them were caught and horribly tortured by French parachutists). Nelson Mandela spent 28 years in prison because he refused to order his followers to abstain from terrorism. The Maccabees were terrorists who went around killing Hellenized Jews. So were the Irgun fighters who in 1938 put bombs in the Arab markets of Jaffa and Haifa in retaliation for Arab attacks. Shlomo Ben-Josef committed a terrorist act when he shot at an Arab bus (and I joined the Irgun when he was hanged by the British).

Generally, terrorism is the weapon of the weak. A Palestinian "terrorist" recently said: "Give me tanks and airplanes, and I shall stop sending suicide bombers into Israel." But big powers, too, can use terror. Dropping the atom bomb on Hiroshima was a terrorist act, designed to frighten the Japanese population into demanding that their government surrender. So was the Nazi blitz on London and the British bombing of Dresden. Churchill and Hitler were as different as day and night, but they used the same method.

Israel has used this method from the day of its inception. In the early 1950s the IDF committed "retaliation raids" designed to frighten the villagers beyond the border in order to induce them to put pressure on the Jordanian and Egyptian governments to prevent the infiltration of Palestinians into Israel. During the War of Attrition in the late 1960s, Moshe Dayan terrorized half a million inhabitants of the Egyptian towns along the Suez Canal into fleeing, so as to put pressure on the Egyptian president to stop attacking Israeli strongholds along the Canal. In the 1996 "Grapes of Wrath" operation, Prime Minister Shimon Peres terrorized half a million inhabitants of South Lebanon by aerial bombardment into fleeing north, in order to pressurize the Beirut government into stopping the Shi'ite guerrillas from attacking the Israeli occupation force and its mercenaries. It is the same method that is used in the army when a commander punishes all the soldiers in a company, so that they will turn against the one who made him angry.

The trouble is, it does not work in conflicts between nations. Generally, it is counterproductive. The Taliban have not turned bin Laden over but have become more extreme in their opposition to America. The IDF blockade against Palestinian villages, which this week denied them water and food, does not isolate the "terrorists," but on the contrary, turns them into national heroes. The devastation caused by the Russians in Chechnya did not break—indeed, it strengthened—the opposing guerrilla forces.

Since terrorism is always a political instrument, the right way to combat it is always political. Solve the problem that breeds terrorism and you get rid of the terrorism.

Solve the Israeli–Palestinian problem and the other flash points in the Middle East, and you get rid of al-Qaida. It will wilt like a flower deprived of water.

No one has yet devised another method.

The Stalemate

January 29, 2005

Perhaps the Second Intifada has come to an end. Perhaps the ceasefire in the Gaza Strip will develop into a general, mutual ceasefire.

For me, the words "cease fire" have an extra resonance. When I was a soldier in the 1948 war, I twice experienced what it means to wait for a ceasefire. Each time we were totally exhausted after heavy fighting in which many of our comrades had been killed or wounded. We hoped with all our hearts that a ceasefire would really come into effect, but did not allow ourselves to believe in it. In both cases, a few minutes before the appointed hour, along the whole front line a crazy cacophony of firing erupted, everybody shooting and shelling with everything they had. To attain some last-minute advantages, as it appeared afterwards.

And then, suddenly, the shooting stopped. An eerie quiet settled in. We looked at each other and left unspoken what we all felt: "We are saved! We have been left alive!"

I understand, therefore, the feelings of the fighters on both sides who are now hoping that the mutual ceasefire will come into effect and hold. After four and a quarter years of fighting, everybody is exhausted.

The first question at the end of the fighting is: Who won?

Naturally, each side will claim victory. The Palestinian organizations will assert that it was only the Qassam rockets and the mortar shells that compelled Israel to agree to a ceasefire. The Israelis will claim that the Israeli army has crushed terrorism and compelled the Palestinians to give up.

So who won? In fact, nobody. The fighting ended in a draw.

The Israeli army has not won, since it did not succeed in putting an end to the attacks, much less in "destroying the terror infrastructure." On the eve of the ceasefire, the Qassam rockets and mortar shells turned life in the town of Sderot into hell. The inhabitants don't hide the fact that they are nearing the breaking point.

Moreover, the organizations reached a new level by undertaking more complicated attacks, real guerrilla actions. The destruction of the army outpost on the "Philadelphi axis" involved blowing up a tunnel beneath it and storming the post on the ground. Similarly, the attack on the Karni checkpoint combined the explosive demolition of a wall with an attack by fighters. These actions were reminiscent of those of the Irgun and Stern Group in the last years of the British mandate.

Our army had no answer to the Qassams and the guerrilla actions. Haven't they tried everything? Brutal incursions. Shelling by tanks, killing fighters and bystanders. Demolition of thousands of homes. Targeted assassinations.

Nothing helped. There remained only the method advocated on TV by Israel Katz, a cabinet minister: to bomb and shell the Gaza Strip towns, open the border to Egypt in one direction and drive hundreds of thousands of inhabitants out into the Sinai desert. (That is what Moshe Dayan did to the Suez Canal towns during the War of Attrition, in the late 1960s.) It has been reported that Ariel Sharon himself proposed, after the Karni incident, the bombing of towns and villages in the Gaza Strip.[69] But nowadays this is not possible: neither the Israeli public nor world public opinion would stand for it.

The simple truth is that the generals are bankrupt. But they have no reason to feel ashamed: no other army has won such a contest in the last hundred years. The French in Algeria arrived at the same point, in spite of torturing thousands of men and women. The same happened to the Americans in Vietnam, in spite of burning down dozens of villages and massacring their inhabitants. Even the Nazis did not succeed in putting down the French resistance, however many hostages they executed.

Our generals, like all the generals before them, made the understandable mistake of thinking in terms of war. But this was no conventional war. A war is a confrontation between armies, and it is fought with methods that have evolved throughout the ages. The confrontation between an army of occupation and resistance forces is quite different. The factors governing that are not taught in officers' courses.

True, the Israeli army tried to improvise, with some success. But it could not win. Because victory means breaking the will of the opponent to resist. And that did not happen.

If that is so, did the Palestinian fighting organizations win?

Interestingly enough, this question is not posed openly, not even by the Palestinians, themselves. First of all, because the idea has been accepted throughout the world that the Palestinian resistance is "terrorism," and who would dare to assert that terrorism had won? The more so since the Palestinians–like the Israelis–committed fearful atrocities.

Also, the propaganda war between Israelis and Palestinians is a kind of world championship of victimhood. Each side presents itself as the ultimate victim. Each side publicizes pictures of dead children, weeping mothers, demolished homes.

Because of this, the Palestinian spokespersons do not boast of the fighting of their compatriots. They avoid pointing to the thousands of their fighters who sacrificed their lives, the children who confronted the tanks, the hundreds of commanders who were "liquidated" and for each of whom a substitute was found, for whom in turn a substitute was found, and so forth. About this, books will be written, songs will be sung, tales will be told in future generations.

Another fact: Palestinian society has not been broken. Israeli tanks roam their streets, hundreds of roadblocks prevent movement from village to village, the economy is shattered, most men are unemployed, hundreds of thousands of children suffer from malnutrition. And in spite of this, miraculously, Palestinian society continues functioning somehow, life goes on; fatigue and exhaustion have not forced it to surrender.[70]

Does this mean that the Palestinian side has won? The organizations can claim that Sharon would not have talked about withdrawal from the Gaza Strip and evacuation of the settlements there if the attacks had not taken place. That is certainly true. But Sharon has not yet begun to consider leaving the West Bank. On the contrary, the settlement activity there is reaching new heights and the land grab is in full swing in the shadow of the "separation fence." One cannot call that a Palestinian victory.

All this points to a deadlock. The Israeli army knows that it cannot vanquish the Palestinians by military means. The Palestinians know that they cannot throw off the occupation by military means.

For the Palestinians, a draw is a huge achievement. The inequality between the two sides is immense. If one takes into account only the strength of arms and the size of forces, without considering the moral factors, the Israeli advantage is astronomical. In such a situation, a draw is a victory for the weak.

We should admit this without hesitation. It is not wise to present the Palestinian side as if it were beaten and broken. Not only because this is untrue, but also because it is dangerous. The boasts of the army propagandists, as if Abu Mazen has folded up under Israeli pressure, are at best stupid, and at worst are intended to demean and provoke the Palestinians to new violence (or to acts of madness). The Egyptian victory at the beginning of the 1973 war set the scene for Anwar Sadat to make peace with Israel. The Palestinian pride in their steadfastness can make it more acceptable for them to keep the ceasefire.

Now, both sides are exhausted. Palestinian suffering is manifest. Israeli suffering is less obvious, but, nonetheless, real. The costs of the occupation amount to tens of billions, hundreds of thousands of Israelis have sunk beneath the poverty line, the social services are collapsing, foreign investment has not recovered, the level of tourism is pitiful. And, more importantly: during the intifada, 4,010 Palestinians and 1,050 Israelis have lost their lives.

That is the background of recent events. Both sides need the ceasefire.

But a ceasefire is only an interlude, not peace itself. If wisdom prevails in Israel (since it is the stronger side) negotiations for a final settlement will start at once, with the general aim agreed in advance: a

Palestinian state in all the territory of the West Bank, the Gaza Strip, and East Jerusalem.

If wisdom does not prevail (and in politics, the victory of wisdom would be something new), this ceasefire will end up like many before: just an interval between two rounds of fighting.

We are faced with a road sign pointing in two opposite directions: one end directed towards peace, the other towards the next violent confrontation.

A Queue of Bombers

March 23, 2002

When a whole people is seething with rage, it becomes a dangerous enemy, because the rage does not obey orders.

When rage exists in the hearts of millions of people, it cannot be cut off by pushing a button.

When this rage overflows, it creates suicide bombers—human bombs fuelled by the power of anger, against whom there is no defense. People who have given up on life, who do not look for escape routes, are free to do whatever their disturbed minds dictate.

Some of the suicide bombers are killed before·they reach their goal, but when there are hundreds of them, thousands of them, no military means will restore security.

The actions of General Mofaz during the last month have brought this rage to an unprecedented pitch and instilled it into the hearts of every Palestinian, whether a university professor or a street boy, a housewife or a high-school girl, a leftist or a fundamentalist.

When tanks run amok in the center of a town, crushing cars and destroying walls, tearing up roads, shooting indiscriminately in all directions, causing panic to a whole population—it induces helpless rage.

When soldiers crush through a wall into the living room of a family, causing shock to children and adults, ransacking their belongings, destroying the fruits of a life of hard work, and then break the wall to the next apartment to wreak havoc there—it induces helpless rage.

When soldiers shoot at everything that moves—out of panic, out of lawlessness, or because Sharon told them "to cause losses"—it induces helpless rage.

When officers order their soldiers to shoot at ambulances, killing doctors and paramedics engaged in saving the lives of the wounded who are bleeding to death—it induces helpless rage.

When these and a thousand other acts like them humiliate a whole people, searing their souls—it induces helpless rage.

And then it appears that the rage is not helpless after all. The suicide bombers go forward to avenge, with a whole people blessing them and rejoicing at every Israeli killed, soldier or settler, a girl in a bus or a youngster in a discotheque.

The Israeli public is dumbfounded by this terrible phenomenon. It cannot understand it, because it does not know (and perhaps does not want to know) what has happened in the Palestinian towns and villages. Only feeble echoes of what really happened have reached it. The obedient media suppress the information, or water it down so that the monster looks like a harmless pet. The television, which is now subject to Soviet-style censorship, does not tell its viewers what is going on. If somebody is allowed to say a few words about it, for the sake of "balance," the words are drowned in a sea of chatter by politicians and commentators acting as unofficial spokespersons, and by the generals who caused the havoc.

These generals look helplessly at a struggle they do not understand and make arrogant statements divorced from reality. Pronouncements like "We have intercepted attacks," "We have taught them a lesson," "We have destroyed the infrastructure of terrorism" show an infantile lack of understanding of what they are doing. Far from "destroying the infrastructure of terrorism," they have built a hothouse to rear suicide bombers.

A person whose beloved brother has been killed, whose house has been destroyed in an orgy of vandalism, who has been mortally humiliated before the eyes of his children, goes to the market, buys a rifle for 40,000 shekels (some sell their cars for this) and sets out to seek revenge. "Give me a hatred gray like a sack," wrote our poet, Nathan Alterman, seething with rage against the Germans. Hatred gray like a sack is now everywhere.

Bands of armed men now roam all the towns and villages of the West Bank and the Gaza strip, with or without black masks (available for 10 shekels in the markets).

These bands do not belong to any organization. Members of Fatah, Hamas, and the Islamic Jihad team up to plan attacks, not giving a damn for the established institutions.

Anyone who believes that Arafat can push a button and stop this is living in a dream world. Arafat is the adored leader, now more than ever, but when a people is seething with anger he cannot stop it either. At best, the pressure-cooker can cool off slowly, if the majority of the people are persuaded that their honor has been restored and their liberation guaranteed. Then public support for the "terrorists" will diminish, they will be isolated and wither away. That was what happened in the past.

During the Oslo period there were attacks too, but they were conducted by dissident fanatics, and the public aversion to them limited the damage they caused.

American politicians, like Israeli officers, do not understand what they are doing. When an overbearing vice-president dictates humiliating terms for a meeting with Arafat, he pours oil on the flames. A person who lacks empathy for the suffering of the occupied people, who does not understand its condition, would be well advised to shut up. Because every such humiliation kills dozens of Israelis.

After all, the suicide bombers are standing in line.

Three Generals, One Martyr

March 27, 2004

Five hundred black- and white-bearded Hamas members were sitting opposite me. Venerable sheikhs and young people. On the side, some rows were occupied by women. I was standing on the stage, talking in Hebrew, with the crossed flags of Israel and Palestine on my lapel.

As I have recounted already several times, it happened like this: at the end of 1992, the new Prime Minister, Yitzhak Rabin, expelled 415 Islamic activists, mostly Hamas members, to the Lebanese border area. In protest, we put up tents opposite the Prime Minister's office in Jerusalem. There we spent 45 days and nights—Israeli peace activists (who were later to found Gush Shalom) and Arab citizens of Israel, mostly members of the Islamic movement. Most of the time it was very cold, and some days our tents were covered with snow. There was a lot of debate in the tents, the Jews learning something about Islam and the Muslims something about Judaism.

The expelled militants themselves vegetated for a year in the hilly landscape, between the Israeli and Lebanese armies. The whole world followed their suffering. After a year they were allowed back, and the Hamas leaders in Gaza organized a homecoming reception for them in the biggest hall in town. They invited those Israelis who had protested against the expulsion. I was asked to make a speech. I spoke about peace, and in the intermission we were invited to have lunch with the hosts. I was impressed by the friendly attitude of the hundreds of people who were there.

Undoubtedly, Sheikh Ahmed Yassin and the spokesman of the expellees, Dr Abd-al-Aziz al-Rantisi (who became Sheikh Yassin's successor last week) would have been present, too, if they had not been kept in prison.[71]

I recount this experience in order to point out that the picture of

Hamas as an inveterate enemy of all peace and compromise is not accurate. Of course, ten years of bloodshed, suicide bombings, and targeted assassinations have passed since then. But even now, the picture is much more complex than meets the eye.

There are different tendencies in Hamas. The ideological hard core does indeed refuse any peace or compromise with Israel. They consider it a foreign implantation in Palestine, which in Islamic doctrine is a Muslim "*waaf*" (religious grant). But many Hamas sympathizers do not treat the organization as an ideological center but rather as an instrument for fighting Israel in pursuit of realistic objectives.

Sheikh Yassin himself announced some months ago in a German paper that the fight would be discontinued after the establishment of a Palestinian state within the 1967 borders. Recently, he offered a "*hudna*" (truce) for 30 years. (Which strongly reminds one of Ariel Sharon's suggestion that Israel would give up the Gaza Strip and retain large parts of the West Bank for an interim phase to last for 20 years.)

Therefore, the murder of the sheikh did not serve any positive aim. It was an act of folly.

The three generals who actually direct the affairs of Israel—Prime Minister Ariel Sharon, Minister of Defense Sha'ul Mofaz, and Chief of Staff Moshe Ya'alon—maintain that "in the short run" the assassination would indeed increase the attacks on Israeli citizens, but "in the long run" it would help to "rout terrorism." They are very careful not to spell out when the "short run" ends and the "long run" begins. Our generals do not believe in timetables.

I take the liberty to tell these three illustrious strategists: nonsense in tomato juice! (as they say in Hebrew slang). Or rather, nonsense in blood.

In the short run, this action endangers our personal security; in the long run it represents an even greater danger to our national security.

In the short run, it has increased the motivation for Hamas to carry out deadly attacks. Every Israeli understands this and is taking extra precautions these days. But the less obvious results are much more threatening.

In the hearts of hundreds of thousands of children in the Palestinian territories and the Arab countries, this murder has raised a storm of rage and thirst for revenge, together with feelings of frustration and humiliation in view of the impotence of the Arab world. This will produce not only thousands of new potential suicide bombers inside the country, but also tens of thousands of volunteers for the radical Islamic organizations throughout the Arab world. (I know, because at the age of 15 I joined the armed underground in similar circumstances.)

There is no stronger weapon for a fighting organization than a martyr. Suffice it to mention Avraham Stern, alias Ya'ir, who was killed by the British police in Tel-Aviv in 1942. His blood gave an impulse to the emergence of the Lehi underground (nicknamed "the Stern gang"), which only four years later was playing a major role in the expulsion of the British from Palestine.

But Ya'ir's standing was nothing compared to the standing of Sheikh Yassin. The man was practically born to fulfill the role of a sainted martyr: a religious personality, a paraplegic in a wheelchair, broken in body but not in spirit, a militant who spent years in prison, a leader who continued his fight after miraculously surviving an earlier assassination attempt, a hero cowardly murdered from the air while leaving the mosque after prayer. Even a writer of genius could not have invented a figure more suited to the adoration of a billion Muslims, in this and coming generations.

The murder of Yassin will encourage cooperation among the Palestinian fighting organizations. Here, too, a parallel with the Hebrew underground presents itself. In a certain phase of the fight against the British, there was much unrest among the members of the Hagana, the semi-official underground army of the Zionist leadership (comparable to Fatah today). The Hagana (which included the elite Palmakh formation) was seen to be inactive, while the Irgun and Lehi appeared as heroes who carried out incredibly audacious actions. The ferment inside the Hagana caused the emergence of a group called "Fighting nation" which advocated close cooperation between the various organizations. A number of Hagana members simply went over to Lehi.

Now this is happening among the Palestinians. The lines between the various groups are becoming more and more blurred. *al-Aqsa* Martyrs' Brigade members cooperate with Hamas and Islamic Jihad, contrary to the orders of their political leadership, saying: "Since we are killed together, let us fight together." This phenomenon is bound to grow and make the attacks more effective.

Hamas' popularity among the population is rising sky-high, together with its capability to carry out attacks.[72] This does not mean that the Palestinian public accepts the aim of an Islamic state or that it has given up the idea of a Palestinian state alongside Israel. Even among Hamas members, many embrace this idea. But the admiration of the masses for the attackers and their actions reflects the conviction that the Israelis understand only the language of force, and their experience proves that without extreme violence the Palestinians will not achieve anything at all.

Unfortunately, there is no real evidence for the opposite. The truth is that the Palestinians have never achieved anything without resorting to violence. Therefore the petitions being signed these days by well-meaning Palestinian personalities, calling for an end to the armed struggle, will have no effect. They cannot point to any other method that will sound convincing to their public. And our government always, without exception, presents such moves as a sign of weakness.

In the even longer run, the assassination of Yassin poses an existential danger. For five generations, the Israeli–Palestinian conflict was essentially a national conflict—a clash between two great national movements, each of which claimed the country for itself. A national conflict is basically rational, it can be solved by compromise. This may be difficult, but it is possible. Our nightmare has always been that the national struggle would turn into a religious one. Since every religion claims to represent absolute truth, religious struggle does not allow for compromise.

The martyrdom of Sheikh Yassin pushes even further away the chance of Israel ever attaining peace and tranquility, normal relations with its neighbors, with a flourishing economy. It increases the danger that future generations of Arabs and Muslims will view it as a foreign implantation, installed in this region by force, with every decent Muslim, from Morocco to Indonesia, duty-bound to strive for its uprooting.

Such insights are far from the capability of our three generals to absorb. Sharon, Mofaz, Ya'alon, and their ilk understand only brute force in the service of a narrow nationalism. Peace does not inspire them; for them compromise is a dirty word. It is quite clear that they will feel much more comfortable if the Palestinian people is led by fanatical religious fighters than by a man prepared to compromise like Yassir Arafat.

You Brought the Boycott upon Yourselves[73]

April 26, 2005

Gush Shalom letter to Bar Ilan University:

To: Professor Moshe Kaveh
President, Bar Ilan University

Dear Sir,
In various media interviews today you expressed anger at the decision of British university lecturers to declare a boycott against the Bar Ilan University, calling it "an unacceptable mixing of politics into academic life." When asked about the "Judea and Samaria College" which your

university maintains at the settlement of Ariel, you stated that this was "an entirely non-political issue" and that said college was nothing more than "the largest of five colleges which Bar Ilan maintains at different locations in Israel."

Indeed, you declared yourself and your colleagues to be proud of the decision to establish the Ariel college, and you felt no contradiction between continuing to maintain that college, at the investment of a considerable part of Bar Ilan's total resources, and the maintenance of extensive ties with universities worldwide, including in Britain.

As an example you mentioned your own ties as a physicist with Cambridge University and your plans to spend some time at Cambridge this summer—plans which, as you stated, remain unchanged also in the wake of the British lecturers' decision.

Surely, a person of your intelligence and experience can be expected to note the obvious contradictions in the above position. As you well know, Ariel is not "a location in Israel." Rather, Ariel is a location in a territory under military occupation, a territory that is not and has never been part of the state of Israel. Moreover, Ariel is a special kind of location: it is an armed enclave, created by armed force and dependent for its continued existence on force, and force alone.

The creation of Ariel is a severe violation of international law, specifically of the Fourth Geneva Convention, which specifically forbids an occupying power from transferring its own citizens to and settling them in occupied territory. On the ground, the creation and maintenance of Ariel entailed and continues to entail untold hardships to the Palestinians who happen to live in the nearby town of Salfit and in numerous villages a long distance all around. Palestinian inhabitants are exposed to ongoing confiscation of their land so as to feed the land hunger of the ever-expending Ariel settlement, and their daily lives are subjected to increasingly stringent travel limitations in the name of "preserving the settlers' security."

The government-approved plans to extend the "Separation Fence" so as to create a corridor linking Ariel to the Israeli border necessitate the confiscation of yet more vast tracts of Palestinian land, depriving thousands of villagers of their sole source of livelihood. Moreover, should the Ariel corridor be completed, it would cut deeply through the territory which the international community earmarked for creation of a Palestinian state, depriving that state of territorial continuity and viability. For that reason, the plan aroused widespread international opposition, not least from the United States, our main ally in the international arena.

In all of this the Bar Ilan University, of which you are president, made itself a major partner—indeed, since a violation of international law is involved, the term "accomplice" may well be used. The "Judea and Samaria College" which you and your colleagues established and nurtured has a central role in the settlement of Ariel, increasing its population and its economic clout. The college's faculty and students are prime users of the "Trans-Samaria Road," the four-lane highway that was created on confiscated Palestinian land in order to provide quick transportation to Ariel. The Palestinian villagers on whose land this highway was built are excluded from using it. They are relegated to a rugged, bumpy mountain trail.

It is you and your colleagues, Professor Kaveh, who started mixing academia with politics. A very heavy mixture, such as few universities anywhere ever engaged in.

You cannot really complain when people in Britain who have different standards for what is the proper moral behavior of academics (or of human beings in general) take action that you do not like. In fact, if you are truly proud of establishing and maintaining the "Judea and Samaria College," you must have the courage of your convictions and take the consequences. Much better, of course, would be for you and your colleagues to sever your connection with the ill-conceived settlement project—and then you can quite rightly demand that the boycott be removed from your university.

Yours
Uri Avnery
Gush Shalom (The Israeli Peace Bloc)

As noted above, not all resistance to Israeli policy is Palestinian—there are a range of Israelis who practice one or another form of resistance to a variety of Israeli policies vis-à-vis Palestine and Palestinians.—SRP

A Tale of Two Demonstrations

April 30, 2005

The day before yesterday, two demonstrations were held, just a few dozen kilometers apart.

One took place at the Homesh settlement, not far from Jenin. Tens of thousands of settlers and their sympathizers came to demonstrate against the planned evacuation of this settlement. The demonstrators swore to sabotage the decisions of the government and the Knesset. One of them declared that they could be removed only in coffins draped with the national flag.

Hundreds of soldiers and policemen were stationed along the route to protect the demonstrators against all eventualities. The official Voice of Israel radio told its listeners that the traffic police were acting on instructions from the leaders of the Settlements Council.

At the same time, another demonstration took place at Bil'in, west of Ramallah.[74] The inhabitants of that and the neighboring villages, together with Israeli peace activists, demonstrated against the "Separation Fence" that is being put up on their land.

This demonstration was savagely attacked by soldiers and policemen, who assaulted them, beat, injured, and arrested them, using old and new weapons. The security people, as the Hebrew expression goes, "had murder in their eyes."

In this area, there is not even the pretense that the Separation Fence serves security purposes. The real aim is evident to anyone visiting the place: to rob Bil'in and the other villages of their land in order to enlarge the settlement of Kiryat Sefer.

I remember that place from some ten years ago. Then, well-kept olive groves were being expropriated and destroyed by bulldozers. At that time, too, the villagers asked us to protest and try to stop this.

Now, a large town of ultra-orthodox Jews has been built there and is growing rapidly. The Separation Fence will pass close to the last houses of Bil'in and cut the village off from the remainder of its lands. On this land new neighborhoods of Kiryat Sefer will be built. Together with the nearby settlements of Modi'in Ilit and Matitiyahu, this is one of the "settlement blocs" that Israeli governments (whether Likud or Labor) want to annex to Israel, with the blessing of President Bush.

The plan of the villagers was to conduct a peaceful demonstration on the path of the Fence and plant some symbolic olive saplings there. But experience in this area has taught us that one must expect the security forces to react violently. Therefore, only activists who know the conditions and are experienced in dealing with them were asked to take part. We were some 200 Israelis, men and women of all ages. The instructions given in the buses, orally and in writing, were to keep the demonstration strictly non-violent.

We expected the buses to be stopped on the way and were prepared for this eventuality. We were, therefore, quite surprised when we reached the village without incident. Only later did we realize that it was a trap.

In the village, we joined some thousand inhabitants of this and the neighboring villages, men, women, and children, and set off together towards the path of the Fence. At the head walked the former Palestinian minister Kadura Fares, the Palestinian presidential candidate Dr Mustafa al-Barghouti, the Arab members of the Knesset Barakeh, Zakhalkeh, and Dahamsheh, the village chiefs and I. We were holding olive branches in our hands, to plant along the path of the Fence. The village youngsters also carried a 50-meter long Palestinian flag. Ahead of us a decorated van was driving slowly, and a Palestinian activist on it announced in Hebrew through a powerful loudspeaker: "This is a peaceful and non-violent demonstration!"

About a kilometer before the path of the Fence, a line of security people stopped us. They wore no insignia, and so we did not know whether they were soldiers or border policemen.

Suddenly, without any warning, a salvo of tear gas grenades was launched at us. Within seconds, we were enveloped by a cloud of white gas, with the thump of bursting grenades coming at us from all directions.

The demonstrators, coughing and choking, dispersed to the two sides. Many of them outflanked the soldiers and continued to move forward over the rocky terrain. They were stopped by a second line and also showered with tear gas.

We, at the head of the demonstration, went on and reached a point about 50 meters from the path of the Fence, when a third line of soldiers attacked us. MK (Member of the Knesset) Barakeh had a heated exchange with an officer, and while they were arguing passionately a soldier fired a gas grenade at point blank range between Barakeh's legs. He was slightly wounded in the leg. Another, particularly ferocious soldier took hold of the poster I was holding in my hands—the Gush Shalom sign of the flags of Israel and Palestine—and pushed me savagely, knocking me over.

At other places, the rampage was even worse. Muhammad Hatib, one of the village chiefs, noticed a man who, with his face covered, started to throw stones at the soldiers. He ran towards him, shouting: "We decided not to throw stones! If you want to throw stones, do it in your own village, not ours! What village do you come from, anyway?" The man turned towards him and attacked him, at the same time calling out to his associates, tearing the handkerchief from his face and donning a police cap.

Thus the secret came out and was also documented by the cameras: "Arabized" undercover soldiers had been sent into action. These started throwing stones at the security people in order to provide them with a pretext to attack us. The moment they were uncovered, they turned on the demonstrators nearest to them, drew revolvers and started to arrest them. Later on, when it became clear that the events had been recorded by foreign television crews, the police officially confirmed that throwing stones is the method used by "Arabized" undercover soldiers so as to merge with the crowd.

In the course of the day, more details about the events emerged: this was a unit that had never before been used for such an action: the prison service unit "Massada," whose normal job is to suppress mutinies in the prisons. This is an especially savage unit, perhaps the most violent in the country, which was supplied with new means of "riot control." Among others: salt bullets that are designed to cause particularly painful wounds. Muhammad Hatib, the man mentioned above, 30 years old and father of two children, got four bullets in his back: large, swollen, black-blue rings the full width of his back.

These salt bullets were brought to Israel from America at the beginning of the 1990s, but until now the army has shrunk from using them, fearing a public outcry. They were tried on us for the first time.

It appears that the army prepared the whole action in advance as a trap. The "Massada" unit tried out its tactics and weapons on this peaceful march of civilians.

The shocking difference between the ways the two demonstrations were treated provides food for thought.

The settlers are openly preparing and trying to paralyze the state, prevent the implementation of government and Knesset decisions, and, in effect, to overthrow Israeli democracy. But Ariel Sharon and his people call publicly to "embrace them," to "love them" and "view their pain with understanding." This is the directive given to the security forces. For peace activists, quite different treatment is indicated.

This throws light on a much more important phenomenon that may determine the future of Israel. Here, people have got so used to it that they accept it as natural. Abroad, people don't know about it.

The fact is that every day, all the Israeli media devote their main news reports to the settlers' propaganda. Every single news program on each of the three TV channels gives exhaustive coverage to the affairs of the settlers, speeches by settlers and interviews with settlers. Often, these reports fill half the news programs.

Between the settlers and the media a kind of symbiosis has come into being—they work "with one head." Every day several events are prepared for the media, which scoop them up greedily, to serve as unpaid propaganda organs of the settlers and the extreme right. Once upon a time, it was usual to give the other side the right of response, for the sake of "balance." Not anymore. There is no other side.

In the news programs, not a word—literally not a word—of criticism of the settlers is ever heard. The establishment "leftists" also speak of the need to "embrace them" and "understand them," and so, of course, do all the spokespersons of the government and the big parties. To people who have an opposite opinion, no opportunity is given to speak about the settlers on the main media of the country.

In this way, Israeli democracy puts all its media exclusively at the disposal of the enemies of democracy. Even in the Weimar Republic, stupidity did not go this far.

Absurd? It only seems so. In reality, it reflects the real situation: in spite of all the loud talk about "disengagement," Sharon's heart is with the settlers. He intends to annex to Israel most of the West Bank settlements—if not all of them.

The present controversy about a handful of small settlements in the Gaza Strip is, in his eyes, a kind of family spat, and will pass quickly. Actually, Sharon might be interested in feeding the commotion, so as to convince the Americans that it is unrealistic to expect him to dismantle the West Bank settlements and outposts. Fact: the army and police have never once used tear gas against right-wing demonstrators, even when physically attacked and injured by them (as happens regularly in Hebron, for example) or when the settlers block vital roads and cause huge traffic jams.

On the other hand, the controversy with us, the peace activists, the real opposition to the government, is a genuine struggle for the future of Israel: whether it will be a state within the Green Line borders, a liberal, democratic state that lives in peace with a viable Palestinian state at its side; or an aggressive, nationalist state, that will hold on to practically the whole of the West Bank and keep the Palestinians in some isolated enclaves.

If one sees it that way, the directives given to the army are quite logical: Embrace the settlers, because they are our brothers, and hit the peace activists, because they are the enemy.

The Magnificent 27

September 27, 2003

A year and a half ago, a small group of Israelis decided to break a deeply entrenched taboo and bring up the subject of war crimes. Until then, it had been self-evident that the IDF is "the most moral and humane army in the world," as the official mantra goes, and is therefore quite incapable of such things.

The Gush Shalom movement (to which I belong) called a public meeting in Tel-Aviv and invited a group of professors and public figures to discuss whether our army is committing such crimes. The star of the evening was Col. Yig'al Shohat, a war hero shot down over Egypt in the Yom Kippur war. His damaged leg had to be amputated by an Egyptian surgeon. Upon his return, he studied medicine and became a doctor himself.

In a voice trembling with emotion, he read out a personal appeal to his comrades, the air force pilots, calling on them to refuse orders over which "the black flag of illegality is waving" (a phrase coined by the military judge at the Kafr Kassem massacre trial in 1957). For example, orders to drop bombs on Palestinian residential neighborhoods for "targeted liquidations."[75]

The speech aroused a strong echo, but the army command succeeded in "damage control." The air force commander, General Dan Halutz, perhaps the most extremist IDF officer except Chief of Staff Moshe Ya'alon, was asked what he feels when he releases a bomb over a Palestinian neighborhood and answered: "I feel a slight bump." He added that after such an attack he "sleeps very well."

It seemed as if Shohat's call had evaporated into thin air—but not any more. The seed has matured slowly. This process accelerated after a pilot released a one-ton bomb over a residential neighborhood in Gaza in order to kill a Hamas leader, abruptly ending the lives of 17 bystanders, men, women and children. Many pilots were deeply troubled by this. Now the conscience of 27 of them has spoken out.

In Israeli mythology, combat pilots are the elite of the elite. Many of them are kibbutz-boys, who were once considered the aristocracy of Israel. Ezer Weitzman, a former air force commander, once coined the phrase "The best boys for flying" (and immediately added, in the typical macho style of the Force, "and the best girls for the flyers.")

The pilots are bought up from an early age to believe that we are always right, and that our opponents are vile murderers. That the army commanders never make a mistake. That an order is an order, and theirs is not to reason why. That professionalism is the highest virtue. That problems have to be solved inside the force. That one does not question the authority of the political leadership. There exists a whole mythology about the part played by the force in the Israeli victories in all our wars: from the tiny Piper planes in 1948, to the destruction of the Egyptian air force in the Yom Kippur war of 1973, and so forth.

The air force does not, of course, take in non-conformists. Candidates for flight training are scrutinized carefully. The force chooses solid, disciplined youngsters who can be relied on, both as to their character and their views, Zionists and the sons of Zionists.

Moreover, the air force is a clan, a sect whose members are

ferociously loyal to the force and to each other, There have never been public quarrels or signs of mutiny in the air force.

All this explains why the pilots struggled with themselves for so long, before they found in themselves the inner strength required for such an extraordinary, morally courageous act as publishing this appeal.

The 27 air force pilots informed their commander that from now on they would refuse to fulfill "immoral and illegal orders" that would cause the death of civilians. At the end of their statement, they criticized the occupation that is corrupting Israel and undermining its security.

The most senior officer among the signatories is Major General Yiftah Spector, who is also a living legend. He is the son of one of the "23 men in the boat," a group that was sent in World War II to demolish oil installations in Lebanon (at the time under Nazi-puppet Vichy French control) and never heard of again. Yiftah Spector was the instructor of many of the present commanders of the air force. Altogether, the statement was signed by one general, two colonels, nine lieutenant colonels, eight majors and seven captains.

Such a thing is unprecedented in Israel. Because of the special standing of the air force, the refusal evoked a much louder echo than the refusal movement of the ground troops, which seems to have leveled out, for the moment, at about 500 refuseniks.

The army establishment, the real government of Israel, sensed the danger and reacted as it had never reacted before. It started a wild campaign of defamation, incitement, and character assassination. The heroes of yesterday were turned overnight into enemies of the people. All parts of the government—from ex-president Ezer Weitzman to the Attorney General (who already has his eye on a seat in the Supreme Court), from the Foreign Office to the politicians of the Labor and Meretz parties—were mobilized in order to crush the mutiny of the pilots.

The counter-attack was headed by the media. Never before did they expose their real face as on this occasion. All TV channels, all radio networks and all newspapers—without exception!—revealed themselves as servants and mouthpieces of the army command. The liberal *Ha'aretz*, too, devoted its front page to a ferocious attack on the pilots, without giving space to the other point of view.

It was impossible to switch on a TV set without encountering the air force commander, and after him a long line of establishment figures who, one after another, condemned the pilots. Army camps were opened to the cameras, loyal officers damned their comrades as "traitors" who had "stuck a knife in our backs." Except for one single interview on Channel 2, the "refusers" were not given any opportunity at all to explain their point of view or answer their detractors.

No doubt: the establishment is worried. Perhaps it may succeed in containing the protest this time and deterring other potential mutineers by spreading defamation, fear, and punishment. But the message of the 27 has been written and nothing can change that.

With this sortie the flyers have served the State of Israel better than any of the hundreds of others in the course of their army service. Some day Israel will recognize the huge debt it owes to the valiant 27.

Vanunu: The Terrible Secret

April 24, 2004

In the darkness of a cinema, a woman's voice: "Hey! Take your hands off! Not you! YOU!" This old joke illustrates the American policy regarding nuclear armaments in the Middle East. "Hey, you there, Iraq and Iran and Libya, stop it! Not YOU, Israel!"

The danger of nuclear arms was the main pretext for the invasion of Iraq. Iran is threatened in order to compel it to stop its nuclear efforts. Libya has surrendered and is dismantling its nuclear installations. So what about Israel?

This week it became clear that the Americans are full partners in the creation of Israel's "nuclear option."

How was this exposed? With the help of Mordecai Vanunu, of course. Throughout the week, a festival was being celebrated around the prisoner, who was released on Wednesday. The Security Establishment has not stopped harassing him even after he has sat in prison for 18 years, eleven of them in complete solitary confinement— a treatment he himself described on leaving the prison as "cruel and barbaric." After he was "set free," far-reaching restrictions were imposed on him (e.g. he is forbidden to leave the country, is restricted to one town, cannot go near any embassy or consulate, may not talk with foreign citizens). All this under the colonial British emergency regulations that were condemned at the time by the leaders of the Jewish community in Palestine, as "worse then the Nazi laws."

Not, God forbid, because of any desire for revenge!

The security people declared from every podium that this is not revenge for all the shame Vanunu caused the security services, and is by no means just more persecution, but an essential security requirement. He must not be allowed to leave the country or to speak with foreigners and journalists, because he is in possession of secrets vital to the security of the state.

Everybody understands that he has no more secrets. What can a technician know after 18 years in jail, during which time technology has advanced with giant steps?

But gradually it becomes clear what the security establishment is really afraid of. Vanunu is in a position to expose the close partnership with the United States in the development of Israel's nuclear armaments.

This worries Washington so much, that the man responsible in the State Department for "arms control," Undersecretary John Bolton, has come to Israel in person for the occasion. Vanunu, it appears, can cause severe damage to the mighty superpower. The Americans are afraid of sounding like the lady in the dark cinema.

(By the way, this John Bolton is an avid supporter of the group of Zionist neo-cons who play a central role in the Bush theater. He opposes arms control for the United States and its satellites, and was installed in the State Department against the wishes of the Secretary of State himself.)

In the short address Vanunu was able to make to the media immediately on his release, he made a strange remark: that the young woman who served as bait for his kidnapping, some 18 years ago, was not a Mossad agent, as generally assumed, but an agent of the FBI or CIA. Why was it so urgent for him to convey this?

From the first moment, there was something odd about the Vanunu affair.

At the beginning, my first thought was that he was a Mossad agent. Everything pointed in that direction. How else can one explain a simple technician's success in smuggling a camera into the most secret and best-guarded installation in Israel? And in taking photos apparently without hindrance? How else to explain the career of that person who, as a student at Be'er-Sheva University, was well-known as belonging to the extreme left and spending his time in the company of Arab fellow-students? How was he allowed to leave the country with hundreds of photos? How was he able to approach a British paper and to turn over to British scientists material that convinced them that Israel had 200 nuclear bombs?

Absurd, isn't it? But it all fits, if one assumes that Vanunu acted from the beginning on a mission for the Mossad. His disclosures in the British newspaper not only caused no damage to the Israeli government, but on the contrary, strengthened the Israeli deterrent without committing the government, which was free to deny everything.

What happened next only reinforced this assumption. While in London, in the middle of his campaign of exposures, knowing that half a dozen intelligence services are tracking his every movement, he starts an affair with a strange women, is seduced into following her to Rome, where he is kidnapped and shipped back to Israel. How naive can you get? Is it credible for a reasonable person to fall into such a primitive trap? It is not. Meaning that the whole affair was nothing but a classic cover story.

But when the affair went on, and details of the years-long daily mistreatment of the man became public, I had to give up this initial theory. I had to face the fact that our security services are even more stupid than I had assumed (which I wouldn't have believed possible) and that all these things actually had happened, and that Mordecai Vanunu was an honest and idealistic, if extremely naive, person.

I have no doubt that his personality was shaped by his background. He is the son of a family with many children, who were quite well-to-do in Morocco but lived in a primitive "transition camp" in Israel before moving to Be'er-Sheva, where they lived in poverty. In spite of this, he succeeded in getting into university and got a master's degree, quite an achievement, but suffered, so it seems, from the overbearing attitude and prejudices of his Ashkenazi peers. Undoubtedly, that pushed him towards the company of the extreme left, where such prejudices were not prevalent.

The bunch of "security correspondents" and other commentators who are attached to the udders of the security establishment have already spread stories about Vanunu "imagining things," his long stay in solitary confinement causing him to "convince himself of all kinds of fantasies" and to "invent all kinds of fabrications." Meaning: the American connection.

Against this background one can suddenly understand all these severe restrictions, which, at first sight, look absolutely idiotic. The Americans, it seems, are very worried. The Israeli security services have to dance to their tune. The world must be prevented by all available means from hearing, from the lips of a credible witness, that the Americans are full partners in Israel's nuclear arms program, while pretending to be the world's sheriff for the prevention of nuclear proliferation.

And the lady cried: "Not you! YOU!"[76]

5
Other Players, Other Wars: The Global Context

Israel and Palestine do not exist in a vacuum. Other countries in the region, as well as world powers—most notably the United States—all contribute to the complexity of the situation. The United States functions as Israel's prime supporter, financially, militarily, and in the UN, having exercised an unprecedented number of vetoes on UN Security Council votes considered harmful to Israel. Most countries in the region have mixed relations with Israel at best. The Saudi Plan for peace has been discussed in Chapter 3. Iraq and Syria have long been enemies of Israel. Lebanon and Iran have a mixed history in their relations with Israel; Israel has invaded Lebanon twice and Lebanon is divided in its sentiments. Iran allied with Israel under the Shah, but is currently one of its prime enemies. Egypt is walking a tightrope between the heavily US-subsidized government and the famed "Arab street"—popular dissent—but currently has a formal peace treaty with Israel (1979–). Jordan, too, has a formal peace treaty with Israel, but is included in this chapter because the "Jordanian option"—the idea that Jordan should be the Palestinian state—is regaining support in Israel after being little discussed since the 1994 peace treaty.—SRP

Two Knights and a Dragon

October 6, 2007

There are books that change people's consciousness and change history. Some tell a story, like Harriet Beech Stowe's 1851 *Uncle Tom's Cabin*, which gave a huge impetus to the campaign for the abolition of slavery. Others take the form of a political treatise, like Theodor Herzl's *Der Judenstaat*, which gave birth to the Zionist Movement. Or they can be scientific in nature, like Charles Darwin's *On the Origin of Species*, which changed the way humanity sees itself. And perhaps political satire, too, can shake the world, like *Nineteen Eighty-Four* by George Orwell.

The impact of these books was amplified by their timing. They

171

appeared exactly at the right time, when a large public was ready to absorb their message.

It may well turn out that the book by two professors, John Mearsheimer and Stephen Walt, *The Israel Lobby and US Foreign Policy*, is just such a book.

It is a dry scientific research report, 355 pages long, backed by 106 further pages containing some 1,000 references to sources.

It is not a bellicose book. On the contrary, its style is restrained and factual. The authors take great care not to utter a single negative comment on the legitimacy of the lobby, and indeed bend over backwards to stress their support for the existence and security of Israel. They let the facts speak for themselves. With the skill of experienced masons, they systematically lay brick upon brick, row upon row, leaving no gap in their argument.

This wall cannot be torn down by reasoned argument. Nobody has tried, and nobody is going to. Instead, the authors are being smeared and accused of sinister motives. If the book could be ignored altogether, this would have been done—as has happened to other books that have been buried alive.

(Some years ago, there appeared in Russia a large tome by Aleksandr Solzhenitsyn, the world-renowned laureate of the Nobel Prize for Literature, about Russia and its Jews. This book, called *200 Years Together*, has been completely ignored. As far as I know, it has not been translated into any language, certainly not into Hebrew. I asked several of Israel's leading intellectuals, and none of them had even heard of the book. Neither does it appear on the list of Amazon.com, which includes all the author's other works.)

The two professors take the bull by the horns. They deal with a subject that is absolutely taboo in the United States, a subject nobody in his right mind would even mention: the enormous influence of the pro-Israel lobby on American foreign policy.

In a remorselessly systematical way, the book analyzes the lobby, takes it apart, describes its modus operandi, discloses its financial sources and lays bare its relations with the White House, the two houses of Congress, the leaders of the two major parties and leading media people.

The authors do not call into question the lobby's legitimacy. On the contrary, they show that hundreds of lobbies of this kind play an essential role in the American democratic system. The gun and the medical lobbies, for example, are also very powerful political forces. But the pro-Israel lobby has grown out of all proportion. It has unparalleled political power. It can silence all criticism of Israel in Congress and the media, bring about the political demise of anyone who dares to break the taboo, prevent any action that does not conform to the will of the Israeli government.

In its second part, the book shows how the lobby uses its tremendous power in practice: how it has prevented the exertion of any pressure on Israel for peace with the Palestinians, how it pushed the United States into the invasion of Iraq, how it is now pushing for wars with Iran and Syria, how it supported the Israeli leadership in the recent war in Lebanon, and blocked calls for a ceasefire when it didn't want one.

All of these assertions are backed up by so much undeniable evidence and quotations from written material (mainly from Israeli sources) that they cannot be denied.

Most of these disclosures are nothing new for those in Israel who deal with these matters.

I myself could add to the book a whole chapter from personal experience.

In the late 1950s, I visited the United States for the first time. A major New York radio station invited me for an interview. Later they cautioned me: "You can criticize the President (Dwight D. Eisenhower) and the Secretary of State (John Foster Dulles) to your heart's content, but please don't criticize Israeli leaders!" At the last moment the interview was cancelled altogether, and the Iraqi ambassador was invited instead. Criticism was apparently tolerable when it came from an Arab, but absolutely not coming from an Israeli.

In 1970, the respected American "Fellowship of Reconciliation" invited me for a lecture tour of 30 universities, under the auspices of the Hillel rabbis. When I arrived in New York, I was informed that 29 of the lectures had been cancelled. The sole rabbi who did not cancel, Balfour Brickner, showed me a secret communication of the "Anti-Defamation League" that proscribed my lectures. It said: "While Knesset Member Avnery can in no way be considered a traitor, his appearance at this time would be deeply divisive." In the end, all the lectures took place under the auspices of Christian chaplains.

I especially remember a depressing experience in Baltimore. A good Jew, who had volunteered to host me, was angered by the cancellation of my lecture in this city and obstinately insisted on putting it on. We combed the streets of the Jewish quarters—mile upon mile of signs with Jewish names—and did not find a single hall whose manager would agree to let the lecture by a member of the Israeli Knesset take place. In the end, we did hold the lecture in the basement of the building of my host's apartment—and functionaries of the Jewish community came to protest.

That year, during Black September, I held a press conference in Washington DC, under the auspices of the Quakers.[77] It seemed to be a huge success. The journalists came straight from a press conference with Prime Minister Golda Meir, and showered me with questions. Almost all the important media were represented—TV networks, radio, the major newspapers. After the planned hour was up, they would not let me go and kept me talking for another hour and a half. But the next day, not a single word appeared in any of the media. Thirty-one years later, in October 2001 I held a press conference on Capitol Hill in Washington, and exactly the same thing happened: many of the media were there, they held me for another hour—and not a word, not a single word, was published.

In 1968, a very respected American publishing house (Macmillan) brought out a book of mine, *Israel Without Zionists*, which was later translated into eight other languages. The book described the Israeli–Arab conflict in a very different way, and proposed the establishment of a Palestinian state next to Israel—a revolutionary idea at the time. It dealt with the "two states for two peoples" solution long before it became a worldwide consensus, and with my proposal for Israel's integration in "the Semitic region." Not a single review appeared in the American media. I checked in one of the most important bookstores in New York and did not find the book. When I asked a salesman, he found it buried under a heap of volumes and put it on top. Half an hour later it was hidden again.

True, I am an Israeli patriot and was elected to the Knesset by Israeli voters. But I criticized the Israeli government—and that was enough.

The book by the two professors, who criticize the Israeli government from a different angle, cannot be buried any more. This fact, by itself, speaks volumes.

The book is based on an essay by the two that appeared last year in a British journal, after no American publication dared to touch it. Now a respected American publishing house has released it—an indication that something is moving. The situation has not changed, but it seems that it is now possible at least to talk about it.

Everything depends on timing—and apparently the time is now ripe for such a book, which will shock many good people in America. It is now causing an uproar.

The two professors are, of course, accused of anti-Semitism, racism, and hatred of Israel. What Israel? It is the lobby itself that hates a large part of Israel. In recent years it has shifted even more to the right. Some of its constituent groups—such as the neo-cons who pushed the United

States into the Iraq war—are openly connected with the right-wing Likud, and especially with Binyamin Netanyahu. The billionaires who finance the lobby are the same people who finance the extreme Israeli right, and most of all the settlers.

The small, determined Jewish groups in the United States who support the Israeli peace movements are remorselessly persecuted. Some of them fold after a few years. Members of Israeli peace groups who are sent to America are boycotted and slandered as "self-hating-Jews."

The political views of the two professors, which are briefly stated at the end of the book, are identical with the stand of the Israeli peace forces: the two-state solution, ending the occupation, borders based on the Green Line, and international support for the peace settlement.

If this is anti-Semitism, then we here are all anti-Semites. And only the Christian Zionists—those who openly demand the return of the Jews to this country but secretly prophesy the annihilation of the unconverted Jews at the Second Coming of Jesus Christ—are the true Lovers of Zion.

Even if not a single bad word about the pro-Israel lobby can be uttered in the United States, it is far from being a secret society hatching conspiracies like the *Protocols of the Elders of Zion*. On the contrary, AIPAC, the Anti-Defamation League, the Zionist Federation, and the other organizations vociferously boast about their actions and publicly proclaim their incredible successes.

Quite naturally, the diverse components of the lobby compete with each other. Who has the biggest influence on the White House? Who scares the most senators? Who controls more journalists and commentators? This competition causes a permanent escalation—because every success by one group spurs the others to redouble their efforts.

This could be very dangerous. A balloon that is inflated to monstrous dimensions may one day burst in the face of American Jews (who, by the way, according to the polls, object to many positions adopted by the lobby that claims to speak in their name).

Most of the American public now opposes the Iraq war and considers it a disaster. This majority still does not connect the war with the actions of the pro-Israel lobby. No newspaper and no politician dares to hint at such a connection—yet.[78] But if this taboo is broken, the result may be very dangerous for the Jews and for Israel.

Beneath the surface, a lot of anger directed against the lobby is accumulating. The presidential candidates who are compelled to grovel at the feet of AIPAC, the senators and congressmen who have become slaves of the lobby, the media people who are forbidden to write what they really think—all these secretly detest the lobby. If this anger explodes, it may hurt us, too.

This lobby has become a golem. And like the golem in legend, in the end it will bring disaster on its maker.

If I may be permitted to voice some criticism of my own.

When the original article by the two professors appeared, I argued that "the tail is wagging the dog and the dog is wagging the tail." The tail, of course, is Israel.

The two professors confirm the first part of the equation, but emphatically deny the second. The central thesis of the book is that the pressure of the lobby causes the United States to act against its own interests (and, in the long run, also against the true interests of Israel). They do not accept my contention, quoted in the book, that Israel acted in Lebanon as "America's Rottweiler" (to Hizbullah as "Iran's Doberman").

I agree that the United States is acting against its true interest (and the true interests of Israel), but the American leadership does not see it that way. Bush and his people believe—even without the input of the lobby—that it would be advantageous for the United States to establish a permanent American military presence in the middle of this region of huge oil reserves. In my view, this counterproductive act was one of the main objectives of the war, side by side with the desire to eliminate one of Israel's most dangerous enemies.

Unfortunately, the book deals only very briefly with this issue.

That does not diminish in any way my profound admiration for the intellectual qualities, integrity, and courage of Mearsheimer and Walt, two knights who, like St. George, have sallied forth to face the fearful dragon.

Baker's Cake

December 9, 2006

No one likes to admit a mistake. Me neither. But honesty leaves me no choice.

A few days after the collapse of the Twin Towers on September 11, 2001, I happened to go on a lecture tour in the United States.

My message was optimistic. I expected some good to come out of the tragedy. I reasoned that the atrocity had exposed the intensity of the hatred for the United States that is spreading throughout the world, and especially the Muslim world. It would be logical not only to fight against the mosquitoes, but to drain the swamp. Since the Israeli–Palestinian conflict was one of the breeding grounds of the hatred—if not the main one—the United States would make a major effort to achieve peace between the two peoples.

That was what cold logic indicated. But this is not what happened. What happened was the very opposite.

American policy was not led by cold logic. Instead of draining one swamp, it created a second. Instead of pushing the Israelis and Palestinians towards peace, it invaded Iraq. Not only did the hatred against America not die down, it flared up even higher. I hoped that this danger would override even the oil interests and the desire to station an American garrison in the center of the Middle East.

Thus I committed the very mistake that I have warned others against many times: to assume that what is logical will actually happen. A rational person should not ignore the irrational in politics. In other words, it is irrational to exclude the irrational.

George W. Bush is an irrational person, perhaps the very personification of irrationality. Instead of drawing the logical conclusion from what had happened and acting accordingly, he set off in the opposite direction. Since then he has just insisted on "staying the course."

Enter James Baker.

Since I am already in a confessional mood, I have to admit that I like James Baker.

I know that this will shock some of my good friends. "Baker?!" they will cry out, "The consigliere of the Bush family? The man who helped George W. steal the 2000 elections? The rightist?"

Yes, yes, the very same Baker. I like him for his cold logic, his forthright and blunt style, his habit of saying what he thinks without embellishment, his courage. I prefer this style to the sanctimonious hypocrisy of other leaders, who try to hide their real intentions. I would be happy any time to swap Olmert for Baker, and throw in Amir Peretz for free.

But that is a matter of taste. More important is the fact that in all the last 40 years, James Baker was the only leader in America who had the guts to stand up and act against Israel's malignant disease: the settlements. When he was the Secretary of State, he simply informed the Israeli government that he would deduct the sums expended on the settlements from the money Israel was getting from the United States. Threatened and made good on his threat.

Baker thus confronted the "pro-Israeli" lobbies in the United States, both the Jewish and the Christian. Such courage is rare in the United States, as it is rare in Israel.

This week the Iraq Study Group, led by Baker, published its report. It confirms all the bleak forecasts voiced by many throughout the world—myself included—before Bush & Co. launched the bloody Iraqi adventure. In his dry and incisive style, Baker says that the United States cannot win there. In so many words he tells the American public: Let's get out of there, before the last American soldier has to scramble into the last helicopter from the roof of the American embassy, as happened in Vietnam.

Baker calls for the end of the Bush approach and offers a new and thought-out strategy of his own. Actually, it is an elegant way of extricating America from Iraq, without it looking like a complete rout. The main proposals: an American dialogue with Iran and Syria, an international conference, the withdrawal of the American combat brigades, leaving behind only instructors. The committee that he headed was bi-partisan, composed half and half of Republicans and Democrats.

For Israelis, the most interesting part of the report is, of course, the one that concerns us directly. It interests me especially—how could it be otherwise?—because it repeats, almost word for word, the things I said immediately after September 11, both in my articles at home and in my lectures in the United States.

True, Baker is saying them four years later. In these four years, thousands of American soldiers and tens of thousands of Iraqi civilians have died for nothing. But, to use the image again, when a giant ship like the United States turns around, it makes a very big circle, and it takes a lot of time. We, in the small speedboat called Israel, could do it much quicker—if we had the good sense to do it.

Baker says simply: In order to stop the war in Iraq and start a reconciliation with the Arab world, the United States must bring about the end of the Israeli–Palestinian conflict. He does not say explicitly that peace must be imposed on Israel, but that is the obvious implication.

In his own clear words: "The United States will not be able to achieve its goals in the Middle East unless the United States deals directly with the Arab–Israeli conflict."

His committee proposes the immediate start of negotiations between Israel and "President Mahmoud Abbas," in order to implement the two-state solution. The "sustainable negotiations" must address the "key final status issues of borders, settlements, Jerusalem, the right of return, and the end of conflict."

The use of the title "President" for Abu Mazen and, even more so, the use of the term "right of return" have alarmed the whole political class in Israel. Even in the Oslo agreement, the section dealing with the "final status" issues mentions only "refugees." Baker, as is his wont, called the spade a spade.

At the same time, Baker proposes a stick-and-carrot approach to achieve peace between Israel and Syria. The United States needs this peace in order to draw Syria into its camp. The stick, from the Israeli point of view, would be the return of the Golan Heights. The carrot would be the stationing of American soldiers on the border, so that Israel's security would be guaranteed by the United States. In return, he demands that Syria stop, *inter alia*, its aid to Hizbullah.

After Gulf War I, Baker—the same Baker—got all the parties to the conflict to come to an international conference in Madrid. For that purpose, he twisted the arm of then Prime Minister Yitzhak Shamir, whose entire philosophy consisted of two letters and one exclamation mark: "No!" and whose slogan was: "The Arabs are the same Arabs, and the sea is the same sea"—alluding to the popular Israeli conviction that the Arabs all want to throw Israel into the sea.

Baker brought Shamir to Madrid, his arms and legs in irons, and made sure he did not escape. Shamir was compelled to sit at the table with representatives of the Palestinian people, who had never been allowed to attend an international conference before. The conference itself had no tangible results, but there is no doubt that it was a vital step in the process that brought about the Oslo agreement and, more difficult than anything else, the mutual recognition of the State of Israel and the Palestinian people.

Now Baker is suggesting something similar. He proposes an international conference, and cites Madrid as a model. The conclusion is clear.

However, this baker can only offer a recipe for the cake. The question is whether President Bush will use the recipe and bake the cake.

Since 1967 and the beginning of the occupation, several American Secretaries of State have submitted plans to end the Israeli–Palestinian conflict. All these plans met the same fate: they were torn up and thrown in the trash can.

The same sequence of events has been repeated time after time. In Jerusalem, hysteria sets in. The Foreign Office stands up on its hind legs and swears to defeat the evil design. The media unanimously condemns the wicked plot. The Secretary of State of the day is pilloried as an anti-Semite. The Israeli lobby in Washington mobilizes for total war.

Take, for example, the Rogers Plan of Richard Nixon's first Secretary of State, William Rogers. In the early 1970s he submitted a detailed peace plan, the principal point of which was the withdrawal of Israel to the 1967 borders, with, at most, "insubstantial alterations."

What happened to the plan?

In face of the onslaught of "the Friends of Israel" in Washington, Nixon buckled under, as have all presidents since Dwight D. Eisenhower, a man of principle who did not need the Jewish votes. No president will quarrel with the government of Israel if he wants to be re-elected, or—like Bush now—to end his term in office with dignity and pass the presidency to another member of his party. Any senator or congressman who takes a stand that the Israeli embassy does not like is committing *hara-kiri*, Washington-style.

The fate of the peace plans of successive Secretaries of State confirms, on the face of it, the thesis of the two professors John Mearsheimer and Stephen Walt, which caused a great stir earlier this year. According to them, whenever there is a clash in Washington between the national interests of the United States and the national interests of Israel, it is the Israeli interests that win.

Will this happen this time, too?

Baker has presented his plan at a time when the United States is facing disaster in Iraq. President Bush is bankrupt; his party has lost control of Congress and may soon lose the White House. The neo-conservatives, most of them Jews and all of them supporters of the Israeli extreme right, who were in control of American foreign policy, are being removed one by one, and this week yet another, the American ambassador to the United Nations, was kicked out.[79] Therefore, it is possible that this time the President may listen to expert advice.

But that is in serious doubt. The Democratic Party is subject to the "pro-Israeli" lobby no less than the Republican Party, and perhaps even more. The new congress was indeed elected under the banner of opposition to the continuation of the war in Iraq, but its members are not *jihadi* suicide bombers. They depend on the "pro-Israeli" lobby. To paraphrase Shamir: "The plan is the same plan, and the trash bin is the same trash bin."

In Jerusalem, the first reaction to the report was total rejection, expressing a complete confidence in the ability of the lobby to choke it at birth. "Nothing has changed," Olmert declared, "There is no one to talk with," and was immediately echoed by the mouth and pen brigade in the media. "We cannot talk with them as long as the terrorism goes on," a famous expert declared on TV. That's like saying: "One cannot talk about ending the war as long as the enemy is shooting at our troops."

On the Mearsheimer–Walt thesis I wrote that "the dog is wagging the tail and the tail is wagging the dog." It will be interesting to see which will wag which this time: the dog its tail or the tail its dog.

America's Rottweiler

August 26, 2006

In his latest speech, which infuriated so many people, Syrian President Bashar al-Assad uttered a sentence that deserves attention: "Every new Arab generation hates Israel more than the previous one."

Of all that has been said about the Second Lebanon War, these are perhaps the most important words.

The main product of this war is hatred. The pictures of death and destruction in Lebanon entered every Arab home, indeed every Muslim home from Indonesia to Morocco, from Yemen to the Muslim ghettos in London and Berlin. Not for an hour, not for a day, but for 33 successive days—day after day, hour after hour. The mangled bodies of babies, the women weeping over the ruins of their homes, Israeli children writing "greetings" on shells about to be fired at villages, Ehud Olmert blabbering about "the most moral army in the world" while the screen showed a heap of bodies.

Israelis ignored these sights; indeed they were scarcely shown on our TV. Of course, we could see them on Aljazeera and some Western channels, but Israelis were much too busy with the damage wrought in our Northern towns. Feelings of pity and empathy for non-Jews have been blunted here a long time ago.

But it is a terrible mistake to ignore this result of the war. It is far more important than the stationing of a few thousand European troops along our border, with the kind consent of Hizbullah. It may still be bothering generations of Israelis, when the names Olmert and Halutz have long been forgotten, and when even Nasrallah no longer remembers the name Amir Peretz.[80]

In order for the significance of Assad's words to become clear, they have to be viewed in a historical context.

The whole Zionist enterprise has been compared to the transplantation of an organ into the body of a human being. The natural immune system rises up against the foreign implant; the body mobilizes all its power to reject it. The doctors use a heavy dosage of medicines in order to overcome the rejection. That can go on for a long time, sometimes until the eventual death of the body itself, including the transplant.

(Of course, this analogy, like any other, should be treated cautiously. An analogy can help in understanding things, but no more than that.)

The Zionist Movement has planted a foreign body in this country, which was then a part of the Arab-Muslim space. The inhabitants of the country, and the entire Arab region, rejected the Zionist entity.

Meanwhile, the Jewish settlement has taken roots and become an authentic new nation rooted in the country. Its defensive power against the rejection has grown. This struggle has been going on for 125 years, becoming more violent from generation to generation. The last war was yet another episode.

What is our historic objective in this confrontation?

A fool will say: to stand up to the rejection with a growing dosage of medicaments, provided by America and World Jewry. The greatest fools will add: There is no solution. This situation will last forever. There is nothing to be done about it but to defend ourselves in war after war after war. And the next war is already knocking on the door.

The wise will say: our objective is to cause the body to accept the transplant as one of its organs, so that the immune system will no longer treat us as an enemy that must be removed at any price. And if this is the aim, it must become the main axis of our efforts. Meaning: each of our actions must be judged according to a simple criterion: does it serve this aim or obstruct it?

According to this criterion, the Second Lebanon War was a disaster.

Fifty-nine years ago, two months before the outbreak of our War of Independence, I published a booklet entitled "War or peace in the Semitic region." Its opening words were:

When our Zionist fathers decided to set up a "safe haven" in Palestine, they had a choice between two ways:

They could appear in West Asia as a European conqueror, who sees himself as a bridgehead of the "white" race and a master of the "natives," like the Spanish Conquistadores and the Anglo-Saxon colonists in America. That is what the Crusaders did in Palestine.

The second way was to consider themselves as an Asian nation returning to its home—a nation that sees itself as an heir to the political and cultural heritage of the Semitic race, and which is prepared to join the peoples of the Semitic region in their war of liberation from European exploitation.

As is well known, the State of Israel, which was established a few months later, chose the first way. It gave its hand to colonial France, tried to help Britain to return to the Suez Canal and, since 1967, has become the little sister of the United States.

That was not inevitable. On the contrary, in the course of years there have been a growing number of indications that the immune system of the Arab-Muslim body is starting to incorporate the transplant—as a human body accepts the organ of a close relative—and is ready to accept us. Such an indication was the visit of Anwar Sadat to Jerusalem. Such was the peace treaty signed with us by King Hussein, a descendent of the Prophet. And, most importantly, the historic decision of Yassir Arafat, the leader of the Palestinian people, to make peace with Israel.

But after every huge step forward, there came an Israeli step backward. It is as if the transplant rejects the body's acceptance of it. As if it has become so accustomed to being rejected, that it does all it can to induce the body to reject it even more.

It is against this background that one should weigh the words spoken by Assad Jr, a member of the new Arab generation, at the end of the recent war.

After every single one of the war aims put forward by our government had evaporated, one after the other, another reason was brought up: this war was a part of the "clash of civilizations," the great campaign of the Western world and its lofty values against the barbarian darkness of the Islamic world.

That reminds one, of course, of the words written 110 years ago by the father of modern Zionism, Theodor Herzl, in the founding document of the Zionist Movement: "In Palestine ... we shall constitute for Europe a part of the wall against Asia, and serve as the vanguard of civilization against barbarism."[81] Without knowing, Olmert almost repeated this formula in his justification of his war, in order to please President Bush.

It happens from time to time in the United States that somebody invents an empty but easily digested slogan which then dominates the public discourse for some time. It seems that the more stupid the slogan is, the better its chances of becoming the guiding light for academia and the media—until another slogan appears and supersedes it. The latest example is the slogan "clash of civilizations," coined by Samuel P. Huntington in 1993 (taking over from the *End of History*).[82]

What clash of ideas is there between Muslim Indonesia and Christian Chile? What eternal struggle between Poland and Morocco? What is it that unifies Malaysia and Kosovo, two Muslim nations? Or two Christian nations like Sweden and Ethiopia?

In what way are the ideas of the West more sublime than those of the East? The Jews that fled the flames of the *autos-da-fe* of the Christian Inquisition in Spain were received with open arms by the Muslim Ottoman Empire. The most cultured of European nations democratically elected Adolf Hitler as its leader and perpetrated the Holocaust, without the Pope raising his voice in protest.

In what way are the spiritual values of the United States, today's Empire of the West, superior to those of India and China, the rising stars of the East? Huntington himself was compelled to admit: "The West won the world not by the superiority of its ideas or values or religion, but rather by its superiority in applying organized violence. Westerners often forget this fact, non-Westerners never do." In the West, too, women won the vote only in the twentieth century, and slavery was abolished there only in the second half of the nineteenth. And in the leading nation of the West, fundamentalism is now also raising its head.

What interest, for goodness sake, have we in volunteering to be a political and military vanguard of the West in this imagined clash?

The truth is, of course, that this entire story of the clash of civilizations is nothing but an ideological cover for something that has no connection with ideas and values: the determination of the United States to dominate the world's resources, and especially oil.

The Second Lebanon War is considered by many as a "war by proxy." That is to say: Hizbullah is the Doberman of Iran, we are the Rottweiler of America. Hizbullah gets money, rockets, and support from the Islamic Republic, we get money, cluster bombs, and support from the United States of America.

That is certainly exaggerated. Hizbullah is an authentic Lebanese movement, deeply rooted in the Shi'ite community. The Israeli government has its own interests (the occupied territories) that do not depend on America. But there is no doubt that there is much truth in the argument that this was also a war by substitutes.

The United States is fighting against Iran, because Iran has a key role in the region where the most important oil reserves in the world are located. Not only does Iran itself sit on huge oil deposits, but through its revolutionary Islamic ideology it also menaces American control over the nearby oil countries. The declining resource oil becomes more and more essential in the modern economy. He who controls the oil controls the world.

The United States would viciously attack Iran even it were peopled with pigmies devoted to the religion of the Dalai Lama. There is a shocking similarity between George W. Bush and Mahmoud Ahmadinejad.[83] The one has personal conversations with Jesus, the other has a line to Allah. But the name of the game is domination.

What interest do we have to get involved in this struggle? What interest do we have in being regarded—accurately—as the servants of the greatest enemy of the Muslim world in general and the Arab world in particular?

We want to live here in 100 years, in 500 years. Our most basic national interests demand that we extend our hands to the Arab nations that accept us, and act together with them for the rehabilitation of this region. That was true 59 years ago, and that will be true 59 years hence.

Little politicians like Olmert, Peretz and Halutz are unable to think in these terms.[84] They can hardly see as far as the end of their noses. But where are the intellectuals, who should be more far-sighted?

Bashar al-Assad may not be one of the world's Great Thinkers. But his remark should certainly give us pause for thought.

Lunch in Damascus

October 7, 2006

Once, while traveling in a taxi, I had an argument with the driver—a profession associated in Israel with extreme right-wing views. I tried in vain to convince him of the desirability of peace with the Arabs. In our country, which has never seen a single day of peace in the last hundred years, peace can seem like something out of science fiction.

Suddenly I had an inspiration. "When we have peace," I said, "You can take your taxi in the morning and go to Damascus, have lunch there with real authentic hummus and come back home in the evening."

He jumped at the idea. "Wow," he exclaimed, "If that happens, I shall take you with me for nothing!"

"And I shall treat you to lunch," I responded.

He continued to dream. "If I could go to Damascus in my car, I could drive on from there all the way to Paris!"

Bashar al-Assad has done it again. He has succeeded in confusing the Israeli government.

As long as he voices the ritual threat to liberate the Golan Heights by force, it does not upset anybody. After all, that only confirms what many want to hear: that there is no way to have peace with Syria, that sooner or later we shall have a war with them.

Why is that good? Simple: peace with Syria would mean giving back the Golan Heights (Syrian territory by any definition). No peace, no need to give them back.

But when Bashar starts to talk peace, we are in trouble. That is a sinister plot. It may, God forbid, create a situation that would compel us to return the territory.

Therefore, we should not even speak about it. The news must be buried in some remote corner of the papers and at the end of the news on TV, as just "another speech of Assad." The government rejects them "on the threshold," adding that it cannot even be discussed until ...

Until what? Until he stops supporting Hizbullah. Until Syria expels the representatives of Hamas and the other Palestinian organizations. Until regime change takes place in Syria. Until a Western-style democracy is installed there. In short, until he registers as a member of the Zionist organization.

The relations between Israel and Syria have a documented history of at least 2,859 years. In the year 853 BC Israel is mentioned—for the first time, it seems—in an authentic document outside the Bible. Twelve monarchs of the region, led by the kings of Damascus and Israel, united against the growing threat of Assyria, The decisive battle took place at Karkar (in the north of today's Syria). According to an Assyrian document, 20,000 soldiers and 1,200 chariots of Damascus fought side by side with 10,000 soldiers and 2,000 chariots of Ahab, king of Israel. It is not quite clear which side won.

But that was a temporary alliance. For most of the time, Israel and Aram-Damascus fought against each other for regional supremacy. Ahab died a hero's death in one of these wars against Aram, just two years after the battle against the Assyrians.

In modern times, the Syrians (although then still under French colonial rule) strenuously opposed the Zionist enterprise right from the beginning. But they also opposed the Palestinian national movement. That is grounded in history: in the Arabic language, the name al-Sham ("the North"), as Syria is called, includes the entire territory between Egypt and Turkey. Therefore, in Arab consciousness, not only Lebanon, but Jordan, Palestine, and Israel as well, are really part of Syria.

When Yassir Arafat created the independent Palestinian national movement at the end of the 1950s, the Syrians demanded to be acknowledged as the protectors of the Palestinian people. When he refused, the Syrians threw the entire Palestinian leadership into prison. (Only the wife of Abu Jihad, Intissar al-Wazir, remained at liberty and took over the command of the Fatah fighters—thus becoming the first woman in modern times to command an Arab fighting force.[85])

Naturally, all the enemies of Arafat found refuge in Damascus, and that is the original reason for the presence of some leaders of Hamas and other organizations there. They were more of a threat to the PLO than to Israel.

In the 1948 war, the Syrian army was the only Arab army that was not defeated. They continued to occupy some Israeli territory. Along this border, many incidents took place (mostly initiated by an officer by the name of Ariel Sharon). In the end, the Israeli army occupied the Golan Heights in the Six-Day War, for the outbreak of which Syria bears some responsibility.[86]

Since then, all the relations between Israel and Syria have been centered on this occupied territory. Its return is a paramount Syrian aim. Israel has applied Israeli law there (which, contrary to the accepted view, means less than annexation). Hafez al-Assad re-conquered it in the 1973 war, but in the end was pushed back to the approaches of Damascus. Since then, the Syrians have been trying to harass Israel mostly by means of Hizbullah.

Once upon a time, the idea of an "Eastern Front"—a coordinated attack by Jordan, Syria, and Iraq—used to cause nightmares in Israel. The prophecy of Jeremiah (1, 14), "Out of the north an evil shall break forth upon all the inhabitants of the land," echoed through the war-rooms of the army high command. Since then we have made peace with Jordan, and Iraq has been blown to smithereens by the Americans, with the enthusiastic support of Israel and its American lobby. But the Syrians are still considered a menace, because they are allied with Iran and connected with Hizbullah.

Is it worthwhile for us to live in this situation in order to keep the Golan Heights? Common sense says no. If we reach a peace agreement with Syria, it will automatically entail an agreement with Hizbullah, too. Without Syrian consent, Hizbullah cannot keep an efficient military force, since practically all Hizbullah's arms have to come from Syria or pass through Syria. Without Syrian support, Hizbullah will become a purely Lebanese party and cease to constitute a threat to us.

Moreover, Syria is a thoroughly secular country. When the Muslim Brotherhood rebelled against Assad Sr, he drowned them in blood. Also, the great majority of Syrians are Sunni. When Syria makes peace with Israel, it will have no reason to remain allied with the fanatical Shi'ite Iran.

So why don't we make peace with Syria?

At this time, there are two reasons: the one domestic, the other foreign.

The domestic reason is the existence of 20,000 settlers on the Golan Heights, who are far more popular than the West Bank settlers. They are not religious fanatics, and their settlements were set up under the auspices of the Labor Party. All Israeli governments have been afraid to touch them.

That is the real reason for the failure of all the attempts to negotiate with Syria. Yitzhak Rabin thought about it and drew back. He argued that we should first of all concentrate on settling the Palestinian issue. Ehud Barak almost came to an agreement with Syria, but escaped at the last moment. The only question that remained open was almost ludicrous: should the Syrians reach the shoreline of the Sea of Tiberias (the situation prevailing before the Six-Day War) or stay at a distance of a few dozen meters (according to the border fixed between the

British, then ruling Palestine, and the French, then ruling Syria). In popular parlance: will Assad dangle his long feet in the water of the lake? For Assad Sr, that was a question of honor.

Is it worthwhile to risk for this the lives of thousands of Israelis and Syrians, who may die in another war?

Until Israel has a government ready to answer this question and to confront the settlers, there will be no agreement with Syria.

The second reason for rejecting peace with Syria is connected with the United States. Syria belongs to George Bush's "axis of evil." The American president doesn't give a damn for the long-range interests of Israel; what is important to him is to achieve some sort of victory in the Middle East. The destruction of the Syrian regime ("a victory for democracy") will compensate him for the Iraq fiasco.

No Israeli government—and certainly not that of Olmert—would dare to disobey the American president. Therefore, it is self-evident that all peace feelers from Assad will be rejected "on the threshold." Tzipi Livni, who last week opened a new front against Olmert and presented herself almost as a peace-lover, opposes the start of negotiations with Syria as well.[87]

This affair throws some light on the complex relations between Israel and the United States: who is wagging whom—does the dog wag its tail or the tail its dog?

Olmert says that we must ignore Assad's peace offers, because we must not help him to escape Bush's wrath. Let's dwell on this utterance for a moment.

An Israeli patriot would, of course, have said exactly the opposite: If Assad is ready to make peace with us—even if only because he is afraid of the Americans—we should jump at this opportunity and exploit this situation to achieve at long last peace on our northern front.

Last week Olmert made a remarkable declaration: "As long as I am Prime Minister, we shall not give up the Golan for all eternity!" What does that mean? Either Olmert believes that his term of office coincides with God's term of office, and he will rule in eternity—or in Olmert's world, eternity extends to four years, at most.

Anyhow, until then, my taxi driver and I shall have to wait for our lunch in Damascus.

So What About Iran?

September 29, 2007

A respected American paper posted a scoop this week: Vice-President Dick Cheney, the King of Hawks, has thought up a Machiavellian scheme for an attack on Iran. Its main point: Israel will start by bombing an Iranian nuclear installation, Iran will respond by launching missiles at Israel, and this will serve as a pretext for an American attack on Iran.

Far-fetched? Not really. It is rather like what happened in 1956. Then France, Israel, and Britain secretly planned to attack Egypt in order to topple Gamal Abd-el-Nasser ("regime change" in today's lingo). It was agreed that Israeli paratroops would be dropped near the Suez Canal, and that the resulting conflict would serve as a pretext for the French and British to occupy the canal area in order to "secure" the waterway. This plan was implemented (and failed miserably).

What would happen to us if we agreed to Cheney's plan? Our pilots would risk their lives to bomb the heavily defended Iranian installations. Then, Iranian missiles would rain down on our cities. Hundreds, perhaps thousands would be killed. All this in order to supply the Americans with a pretext to go to war.

Would the pretext have stood up? In other words, is the United States obliged to enter a war on our side, even when that war is caused by us? In theory, the answer is yes. The current agreements between the United States and Israel say that America has to come to Israel's aid in any war—whoever started it.

Is there any substance to this leak? Hard to know. But it strengthens the suspicion that an attack on Iran is more imminent than people imagine.[88]

Do Bush, Cheney & Co. indeed intend to attack Iran?

I don't know, but my suspicion that they might is getting stronger.

Why? Because George Bush is nearing the end of his term of office. If it ends the way things look now, he will be remembered as a very bad president—if not the worst in the annals of the republic. His term started with the Twin Towers catastrophe, which reflected no great credit on the intelligence agencies, and would come to a close with the grievous Iraq fiasco.

There is only one year left to do something impressive and save his name in the history books. In such situations, leaders tend to look for military adventures. Taking into account the man's demonstrated character traits, the war option suddenly seems quite frightening.

True, the American army is pinned down in Iraq and Afghanistan. Even people like Bush and Cheney could not dream, at this time, of invading a country four times larger than Iraq, with three times the population.

But, quite possibly the warmongers are whispering in Bush's ear: what are you worrying about? No need for an invasion. Enough to bomb Iran, as we bombed Serbia and Afghanistan. We shall use the smartest bombs and the most sophisticated missiles against the 2,000 or so targets, in order to destroy not only the Iranian nuclear sites but also their military installations and government offices. "We shall bomb them back into the Stone Age," as an American general once said about Vietnam, or "turn their clock back 20 years," as the Israeli air force general Dan Halutz said about Lebanon.

That's a tempting idea. The United States will only use its mighty air force, missiles of all kinds, and the powerful aircraft carriers, which are already deployed in the Persian/Arabian Gulf. All these can be sent into action at any time on short notice. For a failed president approaching the end of his term, the idea of an easy, short war must have an immense attraction. And this president has already shown how hard it is for him to resist temptations of this kind.

Would this indeed be such an easy operation, a "piece of cake" in American parlance?

I doubt it.

Even "smart" bombs kill people. The Iranians are a proud, resolute, and highly motivated people. They point out that for 2,000 years they have never attacked another country, but during the eight years of the Iran–Iraq war they have amply proved their determination to defend their own when attacked.

Their first reaction to an American attack would be to close the Straits of Hormuz, the entrance to the Gulf. That would choke off a large part of the world's oil supply and cause an unprecedented worldwide economic crisis. To open the straits (if this is at all possible), the US army would have to capture and hold large areas of Iranian territory.

The short and easy war would turn into a long and hard war. What does that mean for us in Israel?

There can be little doubt that if attacked, Iran will respond as it has promised: by bombarding us with the rockets it is preparing for this precise purpose. That will not endanger Israel's existence, but it will not be pleasant either.

If the American attack turns into a long war of attrition, and if the American public comes to see it as a disaster (as is happening right now with the Iraqi adventure), some will surely put the blame on Israel. It is no secret that the pro-Israel lobby and its allies—the (mostly Jewish) neo-cons and the Christian Zionists—are pushing America into this war, just as they pushed it into Iraq. For Israeli policy, the hoped-for gains of this war may turn into giant losses—not only for Israel, but also for the American Jewish community.

If President Mahmoud Ahmadinejad did not exist, the Israeli government would have had to invent him.

He has got almost everything one could wish for in an enemy. He has a big mouth. He is a braggart. He enjoys causing scandals. He is a Holocaust denier. He prophesies that Israel will "vanish from the map" (though he did not say, as falsely reported, that *he* would wipe Israel off the map).

This week, the pro-Israel lobby organized big demonstrations against his visit to New York. They were a huge success—for Ahmadinejad. He has realized his dream of becoming the center of world attention. He has been given the opportunity to voice his arguments against Israel—some outrageous, some valid—before a worldwide audience.

But Ahmadinejad is not Iran. True, he has won popular elections, but Iran is like the orthodox parties in Israel: it is not their politicians who count, but their rabbis. The Shi'ite religious leadership makes the decisions and commands the armed forces, and this body is neither boastful nor vociferous not scandal-mongering. It exercises a lot of caution.

If Iran was really so eager to obtain a nuclear bomb, it would have acted in utmost silence and kept as low a profile as possible (as Israel did). The swaggering of Ahmadinejad would hurt this effort more than any enemy of Iran could.

It is highly unpleasant to think about a nuclear bomb in Iranian hands (and, indeed, in any hands). I hope it can be avoided by offering inducements and/or imposing sanctions. But even if this does not succeed, it would not be the end of the world, nor the end of Israel. In this area, more than in any other, Israel's deterrent power is immense. Even Ahmadinejad will not risk an exchange of queens—the destruction of Iran for the destruction of Israel.

Napoleon said that to understand a country's policy, one has only to look at the map.

If we do this, we shall see that there is no objective reason for war between Israel and Iran. On the contrary, for a long time it was believed in Jerusalem that the two countries were natural allies.

David Ben-Gurion advocated an "alliance of the periphery." He was convinced that the entire Arab world is the natural enemy of Israel, and that, therefore, allies should be sought on the fringes of the Arab world—in countries such as Turkey, Iran, Ethiopia, Chad. (He also looked for allies inside the Arab world—communities that are not Sunni-Arab, such as the Maronites, the Copts, the Kurds, the Shi'ites and others.)

At the time of the Shah, very close connections existed between Iran and Israel, some positive, some negative, some outright sinister. The Shah helped to build a pipeline from Eilat to Ashkelon, in order to transport Iranian oil to the Mediterranean, bypassing the Suez Canal. The Israel internal secret service (Shabak) trained its notorious Iranian counterpart (Savak). Israelis and Iranians acted together in Iraqi Kurdistan, helping the Kurds against their Sunni-Arab oppressors.

The Khomeini revolution did not, in the beginning, put an end to this alliance, it only drove it underground. During the Iran–Iraq war, Israel supplied Iran with arms, on the assumption that anyone fighting Arabs is our friend. At the same time, the Americans supplied arms to Saddam Hussein—one of the rare instances of a clear divergence between Washington and Jerusalem. This was bridged in the Iran–Contra Affair, when the Americans helped Israel to sell arms to the Ayatollahs.

Today, an ideological struggle is raging between the two countries, but it is mainly fought out on the rhetorical and demagogical level. I dare to say that Ahmadinejad doesn't give a fig for the Israeli–Palestinian conflict; he only uses it to make friends in the Arab world. If I were a Palestinian, I would not rely on it. Sooner or later, geography will tell and Israeli–Iranian relations will return to what they were—hopefully on a far more positive basis.

One thing I am ready to predict with confidence: whoever pushes for war against Iran will come to regret it.

Some adventures are easy to get into but hard to get out of.

The last one to find this out was Saddam Hussein. He thought that it would be a cakewalk—after all, Khomeini had killed off most of the officers, and especially the pilots, of the Shah's military. He believed that one quick Iraqi blow would be enough to bring about the collapse of Iran. He had eight long years of war to regret it.

Both the Americans and we might soon be feeling that the Iraqi mud is like whipped cream compared to the Iranian quagmire.

An Israeli Love Story

July 7, 2007

Not since the resurrection of Jesus Christ has there been such a miracle: a dead body buried in a cave has come to life again.

The "Jordanian Option" gave up its ghost almost 20 years ago. Even before that, it never was very healthy. But in 1988, some time after the outbreak of the First Intifada, it was officially buried by none other than His Majesty, King Hussein, himself. He announced that he had given up any claim to the West Bank.

It was a pitiful death. There was no proper funeral. Shimon Peres, one of its parents, pretended not to know the deceased. Yitzhak Rabin turned his back. From dust it came, to dust it returned.

And now, suddenly, it seems to have sprung to life again. Three wandering scribblers claim to have seen it with their own eyes. Not in Emmaeus, where the three apostles of Jesus saw their resurrected master, but in Washington, capital of the world!

The Israeli love story with the Hashemite dynasty started three generations ago. (Hashem was the founder of the Mecca family to which the prophet Mohammed belonged.)

In World War II, Iraq rebelled against the Hashemite king, who was imposed on them by the British at the time they installed another branch of the family in Trans-Jordan. The Iraqi king and his entourage fled to Palestine. Here he was warmly received by the Zionist leadership, which provided him with a secret radio station on Mount Carmel. Many years later, I heard this from one of the people directly involved, Minister Eliyahu Sassoon.

The British army returned the Hashemites to power in Baghdad. But, as Sassoon added in sorrow, they repaid good with bad: immediately after their restoration they adopted an extreme anti-Zionist line. By the way, the Irgun underground organization was cooperating with the British at the time, and its commander, David Raziel, was killed in Iraq in the course of the operation.

Issam Sartawi, one of the PLO leaders, a refugee from Acre who grew up in Iraq, later claimed that when the Hashemites returned to Baghdad, the British organized a massacre of the Jews in order to gain them nationalist popularity. The documents about this infamous episode are still kept under wraps in the British archives.

But the relations with the Hashemites continued. On the eve of the 1948 war, the Zionist leadership kept in close contact with King Abdullah of Trans-Jordan. Between the king and Golda Meir, several secret plans were hatched, but when the time came the king did not dare to break Arab solidarity, and so he also invaded Palestine. It has been claimed this was done in close coordination with David Ben-Gurion. And indeed, the new Israeli army avoided attacking the Jordanian forces (except in the Latrun area, in an attempt to open the way to besieged West Jerusalem).

The cooperation between Abdullah and Ben-Gurion bore the hoped-for fruit: the territory that was allotted by the UN to the putative Palestinian Arab state was partitioned between Israel and the renamed Kingdom of Jordan (the Gaza Strip was given to Egypt). The Palestinian state did not come into being, and Israeli–Jordanian cooperation flourished. It continued after King Abdullah was assassinated at the holy shrines of Jerusalem, and his grandson, the boy Hussein, took his place.

At that time, the tide of pan-Arab nationalism was running high, and Gamal Abd-el-Nasser, its prophet, was the idol of the Arab world. The Palestinian people, who had been deprived of a political identity, also saw its salvation in an all-Arab entity. There was a danger that the Jordanian king might be toppled any minute, but Israel announced that if this happened, the Israeli army would enter Jordan at once. The king continued to sit on his throne supported by Israeli bayonets.

Things reached a climax during Black September (1970), when Hussein crushed the PLO forces in blood and fire. The Syrians rushed to their defense and started to cross the border. In coordination with Henry Kissinger, Golda Meir issued an ultimatum: if the Syrians did not retreat at once, the Israeli army would enter. The Syrians gave up, the king was saved. The PLO forces went to Lebanon.

At the height of the crisis, I called upon the Israeli government in the Knesset to adopt the opposite course: to enable the Palestinians in the West Bank to set up a Palestinian state side by side with Israel. Years later, Ariel Sharon told me that he had proposed the same during the secret deliberations of the army general staff. (Later, Sharon asked me to arrange a meeting between him and Yassir Arafat, to discuss this plan: to topple the regime in Jordan and turn the country into a Palestinian state, instead of the West Bank. Arafat refused to meet him and disclosed the proposal to the king.)

The Jordanian option was more than a political concept—it was a love story. For decades, almost all Israeli leaders were enamored of it, from Chaim Weizmann to David Ben-Gurion, from Golda to Peres.

What did the Hashemite family have that enchanted the Zionist and Israeli establishment?

In the course of the years I have heard many rational-sounding arguments. But I am convinced that at root it was not rational at all. The one decisive virtue of the Hashemite Dynasty was—and is—quite simple: they are not Palestinians.

From its first day, the Zionist Movement has lived in total denial of the Palestinian issue. As long as possible, it denied the very existence of the Palestinian people. Since this has become ridiculous, it denies the existence of a Palestinian partner for peace. In any case, it denies the possibility of a viable Palestinian state next to Israel.

This denial has deep roots in the unconscious of the Zionist Movement and the Israeli leadership. Zionism strove for the creation of a Jewish national home in a land in which another people was living.

Since Zionism was an idealistic movement imbued with profound moral values, it could not bear the thought that it was committing a historical injustice to another people. It was necessary to suppress and deny the feeling of guilt engendered by this fact.

The unconscious guilt feelings were deepened by the 1948 war, in which more than half the Palestinian people were separated from their lands. The idea of turning the West Bank over to the Hashemite kingdom was built on the illusion that there is no Palestinian people ("They are all Arabs!"), so it could suffer no injustice.

The Jordanian Option is a euphemism. Its real name is "Anti-Palestinian Option." That's what it's all about. Everything else is unimportant.

That may explain the curious fact that since the 1967 war, no effort has been made to realize this "option." The High Priests of the Jordanian Option, who preached it from every hilltop, did not lift a finger to bring it about. On the contrary, they did everything possible to prevent its realization.

For example, during Yitzhak Rabin's first term as prime minister, after the 1973 war, Henry Kissinger had a brilliant idea: to return the town of Jericho to King Hussein. Thus a fait accompli would have been established: the Hashemite flag would wave over West Bank territory.

When Foreign Minister Yigal Alon brought the proposal to Rabin, he was met with an adamant refusal. Golda Meir had promised in her time that new elections would be held before any occupied territory was returned to the Arabs. "I am not prepared to go to elections because of Jericho!" Rabin exclaimed.

The same happened when Shimon Peres reached a secret agreement with King Hussein and brought the finished product to the then prime minister, Yitzhak Shamir. Shamir threw the agreement into the waste bin.

("You face a difficult choice," I once joked in a Knesset debate, "Whether not to return the occupied territories to Jordan or not to return them to the Palestinians.")

One of the interesting aspects of this long love story was that not one of the Israeli lovers ever took the trouble to look at the problem from the other side. In the depths of their heart, they despised the Jordanians as they despised all Arabs.

In the middle of the 1980s, I received an unofficial invitation to Jordan, then officially still an "enemy country." True, I entered with a rather dubious passport, but, once there, I registered as an Israeli journalist. Since I was the first Israeli to go around Amman openly, declaring my identity, I attracted quite a lot of attention in higher circles.

A senior government official invited me to dinner in a posh restaurant. On a paper napkin he drew the map of Jordan and explained to me the whole problem in a nutshell:

> We are surrounded by countries which are very different from each other. Here is the Zionist Israel, and here the nationalist Syria. In the West Bank, radical tendencies flourish, and in close-by Lebanon there is a conservative sectarian regime. Here is the secular Iraq of Saddam Hussein, and here the devout Saudi Arabia. From all these directions, ideas and people flow into Jordan. We absorb all of them. But we cannot quarrel with any of our neighbors. When we move a bit towards Syria, on the following day we have to make a gesture towards Saudi Arabia. When we come closer to Israel, we must appease Iraq quickly.

The obvious conclusion: the Jordanian Option was a folly right from the beginning. But nobody in the Israeli leadership grasped that. As the wise Boutros Boutros-Ghali once told me: "You have in Israel the greatest experts on Arab affairs. They have read every book and every article. They know everything, and understand nothing—because they have never lived for one day in an Arab country."

Old loves do not die. True, the First Intifada pushed aside the Jordanian Option and the leaders of Israel flirted with the Palestinian Option. But their heart was not in the new love, and they acted as if driven by a demon. That explains why no serious effort was made to fulfill the Oslo agreement and to bring the process to its logical conclusion: a Palestinian state next to Israel.

Now, suddenly, people are once more talking about Jordan. Perhaps one could ask King Abdullah II to send his army into the West Bank to fight Hamas. Perhaps we could bury the "two-state solution" in a Jordanian–Palestinian federation that would allow the Jordanians to take over the West Bank again.

The King was appalled. That is just what he needs! To incorporate the turbulent and divided Palestinian population in his kingdom! To open the border to a new flood of refugees and immigrants! He hastened to deny any part in the scheme.

Federation? That is quite possible, he said—but only after a free Palestinian state has come into being, not before, and certainly not instead. Then the citizens may decide freely.

A famous book by the Israeli author Yehoshua Kenaz is called *Returning Lost Loves*. But it seems that this old love is gone forever.

6
Will the Circle Be Unbroken?

This is a question that remains to be answered. Below are some of Avnery's views on the current situation in Israel and Palestine and its global context. —SRP

A Plan for the 21st Century[89]

January 3, 2000

At the beginning of the twentieth century, a few idealists advocated the creation of a "United States of Europe." They were ridiculed. But after two terrible World Wars and tens of millions dead, the European Union was created, a confederacy that practically abolished borders and set up a united economy.

Today I dare to forecast that the twenty-first century will see the creation of a "United States of the World": a global order headed by a world authority.

The last century—like the one that preceded it—was dominated by the national state. This idea won in Europe and expanded from there to all the other continents. Israel, as a "democratic Jewish state" and the coming State of Palestine are late-born children of that era.

We, who were born into this reality, can hardly realize that the national state is a recent human creation. Even at the beginning of last century, the Russian czar, the Austrian emperor and the Ottoman sultan were still potent rulers, each of whom reigned over many peoples speaking many languages.

The national state (as distinguished, for example, from the city-state or the dynastic state) did not come into being by accident. New technologies created a reality that required a (comparatively) big economic, cultural, and military unit. The local market had to be big enough to sustain an economy, population, and territory that could sustain a modern army big enough to defend the fatherland. The national idea satisfied these requirements and gave the masses, together

197

with the new democracy, the motivation and the cohesion that held the new state together.

However, since then the objective requirements have changed with the new technologies. Today's market is global, multinational corporations span the world. Communications, including the Internet, are global.[90] The twenty-first century was ushered in by a celebration that was truly worldwide. English has become the worldwide lingua franca. Tens of millions have left their homelands to look for greener pastures in the developed countries. Nuclear weapons have made old-style wars inconceivable. Humans have walked on the moon; our devices have reached Mars. Not only little states like Denmark and Israel, but even Germany and France, great powers at the beginning of the twentieth century, cannot stand alone any more.

While we Israelis were busy building our national state, the world was already moving from a national agenda to a regional one. Europe was unified, and other parts of the world tried to emulate it. (Some 54 years ago, I tried to apply the same principle to ourselves by creating the idea of a "Semitic union.") But even the idea of regional unions has already become obsolete.

Human consciousness always stumbles behind objective reality. It does so at the beginning of the twenty-first century: While reality does cry out for a world order, consciousness is still nationalistic. Some manifestations are downright ridiculous. For example, France won the international soccer championship and was floating on a wave of nationalist hysteria. But the stars of the French team were foreigners, headed by an Algerian, the likes of whom are viewed by many of the French as subhuman. That did not dampen the spirits of the masses. Neither were they troubled by the fact that French soldiers took part in an action in Kosovo that destroyed one of the pillars of the national state: the principle of "non-intervention in its domestic affairs." (Witness the Holocaust.)[91]

It is impossible to know how the aim of a new world order will be achieved. Perhaps the United Nations will assume the role of a supranational authority. If so, it will have to change completely. In the Security Council, the world government, the veto power of the "permanent members" must be abolished, so that Russia, for example, will not be able to block a Kosovo-like intervention. In the General Assembly, the world parliament, the representation of each member must correspond to the size of its population, so the Fiji Islands will not have the same voting power as the United States.

The UN must have at its disposal a standing army, which owes allegiance to the UN only, and that will be ready for immediate intervention in a Rwanda-like genocide. A world court must be competent to adjudicate all conflicts between states, as our national courts adjudicate conflicts between individuals. A world police must be ready to enforce the world law.

In the European Union, the national states were not dismantled; each kept its flag, language, and traditions. The same will be true in the coming world order. But the national states will be subject to a compulsory world order, much as citizens are subject to the laws of their state.

An unrealistic vision? Not at all. I am quite certain that this will be reality by the year 2100. What a pity that I shall not be around to see it.

A New Consensus

September 24, 2005

In "The Second Coming," the Irish poet W. B. Yeats described chaos thus:

> Turning and turning in the widening gyre
> The falcon cannot hear the falconer;
> Things fall apart; the centre cannot hold;
> Mere anarchy is loosed upon the world,
> The blood-dimmed tide is loosed, and everywhere
> The ceremony of innocence is drowned;
> The best lack all conviction, while the worst
> Are full of passionate intensity.

The defining phrase, as I read it, is "the centre cannot hold." It is a military metaphor: on the classical battlefield, the main force was located in the middle, with the flanks secured by lighter forces. The enemy's aim was to break the center, often by turning the flanks. But even if the flanks collapsed, as long as the center held, the battle was not lost.

That also holds for a political struggle. Everything hinges on the public in the center. If one wants to make a revolution, the stability of the center must be undermined.

That was the aim of the settlers, when they started their nationwide campaign against the Gaza withdrawal. It ended in utter collapse, a defeat of historic proportions. In spite of the dramatic spectacle of the uprooting of the settlements, where everything was planned down to the minutest detail by the rabbis and the army, there was no real public crisis, no national trauma. In Yeats' language: "The centre held."

To understand Israel, one has to comprehend the nature of this center. What convictions hold it together?

A national consensus is not immutable. It changes all the time, but

very, very slowly, in an unseen, unfelt process. Only rarely, as a result
of a dramatic occurrence, does it change rapidly. That happened, for
example, in the 1967 war. A day before the war started, only a few of
us dared to dream that the Arab world would recognize the State of
Israel in its then borders. A day after, the dream had become a nightmare; anyone speaking about the "1967 borders" was considered a
traitor. But that was an exceptional event. Ordinarily, the consensus
moves as silently as a polar glacier.

The consensus of the Israeli-Jewish majority in the fall of 2005 rests
on three pillars.

First: A Jewish state. That is the common denominator of almost all
Jews in Israel. If one does not grasp the centrality of this conviction,
one understands nothing about Israel.

"A Jewish state" is a state inhabited by Jews. True, it is unavoidable
that some citizens will be non-Jews, but their number must be held to the
absolute minimum, so that they are unable to have any influence on the
character and policy of the state. This aim is embedded in the very
substance of the Zionist Movement, which started with a book called *Der
Judenstaat*. It derives its force from the hundreds of years of persecution,
when Jews, helpless and defenseless, were at the mercy of all.

The Jewish Israelis want to live in a state of their own, of themselves alone, where they are masters of their fate. This desire is
anchored so deeply in the hearts of most of them, that there is no
chance for any contrary plan—be it "Greater Israel" or a "bi-national
state." Consequently, there is no chance at all that the majority would
agree to a massive return of Arab refugees to the territory of Israel.

Second: Enlarging the state. The Zionist Movement wanted to take
hold of the country then called Palestine, all or most of it, and to settle
in it.

This, too, is a profound desire, imbedded in the very character of
the movement, a part of its "genes." But this second desire is subordi-
nate to the first one. If there were a possibility of conquering the entire
country and "getting rid" of all the Palestinian population, as proposed
by the extreme right, it would certainly appeal to many. But the majority knows now that this is not a practical proposition. The conclusion
is that the parts of the country with a dense Palestinian population
must be "given up."[92]

Third: Recognition of the Palestinian people. That is a great change.
It contradicts the classic position of the Zionist Movement which was
adopted by all Israeli governments until the Oslo agreement, expressed by
the famous dictum of Golda Meir: "There is no such thing as a Palestinian   people."   When,   in   the   1950s,   we   demanded   the

recognition the Palestinian people, we were considered traitors or fools, or both. But two intifadas, the international situation, and our consistent public opinion campaign have done their work.

The combination of these three principles forms the picture of the present consensus: Israel must annex certain areas of the West Bank and relinquish the rest.

This consensus encompasses the major part of the Israeli political landscape, from Ariel Sharon, Binyamin Netanyahu and Uzi Landau to Shimon Peres and Yossi Beilin.

The disagreements concern only the extent of the annexation. It reminds one—*mutatis mutandis*—of the story attributed to Bernard Shaw, who offered a duchess £1 million if she would sleep with him. When she consented, he reduced his offer to £100, saying: "Now that we have agreed on the principle, all that remains is to settle the price."

Sharon has spoken in the past about annexing 58 percent of the West Bank, comprising the settlement blocs, Greater Jerusalem (with the territory connecting it to Ma'aleh Adumim), the Jordan valley, and the areas between them. He was prepared to leave to the Palestinians their towns and densely populated rural areas. Recently, he has hinted that he might give up the Jordan Valley. He asserts that President Bush has agreed to his plan, but while Sharon talks about "settlement blocs," Bush spoke about "population centers." There is a big difference between the two: a "settlement bloc" includes not only the large settlement itself, but also the smaller ones around it and the area between them. A "population center" means only the large settlement itself, which would leave a much smaller area to be annexed.

At Camp David, Ehud Barak proposed the annexation of 21 percent of the West Bank, in a way that would have cut the Palestinian territory into pieces. He also wanted to "rent" 13 percent more in the Jordan valley. Later, at the Taba conference, the annexation came down to 8 percent, but the tentative accord was repudiated by the Israeli government.

Yossi Beilin was the father of the "settlement blocs" concept, when, long ago, he reached an unofficial agreement with Abu Mazen (Mahmoud Abbas). The more recent Geneva Initiative, proposed by Beilin and Yassir Abed-Rabbo, speaks only about an annexation of 2.3 percent, as part of a 1:1 territorial swap.

The Separation Fence now being built by the Sharon government is designed to further the ongoing enlargement of the settlements. It annexes 8 percent of the West Bank along its western border with Israel. The annexation of the Jordan valley in the East is, for the time being, left open.

These are the boundaries of the present consensus. The debate in Israel, in the near future, will center on the extent and the means of the annexation.

One version has it that there should be no negotiations with the Palestinians, since they will not agree to large annexations. Therefore, Israel should continue with "unilateral" steps, as practiced in the Gaza withdrawal, and annex territories without agreement. The slogan: "Israel itself will fix its borders." The contrary version says that agreement can be achieved on a limited annexation within the framework of an exchange of territories.

The extreme right rejects this consensus. It does not want any compromise. It waves the divine title deed, personally signed by the Almighty, and wants to annex the entire West Bank and Gaza Strip. Without saying so explicitly, this concept means the total expulsion of the Palestinians from Palestine.

The radical peace movement opposes the consensus from the opposite direction. It believes that the future of Israel will only be secure in a lasting peace, based on an agreement between equals and the reconciliation of the two peoples. This camp believes that the agreement must be based on the pre-1967 Green Line border, and that only in the course of negotiations will it become clear if an understanding on fair territorial exchanges can be reached.

However, the main thing is that the consensus is moving. Greater Israel is dead. The partition of the country is now accepted by the overwhelming majority. This means that one can influence public opinion. The "disengagement" affair has shown that settlements can be removed. The public accepted the precedent without flinching. Now the task is to convince the public that real negotiations should be started.

There is someone to talk with, and there is something to talk about.

A Bruised Reed

September 1, 2007

In the year 701 BC, the Assyrian king Sennacherib besieged Jerusalem. The Bible records the words which the Assyrian general, Rabshakeh, addressed to Hezekiah, king of Judah: "Now, behold, thou trusteth upon the staff of this bruised reed, even upon Egypt, on which if a man lean, it will go into his hand and pierce it: so is Pharaoh, king of Egypt, unto all that trust on him."

The writers of the Bible were so impressed by this phrase that they quoted it twice (2 Kings, 18:21 and Isaiah 36:6).

One has to understand the historical context: Egypt was then a great power. For hundreds of years, it had dominated all its neighbors, including the area of present-day Syria, Lebanon, and Israel. The Assyrians, on the other side, were an upstart force. After conquering the Kingdom of Israel in Samaria, the more important of the two Hebrew kingdoms, they tried to occupy the tiny kingdom of Judah, which relied for its defense on mighty Egypt.

Judah held out. For unknown reasons, the Assyrians lifted their siege and retreated from Jerusalem. The kingdom of Judah remained intact for another century—until the Babylonians, who took the place of the Assyrians, conquered it, too. Egypt could not save it. By that time, it had indeed become a bruised reed.

The United States is the modern heir of ancient Egypt. It is colossal, rich, and strong, a cultural, economic, and military power. Pharaoh, king of America, dominates the world as Pharaoh, king of Egypt, once dominated the Semitic region. And like any dominating empire, it is interested in the existing world order and defends the status quo against all rising forces in the world.

Israel, therefore, considers its special relationship with the United States as the foremost guarantee of its national security. No occupied territories nor weapon systems can be a substitute for the umbilical cord that connects Jerusalem with Washington, a connection that has no parallel in the present world, and perhaps even in history.

Many have tried—and are still trying—to explain this special relationship, but nobody has yet succeeded in measuring its full extent.

This relationship has an ideological dimension: the two states were created by immigrants from afar who took over a country and dispossessed the indigenous population. Both believed that they were chosen by God, who had given them the Promised Land. Both began with a beachhead from which they set off on a historic march that seemed irresistible—the Americans "from sea to shining sea," the Israelis from the coastal plain to the Jordan.

This relationship has a strategic dimension: Israel serves the essential American need for the domination of Middle East oil, while America serves the Israeli government's endeavor to dominate the country up to the Jordan and overcome the resistance of the local population.

This relationship has a political dimension: the United States has immense influence in Jerusalem, and Israel has immense influence in Washington. This influence is based on the millions of Jews who emigrated to America a century ago, They now constitute a powerful community, admirably organized, with a political-economic impact on all centers of social power. The combined might of the Jewish-Zionist lobby and the Christian-Evangelical one, which also supports the Israeli right, is immeasurable.

(There is a story about an Israeli politician, who proposed joining the United States as the 51st state. "Are you mad?" his colleagues retorted, "If we were another state, we would have two senators and a few congressmen. Now we have at least 80 senators and hundreds of congressmen!")

Dozens of small countries throughout the world see the way to Washington as passing through Jerusalem. When they want to curry favor with the United States, they first establish close relations with Israel, as if it were a doorkeeper who cannot be passed without a bribe.

This influence is not unlimited, as some believe. The Jonathan Pollard affair has shown that all the assembled might of the pro-Israel lobby is not enough to secure a pardon for one minor Israeli spy.[93] And Israel has just failed to prevent the sale of massive quantities of arms to Saudi Arabia (though of course it is getting even more aid for free).

Neither is the influence a one-way street. When the United States gives Israel a direct order, Jerusalem obeys. For example, when Jerusalem decided to sell China an expensive intelligence airplane, the pride of the Israeli industry, Washington compelled Israel to cancel the deal, causing grievous damage to Israeli–Chinese relations.[94]

But in Washington and Jerusalem there is a deeply entrenched belief that the interests of the two countries are so closely connected that they cannot be told apart. What is good for one is good for the other. These Siamese twins cannot be separated.

Nevertheless, it is worthwhile, from time to time, to come back to the words of the Assyrian general 2,708 years ago. Great powers arise and fall, nothing stands still.

The twentieth century has been called the "American Century." At its beginning, the United States was just another country on the margin of the world system. At its end, after two World Wars that were decided by the rising power of the American giant, it had become the sole world power, the final arbiter of everything. So much so, that a learned professor fantasized about "*The End of History*" under American tutelage.

The twenty-first century will not be another "American Century." One can foresee a slow but steady decline in the status of the United States. Europe is uniting, slowly but surely, and its economic power is growing steadily. Russia is gradually becoming a great power again, helped by its enormous oil and gas reserves. And, most importantly, the two population giants, China and India, are rapidly climbing the economic ladder.

Probably, nothing dramatic will happen. The United States will not collapse suddenly, like the Soviet Union, a giant with feet of clay. It will not go down in military defeat, like Nazi Germany, whose megalomaniac military ambitions were based on a quite inadequate economic base. But the relative power of the United States is in an inevitable process of gradual descent.

The events in Iraq are a small example. America did not enter this adventure only to protect Israel, as the two professors Walt and Mearsheimer assert in their new book. Nor because it wanted to rid poor Iraq of a bloodthirsty tyrant. As we wrote here at the time, it invaded Iraq in order to take hold of the essential oil reserves of the Middle East and station a permanent American garrison in their center. Now it is sinking, as expected, in a quagmire. But a country like the United States, which was able to absorb a shameful debacle in Vietnam, will also absorb the coming fiasco in Iraq. The military might of the United States, unequalled in the world, is based on its unprecedented economic power.

But many small defeats add up to a big one. The war has hurt American prestige, self-confidence, and moral standing (Guantanamo, Abu Ghraib). There was a time when the United States inspired admiration throughout the world. Nowadays, opinion polls show that in almost all the important countries the majority hates the United States. The colossal American national debt also does not bode well.

Is it really good to be tied to the fate of the United States for life and death? Apart from moral considerations, is it wise to put all our eggs— all of them—in one basket?

A cynic might say: why not? America still dominates the world. It will continue to do so for quite a while. If and when it loses control, we shall say goodbye and look for new allies. That is what we did with the British. After World War I we helped them to get the Mandate over Palestine, and in return they helped us to establish the Hebrew community here. In the end, they went away and we stayed. After that, we helped France, and in return they gave us the nuclear reactor in Dimona. In the end they went away, and the reactor remained.

This is called "Realpolitik," the politics of reality. We shall get from the Americans what we can and then, in a generation or two, we shall see. Perhaps the United States will lose many of its assets. Perhaps it will stop supporting Israel when a new reality brings about a change in its interests.

I do not believe that our present policy is wise. Our so-called "realistic" policy sees the reality of today, but not the reality of tomorrow. And after all, we did not found a state for some limited time, but for generations to come. We must think about the reality of tomorrow.

Undoubtedly, the world of tomorrow is not going to be uni-polar, all-American, but multi-polar, a world where influence is divided between many centers, such as Washington and Beijing, Moscow and New Delhi, Brussels and Rio de Janeiro.

It would be wise to start preparing today for this world of tomorrow.

In what way?

I once likened our situation to that of a gambler at a roulette table, who has an incredible streak of luck. In front of him, the pile of chips grows and grows. He could stop at the right moment, change the chips into millions of dollars and live happily ever after. But he cannot. The betting fever will not let go. So he continues even when his fortunes change, with predictable results.

At this moment, we are at the height of our power. Our connection with the United States, which is still all-powerful, gives us a standing much beyond our natural capabilities.

This is the time to cash in the chips for money, exchange our temporary gains for permanent assets. To give up the occupied territories and make peace, establish good relations with our neighbors, strike deep roots in the region, so that we will be able to hold on when the will and ability of America to protect us at all costs has evaporated.

That is even more true if we take into consideration the rise of Islamic radicalism, which is a natural reaction to the actions of the US–Israeli axis. The Israeli–Palestinian conflict is the main cause of this earthquake, which may one day unleash a tsunami. Both we and the Americans would be well advised to start work soon on removing the causes of this natural phenomenon.

America is far from being a bruised reed—now. Those who want to can still lean on this staff for some time to come. But it would be wise for us to make good use of this time to ensure our existence in peace in the coming world.

Inshallah

March 17, 2007

Not only the Palestinians must be breathing a deep sigh of relief after the swearing in of the Palestinian National Unity Government. We Israelis have good reason to do the same.

This event is a great blessing, not only for them, but also for us—if indeed we are interested in a peace that will put an end to the historic conflict.

For the Palestinians, the immediate blessing is the elimination of the threat of civil war.

That was a nightmare. It was also absurd. Palestinian fighters were shooting at each other in the streets of Gaza, gladdening the hearts of the occupation authorities. As in the arena of ancient Rome, gladiators killed each other for the amusement of the spectators. People who had spent years together in Israeli prisons suddenly acted like mortal enemies.

That was not yet a civil war. But the bloody incidents could have led there. Many Palestinians were worried that if the clashes were not stopped immediately, a fully fledged fratricidal war would indeed break out. That was, of course, also the great hope of the Israeli government—that Hamas and Fatah would annihilate each other without Israel having to lift a finger. The Israeli intelligence services did indeed predict this.

I was not worried on that account. In my view, a Palestinian civil war was never in the cards.

First of all, because the basic conditions for a civil war are absent. The Palestinian people are unified in their ethnic, cultural, and historical composition. Palestine does not resemble Iraq, with its three peoples who are distinct ethnically (Arabs and Kurds), religiously (Shi'ites and Sunnis) and geographically (north, center and south). It does not resemble Ireland, where the Protestants, the descendants of settlers, were fighting the Catholic descendants of the indigenous population. It does not resemble African countries, whose borders were fixed by colonial masters without any consideration of tribal boundaries. It certainly had no revolutionary upheaval like those that brought on the civil wars in England, France, and Russia, nor an issue that split the population like slavery in the United States.

The bloody incidents that broke out in the Gaza Strip were struggles between party militias, aggravated by feuds between *hamulahs* (extended families). History has seen such struggles in almost all liberation movements. For example, after World War I, when the British were compelled to grant Home Rule to the Irish, a bloody struggle among the freedom fighters broke out at once. Irish Catholics killed Irish Catholics.

In the days of the struggle of the Jewish community in Palestine against the British colonial regime ("the Mandate"), a civil war was averted only thanks to one person: Menachem Begin, the commander of the Irgun. He was determined to prevent a fratricidal war at all costs. David Ben-Gurion wanted to eliminate the Irgun, which rejected his leadership and undermined his policies. In the so-called "season," he ordered his loyal Haganah organization to kidnap Irgun members and turn them over to the British police, which tortured them and put them in prison abroad. But Begin prohibited his men from using their weapons to defend themselves against Jews.

Such a struggle among the Palestinians will not turn into a civil war, because the entire Palestinian people oppose this strenuously. Everybody remembers that during the Arab Rebellion of 1936, the Palestinian leader at that time, the Grand Mufti Hadj Amin al-Husseini, butchered his Palestinian rivals. During the three years of the rebellion (called "the Events" in Zionist terminology) Palestinians killed more of their own people than they killed of their British and Jewish opponents.

The result: when the Palestinian people came face to face with their supreme existential test, in the war of 1948, they were split and splintered, lacking unified leadership and dependent on the mercies of the bickering Arab governments, who were intriguing against each other. They were unable to stand up to the much smaller organized Jewish community, which rapidly set up a unified and efficient army. The result was the *Nakba*, the terrible historic tragedy of the Palestinian people. What happened in 1936 still touches the life of every single Palestinian to this very day.

It is difficult to start a civil war if the people are against it. Even provocations from outside—and I assume that there has been no lack of these—cannot ignite it.

Therefore I did not doubt for a moment that in the end a Unity Government would indeed come about, and I am glad that this has now happened.

Why is this good for Israel? I am going to say something that will shock many Israelis and their friends in the world:

If Hamas did not exist, it would have to be invented.

If a Palestinian government had been set up without Hamas, we should have to boycott it until Hamas was included.

And if negotiations do lead to a historical settlement with the Palestinian leadership, we should make it a condition that Hamas, too, must sign it.

Sounds crazy? Of course. But that is the lesson history teaches us from the experience of other wars of liberation.

The Palestinian population in the occupied territories is almost evenly divided between Fatah and Hamas. It makes no sense at all to sign an agreement with half a people and continue the war against the other half. After all, we shall make serious concessions for peace—such as withdrawing to much narrower borders and giving East Jerusalem back to its owners. Shall we do so in return for an agreement that half the Palestinian people will not accept and will not be committed to? To me this sounds like the height of folly.

I shall go further: Hamas and Fatah together represent only the part of the Palestinian people that lives in the West Bank, the Gaza Strip, and East Jerusalem. But millions of Palestinian refugees (no one knows for sure how many) live outside of the territory of Palestine and Israel.

If we strive indeed for a complete end to the historic conflict, we must reach out for a solution that includes them, too. Therefore I strongly question the wisdom of Tzipi Livni and her colleagues, who demand that the Saudis drop from their peace plan any mention of the refugee problem. Simply put: that is stupid.

Common sense would advise the exact opposite: to demand that the Saudi peace initiative, which has become an official pan-Arab peace plan, include the matter of the refugees, so that the final agreement will also constitute a solution of the refugee problem.

That will not be easy, for sure. The refugee problem has psychological roots that touch the very heart of the Palestinian–Zionist conflict, and it concerns the fate of millions of living human beings. But when the Arab peace plan says that there must be an "agreed upon" solution—meaning agreed upon with Israel—it transfers it from the realm of irreconcilable ideologies to the real world, the world of negotiations and compromise. I have discussed this many times with Arab personalities, and I am convinced that an agreement is possible.

The new Palestinian government is based on the "Mecca Agreement."[95] It seems that it would not have been possible without the energetic intervention of King Abdullah of Saudi Arabia.

The international background has to be considered. The President of the United States is now busy with desperate efforts to bring his Iraqi adventure to a conclusion that will not go down in history as a total disaster. For this purpose he is trying to bring together a Sunni Front that would block Iran and help to put an end to the Sunni violence in Iraq.

That is, of course, a simplistic idea. It disregards the enormous complexity of the realities of our region. Bush has presided over the setting up in Iraq of a government dominated by the Shi'ites. He has tried to isolate Sunni Syria. And Hamas is, of course, a pious Sunni organization.

But the American ship of state is beginning to turn around. Being a giant ship, it can do this only very slowly. Under American pressure, the Saudi king has agreed (perhaps unwillingly) to take upon himself the leadership of the Arab world, after Egypt has failed in this task. The king has persuaded Bush that he has to speak with Syria. Now he is trying to persuade him to accept Hamas.

In this picture, Israel is a hindrance. A few days ago Ehud Olmert flew to America and told the conference of the Jewish lobby, AIPAC, that a withdrawal from Iraq would be a disaster (contrary, by the way, to the opinion of more than 80 percent of American Jews, who support early withdrawal). This week, the US ambassador in Tel-Aviv hinted that from now on the Government of Israel is allowed to conduct negotiations with Syria—and it may be assumed that this hint will turn into an order before long. In the meantime, no change in the position of the Israeli government is noticeable.

Unfortunately, just at this moment, with a newly formed Palestinian government that has a good chance of being strong and stable, the government of Israel is becoming more and more destabilized.[96]

Olmert's support rating in the polls is approaching zero. The percentage points can be counted on the fingers of one hand. Practically everybody speaks about his political demise within weeks, perhaps after the publication of the interim report of the Vinograd commission on the Second Lebanon War. But even if Olmert manages to survive, his will be a lame duck government, unable to start anything new, and certainly no bold initiative vis-à-vis the new Palestinian government.

But if Bush supports us on one side, and the Saudi king on the other, perhaps we shall after all take a few steps forward. As people in this region say: *in sha Allah*, if God wills.

The Palestinian Mandela

September 15, 2007

The division of the Palestinian territories into a "Hamastan" in the Gaza Strip and a "Fatahland" in the West Bank is a disaster.

A disaster for the Palestinians, a disaster for peace, and therefore also a disaster for Israelis.

The Israeli political and military leadership is happy about the split, according to the doctrine: "What's bad for Palestine is good for Israel." This doctrine has guided Zionist policy right from the beginning. Haim Arlosoroff, the Zionist leader who was murdered by hands unknown on the seashore of Tel-Aviv in 1933, already condemned this doctrine in his last speech: "Not everything that is bad for the Arabs is good for the Jews, and not everything that is good for the Arabs is bad for the Jews."

Will the Palestinians overcome this split?

It seems that the chances for that are getting smaller by the day. The gulf between the two parties is getting wider and wider.

The Fatah people in the West Bank, headed by President Mahmoud Abbas, condemn Hamas as a gang of fanatics who are imitating Iran and are guided by it, and who, like the Ayatollahs, are leading their people towards catastrophe.

The Hamas people accuse Abbas of being a Palestinian Marshal Petain, who has made a deal with the occupier and is sliding down the slippery slope of collaboration.

The propaganda of both sides is full of venom, and the mutual violence is reaching new heights.

It looks like a cul-de-sac. Many Palestinians have despaired of finding a way out. Others are searching for creative solutions. Afif Safieh, the chief of the PLO mission in Washington, for example, proposes setting up a Palestinian government composed entirely of neutral experts, who are members neither of Fatah nor of Hamas. The chances of that are very slim indeed.

But in private conversations in Ramallah, one name pops up more and more often: Marwan Barghouti.

"He holds the key in his hand," they say there, "both for the Fatah–Hamas and for the Israeli–Palestinian conflicts."

Some see Marwan as the Palestinian Nelson Mandela.

Superficially, the two are very different, both physically and in temperament. But they have much in common.

Both became national heroes behind prison bars. Both were convicted of terrorism. Both supported violent struggle. Mandela supported the 1961 decision of the National African Congress to start an armed struggle against the racist government (but not against the white civilians). He remained in prison for 28 years and refused to buy his freedom by signing a statement denouncing "terrorism." Marwan supported the armed struggle of Fatah's Tanzim organization and has been sentenced to several life terms.

But both were in favor of peace and reconciliation, even before going to prison. I saw Barghouti for the first time in 1997, when he joined a Gush Shalom demonstration in Harbata, the village neighboring Bil'in, against the building of the Modiin-Illit settlement that was just starting. Five years later, during his trial, we demonstrated in the courthouse under the slogan "Barghouti to the negotiating table, not to prison!"

Last week we visited Marwan's family in Ramallah.

I had met Fadwa Barghouti for the first time at Yassir Arafat's funeral. Her face was wet with tears. We were crowded among the multitude of mourners, the din was earsplitting and we could not exchange more than a few words.

This time she was calm and composed. She laughed only when she heard that Teddy Katz, a Gush activist who took part in the meeting, had sacrificed a toenail for Marwan: during our protest in court we were violently attacked by the guards and one of them stamped his heavy boot on Teddy's sandaled foot.

Fadwa Barghouti is a lawyer by profession, a mother of four (three sons, one daughter). The oldest, Kassem, has already been in prison for half a year without trial. She is a dark-blond woman ("All the family members, except Marwan, are blond," she explained, adding with a rare smile: "Perhaps because of the Crusaders.")

The Barghoutis are a large *hamula* (extended family), inhabiting six villages near Bir Zeit. Dr Mustapha Barghouti, the physician who is well known for his human rights activities, is a distant relative. Marwan and Fadwa—also a Barghouti by birth—were born in Kobar village.

Marwan Barghouti's family lives in a nice apartment in a condominium building. On my way there, I noticed the widespread building activity in Ramallah—it looks as if new buildings are going on every corner, including commercial high-rises.

Near the door of the apartment, an embroidered sign says in English: "Welcome to my home." The apartment itself is decorated with many images of Marwan Barghouti, including a large drawing inspired by the famous photo that shows him in court, raising his handcuffed arms above his head like a victorious boxer. When the security forces were searching for him, they took possession of the apartment for three days and raised a large Israeli flag on the balcony.

Fadwa Barghouti is one of the few persons allowed to visit him. Not as a lawyer, but only as "close family"—a definition that includes parents, spouses, siblings, and children under 16.

At present, there are about 11,000 Palestinian prisoners in Israeli jails. Assuming an average of five "close family" members, that makes 55,000 potential visitors. Those, too, need a permit for each visit, and many are rejected for "security reasons." Fadwa also needs a permit every time, which allows her only to go directly to the prison and back, without stopping anywhere in Israel. The three sons are not allowed to meet their father any more, since all three have passed the age of 16. Only the young daughter can visit him.

There is hardly anyone who is more popular with the Palestinian public than Marwan Barghouti. In this, too, he resembles Mandela while in prison.

It is difficult to explain the source of this authority. It does not emanate from his high position in Fatah, since the movement is disorganized and there is hardly any clear hierarchy. From the time when he was a simple activist in his village, he rose in the organization by sheer force of personality. It is that mysterious thing called charisma. He radiates a quiet authority that does not depend on outward signs.

The war of vilification between Fatah and Hamas does not touch him. Hamas takes care not to attack him. On the contrary, when they submitted a list of prisoners in exchange for the captured soldier Gilad Shalit, Marwan Barghouti, in spite of his being a Fatah leader, headed the list.

It was he who, together with the imprisoned leaders of the other organizations, composed the famous "prisoners' document," which called for national unity. All Palestinian factions accepted the document. Thus the "Mecca Agreement," which created the (short-lived) Government of National Unity, was born. Before it was signed by the parties, urgent messengers were sent to Marwan in order to obtain his agreement. Only when this was given, did the signing take place.

I took advantage of my visit in Ramallah in order to get an impression of the opinions of Barghouti's adherents. They try not to be swept away by the climate of mutual hate that now governs the leaderships of the two sides.

Some of them strenuously oppose the Hamas actions in Gaza, but try to understand the causes. According to them, the Hamas people, unlike many of the Fatah leaders, have never been in the West and have not attended foreign universities. Their mental world was formed by the religious education system. Their horizon is narrow. The complex international situation, in which the Palestinian national movement is compelled to operate, is quite foreign to them.

In the last elections, my interlocutors explained, Hamas hoped to gain 35–40 percent of the votes and thus gain legitimacy for their movement. They were totally surprised when they won the majority. They did not know what to do with it. They had no plans. It was a mistake on their part to set up a government composed entirely of Hamas members, instead of insisting on a unity government. They misjudged the international and Israeli reaction.

Marwan's adherents do not shrink back from self-criticism. In their opinion, Fatah is not without blame for what happened in Gaza. The movement did not act wisely when they arrested and humiliated the Hamas leaders. For example, they arrested Mahmoud al-Zahar, the foreign minister in the Hamas government, humiliated him, cut off his beard, and called him by the name of a famous Egyptian female dancer. This is one of the reasons for the burning hatred al-Zahar and his colleagues hold for Fatah.

I did not hear denials of the Hamas contention that Muhammad Dahlan, the former confidant and security advisor of Mahmoud Abbas, conspired with the Americans to carry out a military coup in the Gaza Strip. Dahlan, the darling of the Americans (and the Israelis) believed, according to them, that if he were provided with arms and money he could take over Gaza. That pushed Hamas to the decision to act first and carry out an armed takeover themselves. Since the majority of the public supported Hamas and detested Dahlan, who was accused of collaborating with the occupation, Hamas easily won. Dahlan has now been sent into exile by Abbas.

Hamas's center of gravity is in the Gaza Strip. That is the problem of Khaled Mashal, the Hamas leader who resides in Damascus. Unlike his two deputies, he has no roots in Gaza. That's why he needs money to reinforce his standing there. He gets it from Iran.

(I would have liked to give some impressions here of the Hamas point of view, but it is quite impossible to enter the Gaza Strip, while our Hamas interlocutors in East Jerusalem have all been sent to prison.)

How will the Palestinians get out of this bind? How can they re-establish a national leadership that will be accepted by all parts of the people in the West Bank and the Gaza Strip, able to lead the national struggle and make peace with Israel, when peace becomes possible?

Barghouti's followers believe that at the right time, when Israel comes to the conclusion that it needs peace, he will be released from prison and play a central role in the reconciliation—much as Mandela was released from prison in South Africa when the white government came to the conclusion that the apartheid regime could not be sustained anymore. I have no doubt that in order to bring such a situation about, the Israeli peace forces must start a big public campaign for Barghouti's release.

What will happen in the meantime?

There is hardly anyone on the Palestinian side who believes that Ehud Olmert will conclude a peace agreement and implement it. Hardly anyone believes that anything will come out of the "international meeting" that is supposed to take place in November. The Palestinians believe that it is a bone thrown by President Bush to Condoleezza Rice, whose standing has been dropping dramatically.

And if that has no results?

"There is no vacuum," one of the Fatah leaders told me, "If the efforts of President Abbas do not bear fruit, there will be another explosion, like the intifada after the failure of Camp David."

How is that possible, after the Fatah activists have turned over their arms and foresworn violence? "A new generation will arise," my interlocutor said. "As has happened before, one age-group gets tired and its place is taken by the next one. If the occupation does not come to an end and there is no peace, a peace that will enable the members of this generation to turn to the universities, to family, work, and business, a new intifada will surely break out."

To achieve peace, the Palestinians need national unity, much as the Israelis need a consensus for withdrawal. The man who symbolizes the hope for unity among the Palestinians is sitting now in Hasharon jail.

The current situation, in January 2008, is bleak. Just over seven years into the second, al-Aqsa, intifada, Palestinian unity and much of the Israeli peace camp has crumbled. People—civilian and armed forces alike—are exhausted, mistrustful, and angry. Increasingly right-wing governments are being voted into office, even as the same happens in the United States, Israel's sponsor and apologist. The situation is both chronic and acute. The bleeding must be stopped immediately, but that must not preclude immediate action toward treating the malady or the patient will die. Neither Palestinians nor Israelis want the land to die. Perhaps by following Uri Avnery's lead they will recognize what they all have to lose and start the patient on the road to recovery. Whatever form that recovery might take.

Inshallah.—SRP

Notes

Compiled by Sara Powell (ed.)

1. Fatah was the largest of the groups comprising the PLO and, under Arafat's leadership, directed much of official PLO policy for many years. Originally considered a terrorist organization, Fatah is now considered the most moderate—and consequently in much of the world the most legitimate—Palestinian party, despite the fact that it is only one of the groups that comprise the PLO, which, in 1974 was recognized as "the sole legitimate representative of the Palestinian people." The PFLP was a secular, Marxist-Leninist-informed Palestinian nationalist organization under the leadership of George Habbash. Founded in 1967, it became a part of the PLO umbrella organization. The PDFLP split from the PFLP in 1969 under the leadership of Nayef Hawatmeh, and is generally considered to have more of a Maoist approach than the PFLP.

2. Deir-Yassin, a Palestinian village of about 750, was virtually destroyed by Irgun and Stern Gang commandos on April 9, 1948. Over 100 Palestinian men, women and children were killed.

3. Nathan Birnbaum was elected Secretary General of the Zionist Organization at the First Zionist Congress in 1897, but eventually abandoned the idea of political Zionism in favor of a conservationist approach to traditional Jewish culture and religion among the Ashkenazi diaspora in Europe.

4. In 2008, as this book is being edited, the situation is even more vicious, more desperate and more acute as settlements continue to grow, the wall continues to rise, and Palestinians succumb to armed in-fighting under Israeli and international pressure.

5. This phrase has been used by the likes of former Israeli Prime Minister Golda Meir and former American First Lady Eleanor Roosevelt to garner support for the nascent Israeli state, and still (erroneously) informs the American public.

6. *Sonderbehandlung*, literally meaning special handling or special treatment, was a euphemism used in Nazi Germany for the murder of Jews. Avnery uses it here in its literal sense while invoking its previous connotations.

7. The Druze are a religious sect stemming from Islam. Although many consider themselves Muslim, many Muslims consider them a religion apart. They are most prevalent in Lebanon and Syria.

8. It is true that Arab citizens of Israel are accorded the rights of citizens under Israeli law (for example they may run for membership in the Knesset), but the

rights of "nationality" of which Avnery speaks are somewhat different under Israeli law and Arab citizens often find themselves in a different category from other Israeli citizens.

9. This group of "American fundamentalist evangelists" refers most specifically to "millennial dispensationalists," who believe that the Jews must inhabit Israel in order for Armageddon to occur. At that time, those few Jews who convert to Christianity will be saved with those "born again," while the vast majority of Jews, as well as those of all other religions, will be eradicated prior to the "rapture" in which the born-again Christians will be transported directly to heaven.

10. Nonetheless, Herzl was the founder of Zionism. It should be noted that, as were many early Zionists, Herzl was a Jew culturally more than religiously. Like many of his contemporaries, he tended toward the widespread late-nineteenth-century ideas of atheism and nationalism. Many Zionists among the early leaders of Israel came from the same tradition.

11. It should be noted that though many other countries practice many forms of discrimination, no other country with Israel's power and resources has practiced the same kind of ethnic cleansing, at the same intensity, for as many decades, while still commanding much of the world's sympathy. It is a unique situation.

12. In the United States, the situation is quite different. Very little coverage of Palestinian issues is aired, and Palestinians are generally seen as terrorists.

13. *The Protocols of the Elders of Zion* is a long-discredited book of Russian propaganda accusing worldwide Jewry of comprising a controlling cabal. The book is dragged out of obscurity from time to time by people who do not have command of the facts or who wish to use it for propaganda.

14. Originally published in *Ma'ariv*.

15. Originally published in the *International Herald Tribune*.

16. The *kibbutzim* were collectively owned, agriculturally oriented communities; the *moshavim* were similar, but comprised individually owned plots as part of a cooperative union.

17. "The iron wall: we and the Arabs" was the name of an article published by Jabotinsky in 1923 that laid out early ideas that the Zionists must construct an "iron wall" of a strong Jewish nation state in order to realize their vision. Jabotinsky is often cited by voices in defense of the "Separation Wall"; however Jabotinsky, knowing Palestinians would not cede their land, was in favor of full civil rights for the Arab inhabitants of the envisioned Jewish state. For the full text of Jabotinsky's article see http://www.marxists.de/middleast/ironwall/ironwall.htm

18. The first major Palestinian reaction to Zionist immigration to Palestine under the auspices of the British mandate. See Ted Swedenburg, *Memories of Revolt: The 1936–1939 Rebellion and the Palestinian National Past*, University of Arkansas Press, 2003 (2nd edn).

19. Huntington's theory was originally proposed in a *Foreign Affairs* (Summer, 1993) article, then expanded in *The Clash of Civilizations and the Remaking of World Order*, Simon and Schuster, 1996.

20. This essay comprises Avnery's opening remarks from a May 8, 2007 Tel Aviv debate with Israeli "new historian" Ilan Pappe, who argued in favor of one state.

21. For an informed and interesting discussion of the design and intent of

settlements, see Segal and Weizman, *A Civilian Occupation: The Politics of Israeli Architecture*, Verso, 2003.

22. Settlements in the West Bank have more than doubled since the Oslo Declaration of Principles was signed in 1993. Although specifics regarding settlements were withheld from the Declarations, relegating discussion of them to the so-called final status issues, along with Jerusalem and military locations, it was nonetheless understood and expected, based on the general withdrawal that was included in the Declarations, that no new settlements would be built.

23. Levi Eshkol, third prime minister of Israel from 1963–69. Ehud Barak, tenth prime minister of Israel from 1999–2001. A span of 38 out of the then (2001) 53 years since Israel's declaration of statehood—approximately 72 percent of its existence.

24. This essay was written prior to Ariel Sharon's election as Prime Minister in February 2001. During his term in office he presided over huge settlement growth, as well as the withdrawal of settlers from Gaza. See the discussion of the unilateral disengagement plan in Chapter 3.

25. The Oslo Declaration of Principles divided occupied Palestine into three dispersed zones. Area A is that area under full Palestinian Authority control, Area B is under Palestinian "civil" control, but Israeli "security" control, and Area C is under full Israeli control. Area C under full Israeli control comprises almost 60 percent of occupied Palestine. The city of Hebron has special zones. H1 is under full Israeli control because of the settlements in the area, and the borders of H2 are under Israeli control. The situation in Hebron is one of the worst in the West Bank.

26. Teddy Kollek, mayor of Jerusalem from 1965–93 who presided over the Israelization of much of Jerusalem in the wake of the 1967 war and subsequently throughout his term of office.

27. For an excellent discussion of "the planners' ...aim" see Segal and Weizman, *A Civilian Occupation: The Politics of Israeli Architecture*, Verso, 2003.

28. Originally published in *Ma'ariv*.

29. Though this essay is specifically about the destruction of Palestinian homes for not having the proper permits, home demolition is carried out for a number of reasons including to build the "Separation Wall," as a form of collective punishment, and to build new "Israeli only" roads.

30. Though many checkpoints are stationary, some move from place to place, often springing up unexpectedly.

31. The "closed military area" is a tactic the Israeli military sometimes uses that imposes full martial law over the area in question, giving the soldiers on the spot great leeway in their actions.

32. One *dunam* equals 0.247 acres, 370 *dunams* equals 91.429 acres, and 950 *dunams* equals 234.750 acres, a significant amount of land to be appropriated from a densely populated area in the roughly 5,860 square miles of the West Bank, particularly under the circumstances Avnery describes.

33. In a 2004 non-binding opinion the International Court of Justice found the wall illegal.

34. Rachel Corrie, a young US member of the International Solidarity Movement (ISM), was fatally crushed standing in front of a home about to be demolished

in Rafah refugee camp while practicing non-violent resistance on March 16, 2003.

35. Interestingly, the wall being built along the US–Mexico border to keep out immigrants is being built with the aid of Israeli engineers and contractors.

36. Whereas most of those opposed to the wall consider the settlements crucial to determining the wall's path, there are many who consider the location of water aquifers on the West Bank to be equally crucial, and many more who consider the Balkanization or Bantustanization of Palestine to be yet another factor. For a map of the wall see http://www.btselem.org/Download/Separation_Barrier _Map_Eng.pdf. Unfortunately, though maps exist, there are none readily available to the general public that overlay the wall's route with a map of water distribution. Of course, large settlement blocs have been built where water is most abundant. For a good discussion of the geographic considerations of Israeli architecture, see Segal and Weizman, *A Civilian Occupation: The Politics of Israeli Architecture*, Verso, 2003.

37. *Felaheen*: the settled peasant farmers who worked, but did not necessarily own, the land. *Nakba*—catastrophe—is the Palestinian term for the ethnic cleansing of approximately 400 villages in the initial Israeli military occupation beyond the land allotted Israel in UN Resolution 181 which divided Mandate Palestine.

38. The Israeli bulldozers Avnery refers to are typically Caterpillar D-9s. For more information see www.catdestroyshomes.org/. Sharon got his nickname because of his bulldozer tactics and style.

39. Whether or not the "Eastern Wall" will be built is still under question. Currently Gaza is, and has been, completely enfenced. It has been called the largest outdoor prison in the world.

40. As of 2008 there are approximately 11,000 Palestinian prisoners.

41. Gilad Shalit is an Israeli soldier captured near Gaza in June 2006 By January 2008 he had not been released.

42. It is problematic that during prisoner exchanges, Palestinians are released in hugely exponential numbers vis-à-vis Israeli prisoners, giving the impression of either a difference in worth, as Avnery mentions, or a difference in the quality of good faith gestures by either side, because the general public does not realize the gross inequity in numbers of those taken prisoner by either side.

43. Marwan Barghouti is a Palestinian political leader currently serving five life sentences for "terrorist" activities against Israel. See Avnery's September 15, 2007, essay "The Palestinian Mandela" in this volume.

44. There are currently (2008) approximately 4.5 million Palestinian refugees.

45. The right of return for all peoples displaced by war is codified in the Fourth Geneva Convention. The right of return for Palestinians is specifically guaranteed by UN Resolution 194, passed in 1948.

46. Benny Morris became one of the Israeli "new historians" with the 1987 publication of *The Birth of the Palestinian Refugee Problem, 1947–1949*, but gave a series of interviews over the winter of 2003–04 which openly advocated "transfer," an Israeli euphemism for ethnic cleansing through forcing Palestinians out of the country. The new historians are a group of Israeli scholars who used recently declassified documents about the founding of the state of Israel to refute many of its founding myths.

47. See Avnery's essay "The peace criminal" in this volume.

48. For the full story of Avnery's secret contacts with the PLO in the pre-Oslo years, see Uri Avnery, *My Friend, the Enemy*, Zed Books, 1986.

49. As an example, see William Quandt, *Peace Process: American Diplomacy and the Arab–Israeli Conflict Since 1967*, University of California Press, 2005.

50. Though focused on "Barak's generous offer," this essay includes commentary on the Taba talks held in Egypt in January, 2001.

51. See Hussein Agha and Robert Malley, "Camp David: The Tragedy of Errors" in the *New York Review of Books*, Vol. 48, No. 13, August 9, 2001.

52. The Saudi Plan, based on UN Resolution 242, the "land for peace" formula, was proposed by then Crown Prince Abdullah bin Abdul Aziz of Saudi Arabia and later formalized in a unanimous vote at the Arab Summit in Beirut, Lebanon, on March 27–28. On March 29, Israeli forces invaded the West Bank for a prolonged and brutal military occupation in retaliation for a Hamas-claimed attack on a hotel in the Israeli resort city, Netanya, that killed 19.

53. This refers to the present King Abdullah of Saudi Arabia. Avnery notes that it is (also) an allusion to a famous Israeli song.

54. Now King Abdullah of Saudi Arabia. He succeeded his half-brother King Fahd to the throne in 2005.

55. The Conciliation Committee in Lausanne was a United Nations General Assembly committee formed as part of the requirements of UN Resolution 194 to facilitate a final status agreement to end the war between Israel and Palestine. The committee convened in April 1949, and in May an agreement to negotiate final status was signed. However the fundamental issues comprised the same basic issues that are still being negotiated today, including borders, refugees, and Jerusalem.

56. The Palestinians have essentially had a constitution since 1997, although drafts were written as far back as 1968. For a good discussion of the history of the Palestinian Constitution see "The Palestinian basic law." by Adrien K. Wing available at http://www.palestine center.org. The constitution was revised in 2003, consistent with the Road Map's conditions. Israel does not have a constitution, a theme Avnery frequently addresses.

57. As part of the Roadmap, US President George W. Bush met with Israeli Prime Minister Ariel Sharon, Prime Minister Mahmoud Abbas of the Palestinian Authority, and Jordan's King Abdullah in early June, 2003 in Aqaba, Jordan.

58. Otherwise known as the Geneva Accord, the Beilin–Abed-Rabbo agreement was an unofficial final status agreement principally proposed by former Palestinian and Israeli ministers Yassir Abed-Rabbo and Yossi Beilin. This plan has been compared to Avnery's vision for two states, although Avnery puts greater emphasis on Palestinian viability and sovereignty than the Accords do.

59. Sari Nusseibeh and Ami Ayalon published the People's Voice Initiative in 2002, a two-state, mutual-recognition-based peace plan.

60. Sharon's plan of unilateral disengagement is of particular import because it was actually implemented prior to Sharon's stroke in early January, 2006. Its effects are proving deadly in Gaza, as evidenced by a significant amount of coverage in numerous news outlets as well as various human rights reports, and the situation has only worsened since the split in the Hamas–Fatah Palestinian Unity Government.

61. Abu Ala Ahmad Qrei'a—a Fatah leader who served as the Palestinian prime

minister from September, 2003 to July, 2004. He was one of the Palestinian team who worked on the Oslo Declaration of Principles.

62. The questions of safe passage and territorial contiguity for Palestinians were addressed in part in the 2005 Rand Plan, which consisted largely of turning the proposed Palestinian state into a high-speed railway between urban Palestinian areas. The plan effectively cut off agrarian Palestinians from their land, confining them to their cities and the railway between them. The Rand plan died quickly after an initial blitz of US and Israeli hype. Though not discussing the Rand plan itself, Avnery addresses the issue of safe passage in an article entitled "Safe (for whom?) passage," originally published on October 4, 1999 in *Ma'ariv*. The full text is available at http://zope.gushshalom.org/home/en/channels/avnery/archives_article68.

63. Interestingly, Avnery's prediction of the "violent fight" spilling over manifested first in another Lebanon war—this time while Sharon lay in a coma.

64. *Va banque*: play for the whole fortune.

65. Formalin is a compound of formaldehyde.

66. This is a plan proposed by a group of Palestinian political prisoners. For the full text, see http://www.onevoicemovement.org.

67. In early 2007 a unity government was formed due to the US-led rejection of the elected Hamas government. The unity government fell in June, 2007 and serious clashes between Fatah in the West Bank and Hamas in Gaza marked serious dissension among Palestinians. The situation in May 2008 is slightly more stable, but still absolutely critical.

68. Carl von Clausewitz, late eighteenth/early nineteenth-century Prussian soldier, military historian and theorist who wrote *On War* and whose work is still taught and currently being much discussed again in the context of the Bush administration "war on terror."

69. There have been many "incidents" at the Karni crossing between the southern Gaza strip and Israel—a crossing administered by the Israeli airport authority rather than the IDF. The one Avnery refers to here occurred on January 13, 2005, when members of the Palestinian resistance blew a hole in the crossing entrance, ostensibly to smuggle arms and fighters into Israel. Hamas and the al-Aqsa Martyr's Brigade (Fatah) claimed credit.

70. One form of Palestinian non-violent resistance is the concept of *samud*—Arabic for steadfastness. *Samud* involves keeping up daily routine, refusal to flee, refusal to surrender to the occupation.

71. Both Yassin and al-Rantisi were assassinated by Israel, Yassin in March, 2004 and his successor al-Rantisi in April, 2004.

72. Hamas also gained popularity for its social programs and its honest reputation in contravention to Fatah's corruption.

73. Gush Shalom instigated a boycott against products made in Israeli settlements in Palestinian territory in the late 1990s, and are continuing the boycott to include artists and intellectuals operating within the settlements. Here, however, Avnery is referring to a British university decision to impose a boycott on all Israeli artists and intellectuals that was taken during the spring 2002 Israeli invasions into the West Bank.

For the full text of a debate between Avnery and Israeli "new historian" Ilan Pappe regarding boycott within the context of a discussion on one-state (Pappe) and two-state (Avnery) solutions see http://toibillboard.info/Transcript _eng.htm. The British boycott movement is part of an overall strategy being urged by anti-occupation activists around the world that includes BSD—boycott, sanctions and divestment.

74. The Bil'in protestors won a significant victory in September 2007 when the Israeli Supreme Court required that the Wall be moved closer to the Green Line at Bi'lin. However, the Court also retroactively approved another settlement on Bi'lin land.

75. This is a commonly used Israeli euphemism for assassination.

76. Following his April 21, 2004 release from Ashkelon prison in Israel having completed an 18-year sentence, Vanunu is still under extreme restrictions regarding his movements and actions. In April 2008, all restrictions, including being forbidden to leave Israel, talk to the foreign press, discuss nuclear issues at all, or enter the West Bank, were renewed for another year. Additionally, Vanunu has been charged with violating the restrictions imposed on him. His sentencing has been postponed until May 2008.

77. Black September was the month in 1970 when, after a period of escalating tensions, King Hussein of Jordan set the army on the large Palestinian presence. Thousands were killed, and the incident remains a source of tension.

78. Actually, Congressman James Moran (Democrat, Virginia) drew criticism for connecting the Israel lobby with the Iraq war in 2003 at an anti-war forum and again in September 2007 in the Jewish magazine *Tikkun*. His 2003 remark did not specifically cite the lobby, but instead the Jewish community, although contextual remarks made it clear he was referring to Jewish neo-cons and the lobby. Interestingly and atypically, despite lobby efforts to unseat Moran in the elections that followed in 2004 he was returned to his seat in the House of Representatives. His 2007 remarks in *Tikkun* show that he is more careful in his language, and seems to have learned that the US Jewish community and the lobby are not one and the same, but he is still speaking out.

79. John Bolton. One of the neo-cons, he was Undersecretary of State for arms control dealing with weapons of mass destruction leading up to the 2003 invasion of Iraq. He was appointed interim ambassador to the UN in 2005.

80. Hassan Nasrallah, Secretary General of Hizbullah. Amir Peretz, Israeli Secretary of Defense during the 2006 invasion of Lebanon. In the early days of the war Peretz said in a speech that Nasrallah would not forget his name.

81. *Der Judenstaat*, 1896.

82. The Huntington reference is from the 1996 book *Clash of Civilizations*. *The End of History and the Last Man* is by Francis Fukuyama, Harper Perennial, 1993.

83. Mahmoud Ahmadinejad, President of Iran from 2005 to the present (May 2008), known for his vitriolic statements about Israel and the United States.

84. DanHalutz, chief of staff of the Israeli Defense Forces (IDF) 2005–07.

85. Abu Jihad was the nom de guerre of Khalil al-Wazir. Arafat's second in command, he was assassinated by Israel in Tunis in 1988.

86. For a good discussion of the 1967 war see Donald Neff, *Warriors for Jerusalem: The Six Days that Changed the Middle East in 1967*, Simon and Schuster, 1985.

87. Tzipi Livni, Right-wing foreign minister of Israel. She has held several other ministries.

88. In mid-October, 2007, Bush threatened World War III if Iran develops nuclear weapons, which the White House says Iran is doing.

89. Originally published in *Ma'ariv*.

90. The Internet, as part of the information revolution, has significantly changed understanding of the situation of Palestine and Israel because news is no longer controlled by the mainstream media. For the first time people worldwide, and especially in the United States, have access to the Palestinian side of the story.

91. The principle of sovereignty has suffered strong blows ever since, particularly with the US invasion of Iraq, but also in Afghanistan and Haiti, among numerous examples.

92. That is, part of the West Bank and the Gaza Strip.

93. Jonathan Pollard was convicted in the United States of spying for Israel and received a life sentence in 1986. Since he received Israeli citizenship in 1988 there have been numerous attempts by Israel and its lobby in the United States to have him pardoned.

94. Israel does not always listen to direct US orders. In April, 2002, Bush told Sharon to pull back from its military invasion of the West Bank. Sharon ignored Bush, and less than two weeks later Bush received Sharon at the White House, hailing him as a "man of peace."

95. The Mecca Agreement defined the principles for the Palestinian Unity Government. It was decided in Mecca under the auspices of King Abdullah of Saudi Arabia.

96. Formed when the United States refused to deal with the democratically elected Hamas government, the Palestinian Unity Government failed in June, 2007, due at least in part to US unwillingness to deal with Hamas on any level. Fatah regained control of the West Bank, and Hamas regained control of Gaza. In mid-October, 2007, Hamas asked for talks with Fatah prior to the US-sponsored conference called for November, 2007.

Index